MARYSUE WRIGHT

*Ramblings
from
An Old(er)
Broad*

This exercise in rambling would not have happened were it not for the encouragement and help of many.

First and foremost:

The Hubs – In everything in our forty-eight years together, the guy has had my back. And his encouragement gave me the motivation to try my luck at this. Thank you, Dean!

Our son, Bubba, who kept after me to get organized and to get it done. (Probably was sick of hearing my whiney excuses!)

Linda, a grade school, high school, and old(er) broad friend, who, after a pleasant afternoon together, asked, "When did you get kinda good at this? And what are you waiting for?"

Addie, a young friend who gave me critiques, advice, encouragement, and a youthful perspective.

Brenda, my editor and an extraordinary English teacher- friend, who stood at the ready-red pen in hand and encouragement in her heart....

Dirk and Rick, who steered me through the publishing maze.

And all the people in my life that I wrote about-THANK YOU!

Contents

Ramblings from An Old(er) Broad

I haven't ALWAYS been an old(er) broad. But I've ALWAYS had a good memory.... Going back many years, remembering some of the most obscure details, I decided to take pen to paper, or fingers to keyboard, and record some of those memories.

I'm not a reader. Oh, sure, I read magazines, online articles, trashy novels on beach vacations, but the "real" books, I never did. I should be ashamed to admit it, but if Cliff Notes (for an assigned book) in high school were available, I bought them. I just never could sit still and get lost in someone else's story. I'm a do-er. Love to cook, clean, garden, crafts and work on home projects, so if there's any reading to do, it's been about cooking, cleaning, gardening, crafting or home projects.

Luckily, our sons have always favored their dad more in that department. The hubs is a voracious reader. He can have three books going at the same time! Me, I've been known to go to the library, and out of thousands of books, manage to check out the same book I read last year! I don't retain what I've read...which is surprising because I remember so many things in my life! And they always say, "Write what ya know," so that's what I've done!

Yep, had I been a lifelong reader, perhaps this would be a great American novel you're reading. Instead, it's snippets of those memories I've managed to retain.

First in blog form, now I'm putting into book form the ramblings from an old(er) broad. It's my sometimes-skewed way of looking at life as a kid, as a daughter, as a young Mom (and an old(er) one), as a wife, and as a woman. Some pieces are light-hearted, some are heavy handed, some are grouchy, but all are written with love.

I know it's kind of ironic for a non-reader to ask someone to read their book. But I hope you do and that you can relate, smile, reminisce, or just plain enjoy. Thanks for reading *Ramblings from An Old(er) Broad - The Book*

The Kid Years

As a kid, I didn't know how truly blessed I was. I grew up at a wonderful time, in a home with loving parents and four siblings. Life wasn't perfect, I'm sure, but to a kid growing up, it was pretty damn close. It was a time when most moms were at home….when dads supported the whole crew… when kids played outside with neighbor kids…when most families had one car… one TV…one phone….when weekends were family time…at church….or visiting relatives. Yep, my childhood was pretty idyllic.

Simpler Times…

Some days, I can't remember what I had for lunch…or what I wore yesterday. So why is it that I can conjure up some of the most obscure memories from my childhood? Whatever the reason, I've been thinking back to simpler times…

The change in the weather -the cooler temps, the gray skies - had me remembering the days of growing up in the Fall on Allen Avenue....the days of walking home from school with my sister and the neighbor kids who also attended St Ann's...the crunching of the leaves, underfoot, from the big birch tree on Benninghofen Avenue or the pop machine next to the beauty shop on Corwin Avenue that had ChoCola, that awful combination of chocolate milk and cola, in it. (I TOLD you they were obscure!)

Those were the days when most of the moms in our neighborhood were still stay-at-home moms...ready to greet us, after school, with a snack to tide us over til dinner, and to listen, as we'd tell them about our school days. We'd then run upstairs to change out of our school uniforms, and head outside to run off all our pent-up energy.

Summoning our neighbor friends, with an "Oh, Judy" or "Oh, Debbie" at their back doors, was all it took to get a game of spud or tether ball going. We'd have the best time - until the whistle from the nearby auto factory blew- letting us know that all of our dads, no matter where they worked, would soon be home for dinner and we'd be heading for the house.

After finishing up dinner, we kids would clear the table and help wash and dry the dishes. If we were smart, we'd work together to get it done (my sister used to start fights so she'd have to go sit in another room, as a punishment...leaving me to finish the dishes. Some punishment, right?) because, if it was still light outside, we could go out for a little while longer. It was then that you could smell leaves, burning in a neighbor's yard....the best fragrance of the season, in my mind. That enjoyment was short-lived, though, as it was a school night and we had homework to tend to.

The homework completed (some of us took longer...yeah...) we were allowed to watch a program in our TV room, on the only television in the house. Crowded around the console, there wasn't much discussion and never an argument about what to watch, as the choices were limited...but the shows were terrific! And then time for bed! That meant sharing a bathroom with all the sibs to get ready for the next day, when we'd start all over again.

Simpler times...The auto factory's closed now. The big birch tree might still be standing on Benninghofen. Do they even make ChoCola anymore? The fragrance of burning leaves is seldom enjoyed now - legally, anyway. Kids text or use a cell phone to call, instead of an easy "Oh, Debbie." So many moms have to work now because that's what it takes to get by. Organized sports and activities have replaced Spud, and TV shows can now be viewed anywhere and everywhere in the house, via laptops and phones. And life probably IS a lot more peaceful with multiple bathrooms. But I liked the simpler times. I savor the memories and I even long for them some days. Maybe you do, too. But what I'd REALLY like is if someone could please tell me what I wore yesterday!

Pens, Binders and New Shoes

Why is it that the Fall has me wanting to go out and buy new pens? Or a binder? Or new shoes? Must be Back to School time!

It's been over 45 years for me and almost twenty since our boys have been students, but that doesn't stop me from having the urge to report to class. And I'm not sure why. It's not like I was all that studious when I WAS a student...In fact, my interest in the classroom, didn't last as long as those new pens and my enthusiasm waned before I even had a chance to scuff up my saddle oxfords.

As a kid, I guess that, after a long, hot summer, I was ready for some structure in my life. It'd be good to see the same kids everyday... Get the old social calendar revved up again... But with it all, came homework, having to pay attention, needing to sit still and be quiet for what seemed like a long time...none of the things I was (or am) very good at.

I should probably be embarrassed to admit that very few of my grade school memories have anything to do with academics. Oh, an occasional spelling bee that I did well in. I remember that. Or preparing for my First Communion (but I think maybe a lot of my excitement about that was that I got to wear a veil!) I recall saying morning prayers and reciting the Pledge of Allegiance every day. But my memories tend to focus more on the people in my past and the social aspect of academia. Does that make sense?

Like the boy in first grade who used his finger and spit to erase his mistakes (He had a hard time getting anyone to take his damp paper when it was time to pass our assignments up to the front, believe me! Poor guy!) Or the day before school pictures, when a friend and I agreed to "tease" our hair... An exercise that was sure to make us look far more mature than fifth graders.... I came to school with a slight "hair hill" thinking I looked pretty sharp. That was until she (who shall remain nameless) walked into class, sporting a full blown bouffant that was sure to fill the entire photo! Or the walk home from school...six whole blocks! with the other kids heading that way. Or the arrival of spring when we'd be allowed to ride our bikes to school! Here I am...talking about the season that signaled the end of the school year already! And it just began! So you get my drift... I loved school...just not the scholastic part.

I really don't understand my enthusiasm for the whole "back to school" thing at this late stage in my life. Maybe I'll cave this school year and get those pens and binder. Perhaps, I can finally file all these writings into some kind of order. But I think I'd better draw the line on the saddle oxfords. They'd look pretty ridiculous with varicose veins, now, wouldn't they?

Butch,
The
Beauty
Peddler

I was reading an article the other day that touched on who and what defines beauty for us, and it got me to thinking. "What is my first memory of beauty?" Oh, I remember flowers; I had an early appreciation of their colors. I remember thinking my Mom was pretty. How that translates to my early definition of beauty, I don't know. I was young.... And then I read an article about Avon, the perfume and cosmetic company that has been around, it seems like, forever. In fact, I found out that Avon was bringing beauty into women's lives thirty-four years before women got the right to vote! The memories of what was beautiful to a young girl came flooding back.

My personal experience with Avon began before I even started grade school. I remember when the Avon lady came calling. Her name was Butch, an unlikely moniker for a woman peddling such feminine products, wouldn't you say? She carried a black bag and it contained all kinds of creams and potions that she would show to my mom. I can still smell the fragrance of the face cream Mom always bought… (perhaps that is why she still has gorgeous skin at age 95!). "Butch" used to have small samples of the perfume she had to sell. And if she brought mom's order from the last visit, I recall being impressed with the beauty of the containers. One was Topaz, a strong fragrance that came in a tall yellow decanter with a faux topaz gem on the cap. Funny how we remember such things, isn't it? The real excitement came when Butch would acknowledge the young girls in the house and allow us to choose a little white sample tube of lipstick. I suppose we used it when we played dress- up, but just to be given such a grown-up thing, made me feel very…. well, grown up.

We've come along way from the days of the iconic Avon lady, ringing the doorbell of a non-driving mom bringing with her the promise of beauty. Now we are bombarded with ads in magazines, commercials on TV, cosmetic counters in all the shopping malls….all trying to profit from our, perhaps, misconstrued idea what beauty is. I know it's all pretty superficial- striving to improve ourselves outwardly like that, especially if we don't strive to be beautiful inside as well. But I find it pretty humorous now that some of a once young girl's earliest recollections of beauty came from a woman named "Butch".

Ewww…Those Lecherous 7th Grade Boys!

7th Grade boys…I don't know how they are these days but when I was growing up??

We had moved to a new house and a different school was in my future. As a "new kid", the junior high years were going to be interesting. These were the days when we were starting to notice the boy/girl differences and there were some "he "likes" her" stuff going on. But for the most part, we were just a bunch of kids, innocently experiencing life, before the hormones really kicked in. At least that's what the girls presumed.

Some of the boys in our class decided that on Saturdays, whoever -boys and girls -wanted to show up at an old schoolyard, would play a game of touch tackle football. Sounded like fun...

"Time to pick teams"...one of the most dreaded phrases ever muttered, especially to a tall, dorky, un athletic, new girl....As we all lined up, the boy "captains" began their task of choosing up sides. I had no high expectations but prayed that I wouldn't be the last one standing. Names were called out, "I'll take Mike"... "We'll take Greg"... After all the boys had been chosen, the captains started calling out the girls' names..."We've got Linda"..."Marcia, you're over here"... "We'll take Marysue"...What? Drafted so early? I was both surprised and pumped! Must be because they thought I could run like a gazelle! I couldn't -- but with my long legs, maybe that's what they imagined.

The teams were set and for a few Saturdays in the fall of 1965, we had a lot of innocent fun...or was it so innocent? I came to find out, in later years, that it wasn't my imagined running ability that garnered my position on a certain team. One of the "captains" confessed, that the girls who were flat as boards (not "busty") were on his team because the "busty" girls (at least to a 7th grade boy) were a lot more fun to touch tackle. Is there anything worse than lecherous 7th grade boys?

Thinking back on those days, I'm not sure if, had I known their strategy, I'd be more disappointed that the boys didn't think I had gazelle-like moves or that I was flat as a board. It really doesn't matter now. I'm still friends with those lecherous "boys", I can't run (if I ever COULD) and being "flat as a board" wouldn't be the WORST thing for an old(er) broad.

Phys Ed...a.k.a. Misery

Not sure why I've been so nostalgic about my high school years lately. Maybe it's that we've lost quite a few classmates - I don't know... I do know that not everybody looks back fondly at that time in their lives, but I do. Hope you don't mind my going back.

During those years of teenage angst, I guess I fared pretty well....maybe better than many. But I had my times of not fitting in, of trying to find my niche....but it sure wasn't going to be in phys ed! Now I haven't been to a phys ed class in over 45 years- I'm sure they've changed a lot. Just think of the progress that's been made in fitness in that time!

Back in the 70's, in the school I was blessed to attend, we had phys ed every day. We would don these dorky one-piece gym suits, with our last name, emblazoned on our breast pocket....mainly so our tyrannical gym teacher could yell out the correct name when you weren't performing up to par. (My name was mentioned a few times.) We'd wear tennis shoes that we'd return to our lockers after each gym class because, back then, that's the only time you needed them.

We'd then make our way up to the gym for whatever plans "the tyrant" had. Our gym was separated by a big canvas curtain...boys' class on one side, girls on the other. I guess it was because the boys played rougher games, like dodge ball and basketball...or maybe, things were just more separate then. I just know I was grateful because of the aforementioned dorky gym suits!

I remember praying, in the beginning of the school year, that I would have phys ed during the end-of-the- day 8th period. (The things we thought important enough to pray for back then!) That meant you could go home without having to take a dreaded shower. (To this day, the smell of Right Guard deodorant brings back memories...) I always pitied the girls who had phys ed first period - many times, they'd have a kind of "drowned rat" look to take with them the rest of the day. So you get it -my priorities were misplaced and my heart was anywhere but in phys ed.

Girls' sports were woefully lagging behind boys' sports back then. We had intramural games and teams for the real girl athletes. But in our gym class, we did calisthenics, some tumbling, a little bit of volleyball, and we ran laps. I had the athleticism of a rock and was miserable the entire time.

Now, keep in mind that fitness wasn't a big item on anyone's agenda back then. Our folks probably didn't own a pair of Keds. And sweatpants hadn't been invented yet. If you rode a bike, it was to get from point A to point B.... not for the sake of fitness. Funny how things change.

I'm happy to report that my attitude towards fitness has changed, as well. I think that has to do with aging and wanting to prolong my life. But when I think back to my phys ed classes in high school, when a tall, dopey girl had to report to that dreaded class, the only prolonging that was in the equation was my misery.

If you're old enough to remember any of this, I hope I've jogged your memory a bit and you've thought back, fondly or not, to those days of phys ed. And if you're too young for any of this to register, hit your knees tonight and thank the Almighty!

It's in The Genes

I'm not that strong in math. I think that some people are born with a math gene, some are not. And that's okay. I realized early on that I was lacking.

I think I understood early math...you know, the simple addition and subtraction. When multiplication tables entered the picture, I started to lose interest -probably because memorization wasn't a strong suit either. And then they introduced "New Math." Does anyone else remember that?

It was so innovative (and confusing) that classes were offered to parents so they could help their kids with their homework. I remember, sitting with my dad, as he struggled to help me with homework, crying, (me, not Dad) because I just didn't get it. No one else must have gotten it either because it was short-lived. I've always been thankful for that. Taking New Math out of the curriculum probably added years to my dad's life and salvaged our relationship at the same time.

But then...enter Algebra in high school... I struggled with that, too. My teacher agreed to tutor me after school (which meant I had to quit the drill team...don't be too sad. I was only on it for three weeks and my math teacher did both me AND the drill team a favor.) As frustrating as it was for me, it had to be really hard for a teacher who had that math gene, to deal with someone who sooo didn't. I managed to pass that year and was done with math!

Nope - not true! I was quick to find out that math is a life-long thing.....not just something I would struggle with in the classroom. Lots of irony, then, that my first job in the real world was working as a bank teller at our local bank! More irony? That bank is out of business now!

I have found that you need math every day-whether it's adding, measuring, weighing, balancing...a fact of life...but I will go out of my way to avoid its use. And I'm thinking there MUST be many of us lacking the math gene. Why else would they have invented calculators?

A", "A", "A"....

As I'm sitting here, tapping on my iPad, I'm pondering how many hours I spent, learning the keyboard in my typing classes back in the 70's? Too many to count, I bet! And does it even matter now?

I struggled with typing, but it wasn't because I didn't have good teachers. It was one of those classes we took to prepare for the working world back then and I underestimated how difficult it was going to be without lots of practice.

One of the good nuns -Sister Sara Francis - who taught us, was so serious about her subject. We'd sit there, backs straight, our wrists arched a certain way and she'd repeat "a" "a" "a". We were to strike that letter without looking at the keyboard. "I've got this," I thought. We'd go through the alphabet as the weeks went on. Then we started with sentences. "A little peek at the keys won't hurt…" Then paragraphs! "Are you kidding me?" That's when the temptation to look at the keys completely took over. From that day on, I was so screwed!

Our tests consisted of typing from our textbook, as quickly as we could, with no errors....no easy task when you're looking at the book AND the keyboard! Numerous times, Sister would catch me, eyeing the keys, and would correct me. I'd listen to her briefly and what SHOULD have read "The young girl went to the store to buy bread and eggs" came out "rhr youbf gurk webt to (I always got "to" right) rhw drotr to (there's "to" again!) nur bresd amd effs". Then I'd go back to looking at the keys and the book. About twenty words a minute. WOW! What a speedster!

I guess it's pretty sad when you can't even get a secretarial job at a company at which your dad's a vice-president. But no worries. There was a demand for file clerks elsewhere. And if you wait forty-some years, "typing" as we knew it, would become obsolete and tapping your finger on a screen would be just good enough.

The
Demise
of
Home Ec

Is there such a thing as "home ec" in our schools today or did that domestic training go by the wayside?

Home economics, for those who don't know, was a class that was offered to young ladies in the 60's and 70's, to prepare them to be wives and mothers. At least, that's the spiel I gave my folks when trying to talk them into letting me take the class. Really, it was a "filler" for those who weren't motivated to take a third year of Spanish...or Biology... or phys ed. That would be ME! Oh, who was I kidding? It sounded like a fun and easy grade!

I remember the classroom like it was yesterday. Autumn gold appliances lined the room and state of the art (for their day) sewing machines were in the middle of the classroom. This was going to be great!

First up was the sewing part of the course and one of our first assignments was to make a skirt. I remember going shopping for fabric with my Mom and I found what I thought looked very "Bobbie Brooke-ish". A sharp plaid... We found a pattern and I was all set! How hard was this going to be? If you know me, you know I don't like directions and that's what patterns are...directions. And I guess I thought I was some kind of designer, like Vera Wang or something. I didn't need any help. "I've got this..."

Well, I can't even describe how shoddy this skirt turned out! No one told me plaids had to match up on the sides, that zippers were extremely difficult to insert, and that hemming took precision. My Mom, an accomplished seamstress (she made my wedding gown) must have been so disappointed in me.

Our teacher announced that we were going to have a style show to model our wares. I begged for and was given a second chance. Now, my Mom wasn't about to invest any more money on my sewing, so we went to her fabric box, in search of a remnant. We found one - not to my liking but what could I say? I'd ruined a beautiful piece of fabric already. This remnant was olive green, with these chenille-like tufts, almost like upholstery material. When I voiced my displeasure, there was no discussion...only Mom's offer to help me with this one.

This second attempt was at least a little more presentable than the first. Not the Bobbie Brooke-look I was going for but, at least, recognizable as a skirt! I don't remember who the audience even WAS for our "style show"... maybe students from the other classes. I don't know. I just know it was a long walk down that short runway... Lesson learned? If you don't want to parade around, in front of your peers, looking like a sofa, quit being a screw-off, pay attention and follow directions!

I'm pretty sure that, if home ec is no longer a high school elective, sorry performances, like mine, may have been a contributing factor to its demise. Sure, today's young women can learn to sew---probably just by going on-line-- but they'll miss out on the memories, the lessons and the laughs I got out of home ec.

P.S. I neglected to mention that young men also took the class; for them it was called Single Living. Interesting that, in the early '70s, before women's lib caught on, girls taking the class were being prepared to be wives and mothers. Guys taking it were being prepared to be independent. Hmmm...

Anyway, the other part of the class was cooking and baking. Now, I'm not talking about the cuisine we see on the Food Network. I'm talking basic stuff, like measuring ingredients, reading a cookbook, easy foods....Oh, oh, here comes that darn math and the need to follow directions again. With all that knowledge imparted, we were ready to go...cranking out pancakes, french toast, scrambled eggs, like it was our job.

The best part of this class was that we got to eat our creations --that, plus the fact that there was no style show! I wouldn't go so far as to say that students who weren't in our class were jealous, but the aromas, wafting through the school halls, had to be tough to ignore.

After we mastered the breakfast portion, we moved on to more complex dishes - like chocolate chip cookies from scratch, tuna salad, and puff pastry. I remember these dishes because I probably haven't made chocolate chip cookies from scratch SINCE, and my future husband was the guinea pig when I prepared the tuna puffs on my own.

I would never say that home ec made me a better cook, but again, my fellow chefs and I had a lot of laughs and probably did glean SOME information from that class. Who knows? Maybe the tuna puffs played a role in my nabbing that "guinea pig" of many years ago. Nah, they weren't THAT good. But going on 48 years of eating my cooking and he hasn't kicked me to the curb yet!

Yellow, Lined Paper and Cursive Writing

Did I hear right? That there is thought being given to doing away with the teaching of cursive writing? Whaaat? Don't even take into consideration all the time and effort we put in to learning it. Why take something so ingrained in all of us out of today's curriculum?

I remember so clearly the yellow paper tablet that we used in the primary grades. Remember it? It had solid lines that were the starting point. Then you went up halfway to the dotted line, and if the letter had an upper part, you went to the upper solid line. Repetition was key. We wrote "b", "b", "b", Or "n", "n", "n"over and over until it was perfect. I was usually in a hurry but sometimes I nailed it and received an "A" for my effort.

Once we "graduated" to using cartridge pens in the 4th grade, A's were seldom seen in penmanship by yours truly. Cartridge pens. (Do they even make those anymore?) My left-handed-ness had me smearing my way through the 4th grade and I was demoted, by Sister Antonio Pierre, to using a ballpoint pen...I remember feeling a little cheated but my work with the ballpoint was, at least, readable.

I know technology is behind the movement to do away with the need for cursive writing. Technology has already done away with the need for our typing skills, as we were taught. Now, tapping on an Ipad or a Smart Phone is good enough to get by. But do we really want just *good enough*?

I sure hope they rethink all of this. If kids aren't taught cursive writing, how will they read historical documents? Or sign their name to legal documents? And there's something very special about receiving a hand-written love letter, isn't there? Do we really want to lose that?

Let's stop "dumbing down" our kids. Making things easy for them isn't always the best route to take. I'll grant you, cartridge pens outlived their usefulness, but could we please keep the cursive writing??? That's one of the few school subjects this old(er) broad still has a handle on!

Petti Pants
and
Garter Belts

I've been thinking about clothes a lot lately.... mainly because I've been looking for some additions to my wardrobe...with not much success. This then got me to thinking about the things that were in style years ago and have disappeared completely from fashion...and some that are enjoying a resurgence...or never really went away. It's funny how that works.

Remember stirrup pants??? Those cute slacks with the fabric strip that fit under your foot, guaranteeing a smooth leg line (and for tall girls, a low crotch!) I pray they don't come back!

Well, when was the last time you've thought of petti pants? And did you know they were still available? A friend made me aware of their availability and although I won't be rushing out to buy a pair, it was fun thinking back.

Petti pants were popular among school girls in the 70's and for those who aren't familiar, petti pants were a nice alternative to wearing a slip..that undergarment that certainly was named right...mine was always "slip"ping up! Petti pants came in pretty colors (my favorite was a pair of aqua ones), were the same comfortable fabric as a slip, but kind of like Bermuda shorts. They sure were great, worn under a school uniform skirt! Not sure if I'd wear 'em again, but they sure were terrific fifty years ago!

And while we're talking about "unmentionables", who can forget girdles and garter belts? Girdles, garter belts and nylons were what we sported for dressy occasions. Then along came pantyhose. Until the pantyhose industry caught up with tall sizes, I suffered with the aforementioned "low crotch" again and longed for the return of garter belts for the longest time. But let's leave the lingerie department now, shall we?

Turtleneck sweaters, dickies and "poor boys" (those cute, short sleeve sweaters that came with the British Invasion) were must-haves in our high school wardrobes...and they've maintained their popularity thru the years. Dickies, not so much! A blessing, I'd say! Dickies were the top portion of a turtleneck. That was it! Just a fake half/sweater that used to ride up, much like my slip did. I never "got" dickies!

It's funny... Some of the things I wore, years ago, were because they were "in". Now, I must ask, what need was there for a high school junior to wear a girdle? These days, I NEED to wear one and don't want to. I used to wear turtlenecks because they were also "in" years ago. Now I wear them, because, as the late Nora Ephron, who wrote humorous books about aging, stated "The neck and hands don't lie.". Turtlenecks hide, well, "turtlenecks", that crepey condition that comes with getting older.

I have a lot of great memories, tucked away, of fashion from my youth. And that's where they'll stay...tucked away. No need for petti pants, girdles, garter belts, nylons, or stirrup pants for me anymore! Nope, but I'm hanging onto the turtlenecks because... remember, "the neck don't lie."

Not
Being
Flirty

Homecoming at our local school recently had me viewing the many pics on social media, posted by the proud (rightfully so) parents of the current batch of cute attendees. That had me thinking back to the Homecomings of my past.

In the olden days, at my school, preparations for the floats started in the summer. Once school started, some (not mentioning names here) used that float "work" as an excuse to hang with friends on a school night. And then we had to bust ass to finish the float the last week because of that "just hangin' with friends" part.

The senior class had all five floats (Classes were bigger then, I guess) so the fluffing of pomps was a common September task at the homes of kind senior parents.

The parade took place on a Saturday before the game, and folks would line both sides of the main street of our town, as we'd make our way to the athletic field. Spirit was high, as it seemed the whole town was cheering our school on. The mayor of our city, school dignitaries, the homecoming court (girls only then) were all there for a memorable night! After the game, an adult dance was held at the school -when the alumni truly came "home" for homecoming.

Sunday night was when things ramped up for the student dance. (Monday was always a free day for the kids). The gym, was transformed into a dance hall... The junior class was relegated to providing the decorations. Tarps were spread on the floor, to protect them from the high heels we stylishly sported (but walked like Bambi in). Cute suits and dresses were what the gals wore-nothing as "prom-like" as now.....corsages for the girls and a boutonnière, dressed up the fellas' suits.

We'd dance the night away to the music of a local band, pausing, only to have a sip of Coke... or to have a formal photo, taken by a local photographer who was hired by the school. (When the photo packets were ready for pick up, weeks later, sometimes, kids were barely speaking to the dates that shared the photo with them.... one-night stands -teenage edition).

The night would wrap up and we'd head home with our dates or enjoy a sleepover with our girlfriends, sharing details of that fun Fall weekend.

Things have changed, as they always do. I think it's terrific that dates are no longer required. A band of brothers or a group of girls can have just as much fun, without the hassle of a date. There are now pre-dance meals, at friend's homes or local restaurants. We subsisted on chips and pretzels at the dance and saved the meals for the fancier, pricier prom in the spring. And we didn't have group photo shoots all over town, at beautiful sites or friends' homes. There was no social media to share the beautiful pics with the world. Our Dads might take a photo, with a camera, of the nervous couple before they headed out. And the aforementioned posed, professional shot we purchased, would be tucked into a drawer right after we showed them to our friends, parents, and grandparents.

I have many fond memories of homecomings from my past, as will the gorgeous kids I've seen on social media this year. Would I want to relive them? No thanks.

Let's picture this -a group of old women friends, dressed up in their finery, with their hands on their hips, (when did that become a thing?) posing for the pics, before heading out for a night of dancing.

Nah...If I'm in a dress, I'm heading to someone's funeral. And if you see me with my hand on my hip, like the young girls do now, you can bet I'm not being coquettish or flirty; it's probably my appendix's acting up..and the chances are very good, that I'm not going anywhere but home.

Yep, Homecoming always bring back sweet memories...And I'd truly appreciate it if you'd ask YOUR kids to slow it down a bit. Fifty years have flown by fast enough!

"Move Over! We're Going Home!"

I know things have vastly changed in the world of driving since I first got behind the wheel of a car. I'm so far removed from beginning drivers, but I know that they stepped up the requirements to get a license...and that's a good thing. Our eldest granddaughter recently became a licensed driver, so any steps to protect her and the grandkids who follow, is appreciated.

Back in the 60's, getting your driver's license was THE most important thing to a 16-year-old. And that probably hasn't changed. But having that piece of paper represented the freedom of getting out on your own...It meant trust...that your parents would LET you get out on your own (and come back) and responsibility...that you'd take care of the car, yourself and your passengers. But before all of that, there had to be Driver's Training.

For us, it consisted of classroom instruction, watching a gory film (I think it was entitled "Last Prom") about the dangers of not taking your driving responsibilities seriously, and then you got your "temps", the step before you got your real license. We were taken out, as a group, to drive with an instructor who was equipped with a specially outfitted car (a brake on the passenger's side) and an extra bit of human courage. Tough job - I know. The hubs was a driver's ed instructor, to supplement his income as a teacher. Many of our friends benefitted from his tutelage. He's very fond of saying that the reason I suck at driving is because I never had him as an instructor. (Whateverrrr!) Anyway, we 16-year- olds were on our way!

We were encouraged to do extra driving with our parents to get ready for the big driving test. Now, my dad was a patient man, seldom raised his voice, but for a moment in time, I nearly "drove" him to the brink!

On a Sunday afternoon, he thought it was a good idea to go to a new college campus in town and use their parking lot to practice my driving.... show him what I could do. That practice run was in an old Mercury Comet, with a standard transmission...you know...the kind you have to shift. No problem.

It was a cold day and I guess that's why Dad didn't want to turn the old car all the way off. He told me to slide over and put my feet on the brake and the clutch while he walked over to the passenger seat. Good enough plan for me.

I've tried to figure it out, for years...Maybe youthful inquisitiveness? Stupid carelessness? I don't know why but I took my feet off both pedals. This caused the car to lunge forward, almost hitting my Dad, while he was making his way to the passenger side of the car. With that, he flew back around to the driver's side, his face the reddest I'd ever seen! The window was opened just a crack but it was wide enough for me to hear him yell, "Move over! We're going home!" As if the red face and bulging neck vein wasn't enough for me to get the message...

We returned home in silence, Dad relayed to Mom my stupid move and a swift call to a local driver's ed instructor was made. I finished my training with Benny and passed the test on the first try.... something that I'm sure shocked dear old Dad.

Through the years, "my knuckleheaded move" (his words, not mine) was mentioned. Dad would smile and still question, "What were you thinking?" I still don't know, but I DO know this. I never wanted to see that expression on the old man's face again. And I never did! Okay, maybe I did...a few more times... But let's save those for other stories.

Christmas Childhood Memories

I'm the nostalgic type to start with. Thinking back to simpler times is always a comfort to me. But there's nothing that makes me more nostalgic than the Christmas holidays.

Like when....

We would go to the Miller's Root Beer Stand lot or Couch's Market to pick out a tree. The fragrance of the freshly cut trees was wonderful!

Like when....

The cardboard box of shiny glass ornaments and tangled lights was brought up from the basement to adorn that fragrant tree.

Like when....

We would pile into the car to look at the beautiful lights uptown. The city building was aglow, and the storefront displays were all so beautiful and colorful.

Like when....

We would stop at the First Church of God on Pleasant Avenue to see the live Nativity scene.

Like when....

We would go to Fritsch's on Pleasant Avenue, where Santa would be passing out candy canes in the parking lot to all the excited kids.

Like when...

We would check out the Nativity set on the porch of the Zettler Funeral Home.

Like when....

Our classrooms at St Ann's were filled with green and red construction paper artwork that would serve as "gifts" for our folks.

Like when....

Dad would take us to Roemer's Hardware to do some Christmas shopping. The first gift I remember which found me on the giving end, was a cookie jar for Mom. (which really was a gift for us kids - the cookie eaters.)

Like when...

Mom would help us pick out gifts like gloves or a flashlight for Dad at Sears uptown.

Like when....

Our house was all decorated, ready for all the family that made their way there on Christmas Eve.

Like when....

We'd go for a ride and return home to find that Santa had come!

Like when....

The baby dolls, roller skates, baking set, play telephones and stoves took over the living room floor (not all in one year, mind you -that would've been excessive!)

Like when....

Mom seemed so moved when she'd open Dad's gift - the cobalt blue gift set of Evening in Paris parfum (I never knew the significance until I learned that Paris was where Dad served during the war.)

Like when....

The house would be filled with the squeals of the Bruner Kids - "I knew Santa'd bring this!" "Look what I Got" - as if Mom and Dad didn't know!

Like when....

All the tasty cookies and candies were on display, just waiting for my grubby little hands to sample.

Like when....

We'd get ready for church, our dressy attire provided by a Mom who loved to sew...

Like when....

It was all over and we knew it'd be awhile before the magical sights, smells and feelings would return.

I hope your Christmases are always as special as it was when we were young!

Toy Story

As Christmas nears, I'm sure everyone's kids and grandkids are making their lists. No doubt, they have the old standbys, like dolls and bikes, on them. And I'm sure technology is represented on a lot of their lists, too. With that thought in mind, how do you think they'd feel about receiving a Slinky or a Magic 8 Ball instead? I'm pretty sure their excitement wouldn't match mine the year I found those items under our tree!

I've been thinking about how far we've come in today's toy departments. Who wants to join me on a Christmas shopping trip to a toy store of the 60's, 70's and 80's? Let's go!

Today's kids have iPods on which to hear their music. We had phonographs or record players on which to play our 45's. Kids today may have cameras and smart phones with cameras in them. We had the View Master, that "viewer" that allowed us to look at slides of vacation spots or the characters of our times, like Quick Draw McGraw or Superman... and who can forget ColorForms, those plastic shapes that magnetically stuck to a board?

Kids today can play games like Candy Crush or Heads Up on their phones and tablets. We played board games like Mouse Trap and Operation. If we wanted to be really active, we had Twister, the game that had us contorting into all kinds of positions, according to whatever came up on our spin of the wheel.

I always wanted an Easy Bake Oven until I found out from a neighbor girl, who received one for Christmas, that it took about two hours to bake a cake with that lightbulb! (Patience has never been one of my virtues-nor is baking one of my talents.) I never mastered the Etch A Sketch either, that magnetic screen with the knobs, but I thought they were silly anyway. If you wanted to get really creative, there was always Mr. Potato Head, that goofy toy that had you inserting plastic face and body parts into a real potato. Good lord...

Recollections of toys from the past wouldn't be complete if the list didn't include Barbie Dolls and Chatty Cathy dolls. They were both pretty innovative in their day because one had a very womanly shape and the other one blathered on, at the pull of a string. Hmmm... Sexist stereotyping? Maybe, but, as a little girl, I received a doctor's kit one Christmas so, maybe not.

Kids today seem a lot more sophisticated with their toy choices than we were. But I think that, without the toys of the past, there wouldn't have been the evolution into the toys we have today. So, kids of today... you're welcome!

Snow Days

As I sat watching TV one recent nasty wintry night, I couldn't help but see the scrolling names of the schools that would be enjoying a day off the following day. Of course, this got me to thinking back to the days when the words " snow day" was cause for real excitement in our house on Allen Avenue.

I don't know if we had less snow back in the 50's and 60's...or if it's that, now, having so many school busses and having the roads cleared for them, is the problem... Or if kids just aren't as tough these days. But I sure can't remember a year when we would've used up five days for snow, as the schools are allowed now. Few and far between, snow days were seldom and celebrated!

So many of the kids walked to neighborhood schools, or had dads drop us off in front of the school. Oh, sure, there were "bus people"...kids who lived in the outreaches of our school neighborhood - and who we used to be jealous of because they got to leave class to board the bus earlier than us walkers. Okay, it was only ten minutes earlier, but to a kid who wasn't a big fan of sitting still or of academics, that's a long time!

Long before there was the technology today that tells us, days in advance, of impending weather, there was the TV weatherman, who would hazard a guess as to whether or not we'd have snow. And it was anyone's guess, how much. The next morning, if there was snow on the ground, we'd anxiously sit in the kitchen, listening to WMOH on the radio, just praying that "St Ann's -CLOSED - would be the next words out of the announcer's mouth. And if they were, there'd be whooping and hollering at the great news! Not sure how we were going to spend that free day, but we were pretty sure boots, mittens and hats were going to be in the mix!

It's strange, how much quicker a day OFF school went than one spent IN school. The neighbor kids would gather to build snowmen and forts, have snowball fights and pull each other around on sleds. There were no hills for sled riding on our side of Pleasant Avenue, so unless you were old enough to cross some busy streets, pulling or being pulled around would have to do. When we got too cold, too wet or too tired, we'd go in to warm up, dry off and rest up, much to the chagrin of our moms, who were getting tired of mopping up melted snow... tired of putting mittens and boots back on or tired of feeding the huddled masses. But that day would fly!

It's funny...I notice the scrolling of school names across our TV now, knowing that some kids, somewhere, are plenty excited over a snow day. Me? There's a certain delight in knowing when you're old(er) and pretty much retired, EVERY winter day can be a snow day... and I rather like that!

Winter Fun...
An Oxymoron?

When did I start disliking winter so much? Is it because now these old bones feel the cold and respond with creaks and aches? Is it because the thought of flying down a hill on a piece of wood doesn't hold any charm anymore? Is it that driving on ice and snow isn't my idea of a good time? (I'm not a great driver on DRY pavement!) I really am not a fan now, but you know what? Some of the best memories from my childhood took place in the winter months.

Need I even mention Christmas? Time off school, gifts under the tree, spending time with family, the festive foods, the cookies...what wasn't to like?

But my acceptance of winter, years ago, went deeper than loving Christmas. Maybe it was that my dad was a lover of all things winter and we were recruited to join him at an early age. Back when liability wasn't a concern of the city, Potter's Park was opened for sled riding and ice skating...they even furnished a fellow to keep a campfire going so we could warm ourselves. So, on weekends, if it was cold enough or there was snow, we'd pile into the car and head to Potter's. When we got cold, we'd huddle around the fire, and to this day, I can't smell the aroma of a campfire and not think of dear winter-lovin' Dad or the fun we had on those winter days.

Having a day off school because of snow was probably another reason I tolerated winter years ago. We'd haul out the heavy coats, mittens and boots (not the fashionable boots of today but ugly black things with those awful metal buckles!) and head outside. We'd take turns, pulling each other on the sled...have impromptu snowball fights... and when the fun was over, (or someone got hurt) Mom had hot chocolate waiting for us. I remember that those days went a lot faster than the ones we spent in school.

Now, the winter nights find me bundled up in an old-lady robe, checking the thermostat frequently, convinced that the hubs has changed it again. Where have the years gone and when did I get so...not young?

I know that one of the benefits of having so many winters behind me is that I appreciate things more. Christmases, friends, good times...even winter. But ice skating's probably a memory...so is sled riding...almost every day is a day off... I miss the fun that came with winter. But I'm thinking, that watching others enjoy winter sports is a smarter (albeit safer) option these days... now where's that robe?

A Touch of Pagan in Me....

As Easter, the celebration of the Risen Lord, approaches, I got to wondering when and why did the Easter Bunny and Easter eggs, enter the mix? I did some investigating and found out that, in the pagan world, the bunny is representative of spring - that makes sense -and the eggs represent new life. Simple enough.

Easter, as a kid, was certainly a religious event in our home. My parents saw to it! Giving up something during Lent...Going to church in the evening on Holy Thursday, where the priest had his feet washed... Stations of the Cross on Fridays...fasting and abstaining on Good Friday. All to prepare for the most important day in the Christian faith -Easter Sunday.

Looking back, I have to say, I must have had quite a bit of pagan in me, too. As much as Easter was a celebration of my faith, my memories of Easter always go back to the fashion and food. (Go figure!).

My Mom, the seamstress, always made sure her girls had new dresses for Easter. Some years, we even had spring coats. My favorite part of the ensemble was always the "bonnet"! I love hats and, if I thought I could wear one now, without folks thinking I was a goof, I'd be wearing one this year. New patent leather shoes were also an Easter staple. Loved the new shoes, but was not a fan of the socks we had to wear with 'em. I look back, in amazement, at how my parents outfitted five of us in Easter finery... and am pretty sure they could've done without a second-grade daughter, pouting over a pair of lacy anklets...which I did.

Our Easters meant trips to both grandparents' homes, for wonderful meals, that always included ham and all the trimmings. We'd join in egg hunts with our many cousins. There were plenty of eggs and lots of candy to go around but certain cousins were always a bit pushier than we were and ended up with more loot than the Bruner kids. No worries. We'd make up for it at the NEXT grandparent stop where WE were the pushy ones.

I remember, on Easter Monday, we'd hide our eggs over and over again, having day-long neighborhood egg hunts. I'd take part, that is, if I felt well enough. I say that because there were few Easter Sunday nights that I went to bed without a bellyache. So many marshmallow eggs, so little time! I was an Easter candy binge eater, for sure. Good thing we didn't have school on Easter Monday because I doubt I'd have been in class most years.

Years go by and some things never change...and luckily, many things do. Faith is a big part of my life...all year round... still. And, although I don't get as dressed up for Easter as I used to, I sure appreciate my parents' sacrifice and talents more now (but I don't have to wear those darn anklets, Mom!)

This Easter, I'll indulge in some delicious ham, some hard-boiled eggs, chocolate, in the form of bunnies and crosses, marshmallow eggs, malted milk eggs, jellybeans and some marshmallow Peeps, for sure! I TOLD you some things never change!

On My Honor, I Will Try...

I'm sure it wouldn't have ANYTHING to do with the fact that I've consumed a box of Girl Scout Thin Mints that got me to thinking back to my scouting days. Yes, I was a Girl Scout...but I'm getting ahead of myself here - first, I was a Brownie.

St Ann's, the grade school of my early years, had some terrific scout leaders. I remember the patience and attention of Mrs McCool and Mrs. Fruttoso, trying to ride herd on a group of young, rambunctious girls. After school, on Mondays, we'd descend to the cafeteria for our meetings. They always opened up with the Pledge of Allegiance and the Brownie/Girl Scout pledge.

On my honor, I will try:

To do my duty

To God and my country,

To help other people at all times,

And to obey the Girl Scout Law.

We then would hear about scouting business, pay our dues, begin our craft project and then enjoy a treat. In addition to the lessons learned about patriotism, self esteem, commerce (had to sell those cookies!) and teamwork, the giggling, camaraderie, and the treats prepared me, I think, for the great relationships I have with my treasured women friends now. (We still giggle and eat...)

After a few years as a Brownie, it was time for us to "fly up". Not sure why that term was used but it meant we were advancing to the big leagues - The Girl Scouts! I was always partial to the light brown color of the Brownie uniform, but I was ready to don the green of the Big Girls. And although it was still fun, life as a Girl Scout got a bit more serious. We had to work on getting merit badges - that reward that came after you performed certain tasks in a specific field. "Homemaking" is the only one that stands out in my memory (go figure!) but I'm sure there were a few more I earned. I DO know that my older sister's sash had more badges, but hey, she stuck it out longer.... and probably worked harder at it.

I'm not sure why my time as a Girl Scout came to an end. Maybe because we moved to a new school. Maybe my propensity to quit things reared its ugly head again (I've told you before about my short attention span). Maybe it was when Mom wanted me to sew the badges on my sash myself - and glue guns weren't invented yet. I can't remember. But I do know that scouting - then and now - is a great organization - and that the lessons I learned, as a young girl, were invaluable ones.

Now, where's that last box of Thin Mints?

P.S. And thanks to my old(er) sister for her help in remembering the Girl Scout pledge... You didn't think I, with the short attention span, could recall that, now, did ya?

Salvation

or

Fashion?

As I was sitting in church -the church of my youth -St Ann's - some memories came flooding back. (Forgive me, Lord, for letting my mind wander...). I got back to doing what I was in church for but after Mass, I continued my reminiscing.

My thoughts centered around a childhood friend...well, really, she was my older sister's best friend. They included me occasionally -usually when something needed to get done that would get those two in trouble. Like calling boys to find out if those boys "liked" either of them. Or if they needed a scapegoat for anything mischievous, they'd get into.

To say this Allen Avenue friend was ornery would be an understatement. Nothing really hurtful, but as the youngest in her family, with older parents, she got away with a lot!

On one occasion, "she" (I really shouldn't use her name...) convinced my naive sister that a bonus item that came with a nail polish purchase at Avenue Pharmacy, the old neighborhood drugstore on Pleasant Avenue, was free...WITHOUT the purchase. When my sister proudly showed our horrified mom her "free" bounty, Mom marched them back to the drugstore to apologize to the store owner. (Can you say "shoplifting"? Kids today would probably get a rap sheet out of that kind of move!). Throwing rocks at, and ultimately, breaking a streetlight? Dad escorted them to the corner, with brooms in hand, to clean up the result of their rock-throwing. (The rap sheet would grow.)

The reason I thought of this friend in church the other night was that we are Catholic. "She" was not. But she was always up for going with us to the summer novena or benediction or Stations of the Cross at our church. I think Mom thought of her inclusion in these services as some kind of salvation, but I'm convinced that she went because she thought she looked good in a chapel veil or a mantilla.

My sister's best friend moved away when she was in the sixth grade. It was a sad day at our house, but we joke now that her moving probably kept my sister out of the juvenile detention center!

My sister and her friend remained close -despite the distance - for years. She passed away a while ago, after suffering a debilitating illness for years. She outgrew her orneriness, but she always had that twinkle in her eye that said she was up to something!

I like to think that those hours spent in church with us erased all the trouble "she" got herself (and my sister) into, those many years ago. I hope that's the case. And I'm thinking, the next time I'm in church, I'll probably think of her again. And I'll tell her she really DID look pretty good in a chapel veil.

A Rite of Spring

When I think back to the springs of my youth, my thoughts always go back to the neighborhoods I was blessed to live in. After the long winters, emerging from our homes on Allen Avenue, to be greeted by the neighborhood kids who'd also been in seclusion, was always welcomed. Oh, sure! We'd seen them throughout the winter, but there was something special about the freedom that spring, and nicer weather, brought us.

We didn't have a garage at our home in Lindenwald so the first order of business was for Dad to get the bikes up from the basement. I can remember the excitement when our bikes were tuned up and ready to go. "Where would they take us this spring"? If it was only crossing the street, to explore the other part of our neighborhood, it was spring and life was good.

Roller skating was another mode of springtime transportation. We didn't have the kind of shoe skates the roller rinks had, of course. Ours were metal skates that fit over our shoes and could be adjusted to many sizes, as long as you had the key that came with them. That key assured us that we'd have those skates for a few springs, no matter how much we grew. I can remember all the cracks and bumps in our neighborhood sidewalks. Avoiding them was a necessity if we were to remain scrape and bruise-free....no easy task.

Walking definitely made it easier to converse with friends than biking or skating ever did. And for that reason, it was, and still is, my favorite way of getting around. Whether it was walking to school, clenching a bouquet of lilacs for the May altar at St Ann's (you're never too young to start getting in good with your teacher, you know...) or walking home from school, loaded down with homework (a lot of good that sucking up did, huh?) being outside with school friends and neighbors was what we'd been waiting for.

Seeing folks, out and about in the spring, enjoying everything that this wonderful season has to offer, takes me back to a much simpler time...and as an old girl who has seen so many springs, I never tire of it. So, get out your tennies, your bike, your skates, or whatever! Just get out there! I hope your springs are as glorious as they used to be!

May I
Have
This
Dance?

I have to ask. Do high schools still have dances? Now, I'm not talking about date dances, like homecoming or proms. I've seen plenty of darling pictures the proud Moms post on social media of those special occasions.

I'm talking about just regular dances on a Friday or Saturday night...to give the kids something to do...to help them learn how to act around the opposite sex. (Gosh! Did I just sound really old?) The reason I even ask is because some of my fondest high school memories are of the dances we enjoyed as teens...and if today's kids don't have these opportunities, they're missing out on some great memory-makers.

Most of our school dances took place in the school's cafeteria. Nothing fancy... Different clubs or groups would sponsor them as fundraisers. The tables and chairs would be cleared away, making room for a dance floor. A band, a sound system, or just a record player would be brought in...and teachers and parents acted as chaperones. Let the fun begin!

Because we wore school uniforms during the week, we got to wear our "good" clothes to dances and social things. Skirts, sweaters, hose, loafers, Wind Song or Emeraude cologne...we were all set! When we'd arrive at the dance, the excitement would set in! "Who was going to be here?" "Would so-and-so ask me to dance?" "Do I look okay?"

The cafeteria was dark, except for the lighting that came with the music. Good! It was easier to blend in, as we'd lean against the wall, waiting to be asked to slow dance...or until a group of girls, got up the nerve to go out on the dance floor to fast-dance, anxious to try out the moves we saw on Bandstand or Soul Train the week before. (Yeah right! Like we could do THAT!!) Funny, but the guys weren't into fast dancing back then....well, it was their loss.)

The music and laughter of these school dances had kids meeting kids they didn't get to know in class. The need to summon up the courage to ask a girl to dance or the disappointment of being a girl who didn't get asked, were hard lessons we learned at those dances. All part of growing up... The night always seemed to go quickly until there'd be one last song played before the lights came back on, signaling the end of a fun night.

When we were in the lower grades, somebody's dad would pick up the group for the ride home...we'd recount the evening's happenings and get dropped off, with memories of a good time, fresh in our minds. When we were older, if we had someone in our group who had their driver's license, we'd all pile into a car and go somewhere for a Coke and conversation... probably about "who liked who" or what somebody wore that night.

This would probably sound pretty dorky to the kids growing up now, but those high school dances were a big part of our social lives back then. And I can't help but wonder how many sweet, young romances got their start with a "May I Have This Dance?" in a high school cafeteria those many years ago?

Summer Days at The Playground

Summer, as a kid, was my favorite time of year! My mind always goes back to the days when we enjoyed many a summer day at our neighborhood park.

Those were the days! A summer day, heading to the park with the neighbor kids, not a care in the world....Who wouldn't want to go back in time to that?

Sure, our park had playground equipment that would be deemed unsafe by today's safety standards. We didn't know any better back then, I guess, and despite some scrapes and bruises, we all lived.

One of the less-safe rides was the merry-go-round. We would all get on, and someone, (usually someone who took delight in scaring the heck out of kids) would make it go round and round fast. We hung on for dear life and when it came to a stop, we'd be dizzy and laughing.

The teeter-totter was for suckers...or extremely trusting kids. You'd sit on one end and another kid would sit at the other, and you'd go up and down. The kid who weighed the most pretty much decided who would be "up" most of the time. Our park had some smart alecks who would jump off their end, when you were on the "up" part of the ride... Your side of the teeter-totter, and your fanny, would hit the ground...hard! (Maybe some of our current back problems come from being slammed down, onto the hard ground, by the smart alecks' antics? Maybe....)

The swings seemed safe enough -unless someone would push you and you'd go sky-high. The daredevils would jump from the swing when it was at its highest point. Needless to say, I never jumped.

The slide was my go-to ride...it seemed the most laid back of all the rides. I remember the only downside was, in the heat of the summer, the shiny metal would scorch the back of your legs... that, and the puddle that always seemed to be at the bottom of the slide.

Come to think of it! There always seemed to be puddles everywhere at the park...under the swings, around the merry go round...everywhere young feet had worn paths into the hard ground. That's right! We had the hard earth as our play surfaces. No rubberized products...no wood chips...just good old dirt, or mud, depending on the weather that week.

Our park had park leaders, teenagers who were hired by the city to ride herd on the neighbor kids. Sometimes there were crafts, sometimes games, organized for us to play, but the highlight of the week was Park Pool Day. That's when the park leaders would walk us to the neighborhood pool, where we'd sing our "park song" for free admission and splash around with the same hooligans we played with at the park.

Another highlight of summers at the park were when The Show Wagon would make a stop for those brave enough to perform for the other kids and their parents. Some would sing, some would dance, some would twirl batons....any of the talents they wanted to show off. I was never brave enough to sign up and kind of admired the kids who did. It was a fun night, but I'm pretty sure, there were no major talent discoveries in Lindenwald those nights.

Times are different now...kids have so many things to occupy their time. But summer days, spent at the playgrounds of our town, in the 50's and 60's, would be hard to beat. And I'm so glad I was there.

June Coppertone, Baby Oil and Charley...

As the weather starts to warm up, my childhood memories always go back to the public swimming pool in our neighborhood. That was the center of the universe for the kids of Lindenwald, in Hamilton, Ohio, in the summers of the 60's.

There really was no discussion. Siblings, friends, neighbor kids -we would all head to the pool, usually walking there. Standing in line with our quarter in hand, we'd enter the place, put our belongings in the metal baskets which were found in the dressing rooms. We'd turn the basket in to the desk and get a pin with a number that corresponded with the number on the basket. Pinning it to our swimsuits, we knew our belongings were safe for the afternoon.

Our folks were comfortable turning us loose there every day, unaccompanied, because the gentleman who was in charge, Mr. Sharp, (that name just sounds like someone in charge, doesn't it?) ran a tight ship. "No running! No horseplay!" (What does that word MEAN? I've never understood that word!) "No food or drink in the pool area." A few of the rowdier boys didn't get the memo and spent a lot of time on the penalty bench for not following the rules.

One of those guys was particularly pesky. I'd better not mention names (maybe he straightened up, is a successful lawyer now and would come after me for defamation of character) but let's say, for the sake of this story, his name is Charley. Charley was the pest who would dunk the girls, splash them when they walked by, and cut line at the concession stand. He was such an annoyance! A good day at the pool for us was when Charley spent the better part of it on the penalty bench! I often wonder what ever happened to Charley. Haven't seen his name in the police blotters, but If there's any justice, he had to raise five sons who were as big a pain as he was!

"Pool breaks", when the pool was emptied of kids and the adults could swim in peace, were touted as a chance for the kids to rest. I really think it was a conspiracy to up their profits at the concession stand because that's where we all headed. Back then, the big decision of the day was whether to get a pop and popcorn or switch the popcorn out for a frozen Zero candy bar. Either way, for twenty cents, it was a win-win situation. When the whistle was blown again, it was back into the pool!

Not so for the older girls. They, with their train cases (that small boxy piece of luggage) in hand, would spread their towels, get out their baby oil and Coppertone, and be all set to talk and tan. They didn't get in the pool very often...Didn't want to muss their hair, I guess....and with good reason. The teenage boys who were too cool for the pool hung on the chain link fence, ogling the girls in their cute swimsuits.

All the pools in our town are gone now. High maintenance costs, liability, folks having their own pools...I know you can't go back in time, but such a big chunk of our summertime was spent at those pools, that their closings made me sad. Splashing around, being with friends, even having to deal with the "Charleys" of the world... Life, in the 60's, at a public pool in Lindenwald, was good.

Wrinkles
Command
Respect

We had the good fortune of heading south for a few weeks recently - I always feel blessed to be able to warm up the old bones a bit in February. It turns out those we left behind in Ohio had pretty nice weather, so that was good, too. (I'm not one to be overbearing about my good fortune...ha!)

Anyway, it was seeing a little one at the pool, being slathered in sunscreen, by her Mom, that took me back to a much simpler time than now...a time when we were ignorant to the damaging rays of the sun. (Why is it that things that feel so good, like the sun on our skin, have to be bad for us?)

My mind wandered back to the days when we would slather on our own concoctions, be it a mixture of mercurochrome and baby oil (remember that?) or Crisco (we'd smell like french fries after a sunbathing session!) Or the store-bought Coppertone, still one of my favorite summertime scents.

For us, Good Friday seemed to be the start of sunbathing season (or laying out as we called it back then.) Not sure why, but I remember spreading our towels on the patio of our childhood home, our sunbathing aids at the ready, and letting the sunlight work its magic. What kind of tan we thought we'd get in March or April is beyond me, thinking back, but I'm sure that wasn't the dumbest thing we ever did! And it felt so good!

Yep, all this, in our quest to be brown (or red) and beautiful. And for what? Well, that warm glow of our youth has turned into wrinkles, sun damage or worse, now. Dermatologists are thriving! And still the sun calls to us!

My Mom seldom sunbathed - she always wore a sunhat if she did...and, at 95 years of age, has the complexion most fifty year olds would envy. That ship has sailed for me - Oh, sure, I slather on the sunscreen now, wear a ball hat, if one's handy. But the damage is done, and sunshine still has a way of making me feel better than most anything... and I can't resist!

Aside from the medical impact of sunbathing, (skin cancer is no joke!) I guess I'm past caring about the wrinkles and sunspots. Age does that to one, perhaps. I think we should, instead, start a movement. "Wrinkles Command Respect!" can be our rallying cry. We've lived, loved, sunbathed (or laid out) plenty. And we have the wrinkles and leathery skin to prove it!

That little girl by the pool, who was resisting her Mom's attempt to protect her with sunscreen probably won't have such issues. When she's our age, there will probably be procedures and products that will have her looking fine forever. I hope so.

I loved those simple days of spreading out a beach towel, spending time with friends, and soaking up the sun. But now, as an old(er) broad, I must ask: Why does something that feels so good have to come with such a cost?

Rewind the Tape, Please...

It's funny how the memory works...I just wish that our memories were like the old video tapes we used to have in the 70's. Rewind the tape and see things in order, as many times as we want.

I received a phone call one night from my aunt, telling me about the death of another, older aunt. In her 90's, my aunt had a very rich life, made fuller by the nine kids she bore and the farm she helped to run. I felt bad for her kids, but selfishly, I was sadder about how time is going so quickly and how things change.

She was Dad's older sister and since my dad's death, our time with her family hadn't been what it used to be. We've all grown up and gone different directions-and that's sad…but without the older-generation-glue holding us together, it was inevitable- and that's even sadder.

But we're blessed to have the gift of memory. That city slicker/country cousin memory tape would be a lot of fun to watch now, if it only worked that way. The city slicker kids of my branch of the family always knew that if we went to the farm, we were in for adventures. And the country kids from the other branch of the family never disappointed! The sheer number of the kids in that family guaranteed it.

Whether it was swimming in a pond (something totally unique to kids, used to swimming at a public pool in Lindenwald) ....swinging on ropes in the barn (that about caused our Dad to have a coronary) ... throwing pitch forks at bales of hay (another coronary for Bob) ...chasing after farm animals... chemistry set experiments before we were ready for them... Gosh, we had a lot of mischievous fun with those cousins!

The country cousins seemed to have a freedom that we lacked…maybe because they so greatly outnumbered their parents…maybe the size of the farm aided their getting away with stuff…maybe we city kids were more sheltered than we should have been. I just know our cousins probably thought we were wimps when we were there…and I remember the scoldings we got in the car, on the way home, for some of the stunts we pulled.

Life isn't a video machine, sadly…and different happenings in our lives can't be re-wound. But if all that WERE true, I know one of those "tapes" that would be played plenty. And those fun, exciting days with our country cousins would come to life again!

Smart TV and Me -
Another Oxymoron

We knew her time was about up...squiggly lines all over the place...she was getting temperamental. She'd entertained us for years, but it was time for her to go. Our TV gave us the signal that she was finished and we obliged her. She was headed to the TV graveyard. Now, there's never a great time to replace something like a TV, but it had to be done.

The hubs and I researched, shopped, and finally zoomed in on a Smart TV. I still don't know what's so "smart" about it...maybe because I feel dumb every time I turn it on? That it's smarter than me? It has so many options, so many icons on the screen, so much stuff. It took a fella to come to the house to set it up, program it, and leave a manual for us to digest. There are no Cliff Notes with a Smart TV. No short cuts... You have to read the whole darn manual. All of this made me long for the days when installation meant you took the plug and stuck it in the outlet. Remember those days?

I remember, as a child, our TV was as much a piece of furniture as it was just a television. The finely crafted wood...the shiny finish...TVs had simple dials that were marked for channels 1-12, volume, and a fine tuning one for adjusting horizontal and vertical. So simple anyone could use it, but just because it said 1-12 didn't mean we had programs on every number. Back then there were three channels (five, if you got good reception for Dayton stations, too.). And don't count on the "vertical" or "horizontal" to make that big a difference unless you had a decent antenna. Poor reception, by today's standards, was the norm for many TV viewing nights. Oh, and it was in black and white.

We didn't have a color TV until later in the game. I remember being invited to a friend's house to watch "The Wonderful World of Disney" in "living color" (versus "dead color?" What did that even mean?) Well, it didn't matter. For one night, I was able to witness a program in glorious living color." Television viewing was never going to be the same again. I remember even being a bit jealous when I had to return to the old black and white television at our house.

It's funny... we had fewer channels to pick from, but some of the best programming in TV history were on those few channels. And we had one television, which made whatever room it was in a central gathering place for family and friends. TV viewing was an event that was shared and talked about. Even the commercials were enjoyed. Some days I miss that.

I know...I get the warm fuzzies, thinking about television in the past. You can't deny that on today's TVs, the reception...the features, like starting and stopping programs so you can view at your leisure...the vibrant colors... are all terrific. But some days, I just wish the new TVs didn't have to be so "Smart" about it.

The Top 40 Countdown

I was messing around with my iPhone, downloading some music, and that got me to thinking of the advancements in technology, where music's concerned. I don't know how it all works but it's really something... you can "drag" a song from one place, like my iPad, to my MP3 player. Amazing!

It hasn't always been that easy. I remember, as a young girl, going to music stores or the record section at a department store, with my hard-earned allowance in hand, ready to purchase the latest hit. That "45" or "single" would be played over and over on our record player, to the point of our being sick of it within the week...then we'd move onto another favorite song.

We seldom purchased albums... first, because they were pricey, and you had to play through some crummy songs before you got to the one you liked.

It's funny how, when you think back to a memory and that spawns another one. In this silly memory, I'm waiting with my sister, for the popular radio station, WSAI, to play the Top 40 - a countdown of the most popular music of our day. It took place on Saturday mornings. We were supposed to be cleaning our room, but in between the dusting and the straightening, we had another task to tend to. We'd take turns, writing down the names of the songs, as they were played. By the time our room was done, we'd have a list of the top records in the listening area. (The term losers wasn't used back then, but I'm pretty sure it would have applied in this instance.) What were we even going to do with that silly list?

Someone eventually got the idea to print the list, sell advertising space, and distribute the countdown sheets through music stores and restaurants... to boost record sales and sell whatever they were advertising. Shoot! We missed an opportunity! Instead of doing chores, we should've been hawking advertising and printing out our own lists! Who knows where we'd be today?

Really, we were glad someone came up with the concept and we were sure to pick up the "Top 40" sheet at Imfeld's Music Store or at The Country Kitchen when we were uptown. But cleaning our room sure wasn't as much fun as it used to be!

Princess Phones and Party Lines...

Anyone who knows me knows that I was slow to join the Smart Phone trend. I joke that "smart phone" and "Marysue," uttered in the same sentence was an oxymoron, much like Marysue and a Smart TV. They just don't go together. Now, don't go thinking I'm a Neanderthal. I finally have a smart phone, but I don't have to like it! The plan is that, should I need a phone when away from the real phone at home, it's there.

This got me to thinking how far we've come in the phone business. What now is a palm-sized accessory that goes everywhere with us, got its humble beginnings as a rather substantial item that was found in our homes. The phone in my childhood home was black, with a numbered dial, that hung on the wall in our dinette. That way, Mom could keep an eye on things in the kitchen or have a seat while conversing. She and Dad could also monitor who was on the phone and for how long. Yep, Twinbrook-22642. (Not sure why I remember our number!).

It was a big deal to have a phone in a bedroom and that didn't happen in our house for years-a real luxury. We didn't have to go any further than my grandma's house, though, for that luxury. She had phones in her bedrooms. One was the first princess phone I ever saw (in pink, no less.) The princess phone was sleek and pretty, and it had push button numbers, instead of that dial that we had at home. (How's THAT for new technology?!) I thought that was really something. A bedside phone! But, needless to say, that wasn't going to happen in OUR house anytime soon.

I'm old enough to remember party lines. Remember those? When we shared a phone line with someone else in town and you couldn't make a call until they were off the phone? Now, THAT was Neanderthal! And if you had a party line partner who was a blabber head, you were screwed! Luckily, the party line deal was short-lived in our house.

The next step to phone mobility was the cordless phone. What? You could be on the phone and actually walk away from it? No black curly cord to contend with. That was living! Next up came car phones...those dandy appliances that were about as big as your head and were wired into your car so you could chat away when en route to somewhere. Then answering machines came along, allowing us to be away from the phone and not miss a thing.

And soon came cell phones, smart phones, and don't even get me started on texting! With the earliest concept of a typewriter showing up in the 1700's (a precursor to texting) and telephones following in the 1800's, it seems to me we're going backwards! What's next? Smoke signals?

Fast forward to now. EVERYONE has a cell phone or a smart phone. Even young kids! They really have changed the way we live, but have they improved communication? With texting, sarcasm is easily misunderstood... and with a voice missing, are true feelings conveyed? And the appearance of self-importance, with everyone looking at their phones all the time, really bothers me. Having all calls (and texts) right there, at all hours of the day and night? To me, that's as bad as sharing a party line with a blabber head. Okay, I AM a Neanderthal! But I am a Neanderthal who loves face-to-face conversation. Getting away from being in touch ALL the time. Not having to be so "smart." Maybe those big old black wall phones weren't so bad, after all. Just sayin'...

How'd We Ever Make It?

A friend of mine recently posted a picture of an old station wagon on social media and wrote about how there were no seat belts in our cars, years ago.

That got me thinking back to family car trips and how different things are now. We have these spacious vehicles, equipped with seat belts, air bags, laws about car seats for kids. All of these have made a difference in the number and severity of injuries and one must ask...how'd WE ever make it?

I remember our family of seven, piling in a sedan for our trips...always three in the front - four in the backseat. My baby brother would be sitting up front with the folks, in what amounted to a seat made of a steel frame, with a thin plastic covering the thin seat. And what would protect his sweet face, in case of a fast stop, or heaven forbid, an accident? Oh, that would be a play plastic steering wheel, complete with a red rubber horn in the middle! Yeah, like that would save him! A far cry from the requirements now that have kids sitting in infant seats for years!

Once my brother outgrew that car seat, he had to join us in the back, while the oldest sister took her place, upfront with the folks, minus the baby seat, of course. And with no seat belts...

I remember, like it was yesterday, how my brother used to stand in the back directly behind my Dad - and good thing! There wasn't any more seat room for one more kid to sit! But standing in a car would be a no-no these days, for sure! And with good reason.

I also remember so clearly some of the tiffs that would take place, no doubt because of the cramped condition of the backseat occupants. I don't recall Dad ever threatening us with, "Do you want me to turn around and go home?" Or "If I have to pull over, somebody's gonna get it!" But I DO remember the swinging-arm-of-the-law, a maneuver, perfected by Dad, that would have his arm, hanging over the seat, ready to crack the leg of the instigator. He didn't have to use it often -maybe someone had the audacity to cross into somebody else's space or an argument ensued over whose turn it was to sit by the window. But I'm no dummy and for the better part of two years, I'm pretty sure I sat on my feet every time we got in the car. "Hah, foiled ya, Dad! Swing away!" (Yeah, like I'd have said -or even THOUGHT it!)

As the years went on, and we kids got older, the number of "riders" in Dad and Mom's car diminished...no need for "the-swinging-arm-of-the-law" and still no seat belts in the car...I really do have to ask, "How'd we ever make it?" But I certainly feeling blessed that we did!

Music to Someone's Ears....

Is anyone else paying attention to the voices of the youngsters on shows, like "The Voice" or "American Idol"? I'm talking, 12, 14, 16-year olds! Where are they coming from?

The way they handle a song is way, way beyond their years. I am always amazed when I hear that kind of talent.

It's a far cry from when my sister and I would stand on our basement steps, singing "Johnny Angel" using hairbrushes as microphones. Sorry to out you, sister, but we were AWFUL! We would have heard "You were pitchy" all over the place back then. We would've been told to keep our day jobs by one of the meaner judges of those shows. But you know what? It wouldn't have silenced us!

To this day, music lightens my mood and singing along to an oldie is sometimes just what I need. My voice is thinner now -they say as we age, that happens - (and might I add, that's the ONLY thing that has thinned as I've aged!) but I can still sing in the car or the shower with the best of 'em!

I'll never be on a singing talent show...I've resigned myself to that fact. Hmmm...maybe "Dancing with The Stars" will call?

If
They
Only
Knew...

I remember how much fun watching TV was, as a kid-still in pajamas, eating cinnamon toast, drinking chocolate milk, and watching Captain Kangaroo, Uncle Al, or Saturday cartoons. In the afternoon, when Mom would be ironing, we'd watch game shows, like "Beat the Clock" or "The Match Game." In the evening, after the dishes were done, our family would gather around the set to watch comedies and variety shows like "I Love Lucy" or "The Ed Sullivan Show"...or dramas, like "Perry Mason" and "Gunsmoke."

Back when we were kids, the TVs weren't much bigger than a microwave is now. We had, maybe four TV stations, and those were made possible by an antenna or rabbit ears that we had to manipulate to get a clear picture. After the news, those stations would go off the air until the following morning. And black and white TVs were what most of us had... getting a color TV was a sure sign that you had arrived.

Don't those memories beg one to ask the question, "When did things become so different?"

We have big beautiful screens now - cable, satellite, or dish - that assure us bright, clear and colorful images. The technology is astounding. Countless channels that allow us to watch something any hour of the day or night, but is it any better?

Looking back can trick us into thinking that things were better -even when they weren't. I get that. But many nights now, we surf through so many stations, just hoping that something worth our time, is on. And did we ever think we'd be paying to watch television? It used to be the initial outlay of cash for a TV set and the little you had to pay for the electricity to power it, was all it took. Now, some TV viewers pay as much every month for the privilege of watching TV as they do for their utilities. And for what?

I know there is some terrific programming out there now. But, to me, reality shows, TV shows with outlandish story lines, and countless reruns and copy-cat shows are more the norm. It just seems we pay more for less now.

I think it's kind of funny that our kids will look back on these current times as their "good old days." If they only knew...

Those Were the Days....

On a recent coolish July Saturday morning, I loaded the dog into the car for a visit to our town's Farmers' Market. It's become a part of my normal routine...supporting the local farmers and enjoying their fresh produce and baked goods. It gets us out for some exercise and some pats on the head from the vendors and other patrons-the dog's head, not mine.

The weather was so delightful that morning that we extended our walk - our city really IS a walkable town - checking out the new projects going on-the new businesses that have replaced the old-and thinking back.

When we walked past what used to be a favorite, former department store, the memories came flooding back. Oh, I'm glad that there's a new tenant there now. The malls, in outlying areas, pretty much guaranteed our department store's demise and to see it sit vacant was sad. But I sure do miss our town's anchor store.

I remember the excitement that came with the new store's arrival. Sure, we had Wilmer's, J.C. Penney's, Lerner's, Martin's and smaller shops, like Marilyn's and Russell's. But this was new! Three floors of newness! Even the iconic antique scale was left at the old Wilmer's store. Remember that thing? The placement of that scale was evil! After unsuccessfully trying to find something in the junior department in the old Wilmer's building, (seems I was never a "junior") I'd head down the escalator and there was that damn scale! Maybe it would've been more helpful to me, personally, if they'd placed it closer to the candy department! Ha!

Those were the days when stores had hosiery departments (my mother-in-law, Fran, worked there for years) before Leggs changed things forever in the pantyhose realm...the days of a bridal registry department, where, as a young bride, I let my wishes be known for shiny cookware, beautiful china, a fondue pot, and plush new towels...the days of the candy department, where delicious chocolates and old time candies were displayed behind glass...the days of a Formal Department, where Mrs. Wilder would kindly allow a high school girl to try on elegant dresses, all to her heart's content, knowing that that girl had no intention of buying...just imagining and pretending...the days of a jewelry department, where I could look and not afford the gorgeous pieces...the days of the perfume and makeup department (my personal favorite) where, if you hit it at a certain time, you might snag a free sample of something glorious. The days of a millinery department, (a fancy word for hats) where I tried them on, thinking I was someone glamorous, for just a few moments...the days of racks and racks of fashionable clothes for men, ladies, babies, juniors, (Boo!) and kids.

As I was walking the sidewalks in front of the store on that recent July morning, my mind went back to the annual promotion of Old Fashioned Days, when the employees would dress in vintage clothes and prices were slashed. And when the stores, sidewalks, and streets were full of shoppers.

Fast forward to now. Our town is enjoying a rebirth. We'll not have the department stores of old- I know that - but we have a newness again, much like the newness of that new department store, but this time, a reinvention of what's needed in this town. A youthful energy that was missing is back.... and good for us!

But, on that coolish Saturday in July, this old(er) broad sure was missing the "old fashioned days" when I was younger and that old favorite shopping destination - and my future- had so much in store.

The Old Filling Station

Who else remembers "Service with A Smile" when filling up the car with gas? When the filling station attendant rushed out to greet you? When he tediously cleaned the windshield with a squeegee and a cloth and checked the oil and the water in the radiator? Does anyone else miss that?

Oh, I get it! With more cars on the road, credit cards and everything else going self-service, it was only a matter of time. But it sure was nice, being able to sit in your car and be waited on, wasn't it? And as the years go by and the bones get creakier, it's becoming even more desirable.

I remember when gas stations were on many corners of the Lindenwald neighborhood I grew up in. Our folks, more than likely, knew the owners and their employees, by name. And many a high school fella had his first job pumping gas. These places were usually also the place where our cars were worked on...and our dads (and many of us) paid in cash.

I miss those days of driving over a tube that signaled the employee, with a bell, that you were there. I remember that tidbit because, when we'd ride our bikes near the Sohio station on Pleasant Avenue, we'd deliberately ride over those things. And it usually meant we'd be getting hollered at by the owner, who mistakenly thought he had a customer arriving. (Looking back, that was pretty bratty of us.)

You can never go back-I'm aware. But as I sit in my car now, it's because someone is in front of me, pumping their gas, not because I'm going to be waited on, like in the olden days. And I'll pull myself out of my car, stick my credit card in the slot, put the gas pump nozzle where it belongs, fill'er up and be on my way (a lot poorer than in the olden days, too, I might add!)

No human contact-just doing what's necessary to stay on the road. Do it yourself and be on your way. It has to be done; what else are you gonna do? But that doesn't mean I can't miss the sound of that bell, the greeting of a man who's truly glad to see me, and is ready to provide me with "service with a smile." And I DO miss that.

Uptown, Downtown.....

Being stuck in traffic on the main street of our town had me thinking back to the time when our town was such a bustling one. So many things to do and places to go. I know that, looking back, things seem better and look bigger, but that's not always the reality. But in the case of my hometown, it truly is.

A lot of my memories are centered...well...in the center of our town. Some called it uptown, some called it downtown. It didn't matter. It was such a vibrant place...back then.

I remember, so well, the city busses that would take us all over the place. Riding with my mom, as a child, I remember how she'd let me pull the rope that would signal the driver that our stop was coming up. Once uptown, the countless stores awaited our business. Dress shops, movie theaters, lots of restaurants, department stores, and drugstores all lined the street of our thriving town.

I'm not sure why, but I vividly recall the fragrance of roasting cashews when we'd enter the Sear's store in search of bargains. Their candy counter was next to the escalator that we HAD to pass to get to the second floor and that usually meant a small bag of candy for me. On to Penney's, where I remember waiting impatiently, in the fabric department, while Mom pored over the bolts and bolts of material, just hoping she'd pick SOMETHING so we could move on. Occasionally, we'd pay a visit to the more upscale Martin's or Robinson Schwinn (where I saw my first elevator attendant- can you imagine THAT job? As a claustrophobic, it certainly wouldn't be on my list of Career Day choices!) A special treat, before boarding the bus for home, was a cold Coke at the lunch counter of one of the five and dime stores on the main street of our town.

When we were pre-teens, riding the bus uptown was the first real breaking away from home for a lot of us. Leaving the safe neighborhood that we grew up in, for parts of town that were different, was a big step. A group of girls on our own, without supervision, going uptown gave us freedom that had us spending our allowances and our babysitting earnings on things with little approval, except of those we were with. "Should we go to Imfeld's Music Store to buy a Beatles record? Or maybe Woolworth's for that pretty shade of lipstick we had seen in "Seventeen" magazine?" If I'd had a very lucrative week at babysitting or had managed to save up some loot, (something that seldom happened!) maybe I could I spring for that sweater in Miller-Wohl's window? Or was the one at Wilmer's cuter? We'd compare our purchases when we all sat down in a booth at Country Kitchen, a hangout, where we felt more mature, just stepping in the door. Every booth had a small jukebox, which, thinking back, was kind of silly. Sure, you got your choice of tunes, as long as you didn't mind hearing your Beach Boys song, mixed in with Aretha Franklin and Petula Clark , the choices of your booth-neighbors. After sharing fries and a Coke, laughing and talking, we'd step outside to the bus stop for our ride home.

As a young Mom, the city busses lost their significance to me-and to a lot of other folks. Driving uptown with kids in tow and running into a store, for this or that, replaced the carefree fun of making those frivolous decisions about lipstick and records. And when the big malls came along, the shoppers followed, the stores we frequented as kids closed and our fine city center hasn't been the same since.

And I hate malls for that. I probably shouldn't be so hard on them. They were new and shiny and they offered everything one could want or need-something our "downtown" or "uptown" could no longer do. Maybe something new will come along and malls will be replaced by something else and the kids who enjoyed them will mourn their demise, too. Life's like that. We think our memories are the best, that our pasts are richer because of certain events or places. But it would be hard to argue that my town wasn't the absolute best in its day! And I truly miss it.

Where Are All the Kids?

I asked myself that question when I was driving through our neighborhood on a recent summer day. The weather was way too nice for them to be inside. Where were they?

I know that, today, so many Moms have to work. Not for frivolous things, not for personal fulfillment, but just to make ends meet. And that makes me sad.

I, along with most of the kids I grew up with in the 50's and 60's, had stay-at-home Moms-and I always felt very blessed. Sure, we had some pre-women's lib pioneers, but for the most part, our Moms were home all day. And that made for a terrific childhood!

Life was a lot simpler then. Dads went to work, the kids did their chores, and then were outside most of the day. Most of the homes in our neighborhood had three or more kids per house. It was a lively neighborhood, for sure!

There were kickball games to be played, lemonade stands to be tended, doll carriages to be pushed with our neighbor friends, bikes to be ridden... Oh, it wasn't always Utopia though- we were kids, after all. Sometimes, disagreements would break out and the lines would be drawn. But the three kids who weren't getting along with three other kids one day would eventually make up and the next tussle might have a totally different group of kids siding with former enemies against their former friends. We were kids and we worked it out.

It seems that there was always something to do in our neighborhood. If it was just sitting around, talking about what we were going to do the next day, we were outside. Later in the day, we'd all head home for dinner, and with that behind us, the kids would be back out for more fun. Playing dodge ball, spud, jump rope, catching lightening bugs...then the street lights would come on-the universal signal that it was time to say, "So long" and head for home. But we knew that tomorrow would offer more of the same-neighborhood kids and good times.

Back then, everyone knew their neighbors. And we looked out for one another. If you were getting into something that wasn't approved of, it wasn't unheard of to get a correction from a neighbor kid's mom. And that was okay.

Now, I'm not saying that today's home lives and neighborhoods aren't terrific- it's just different now. But I feel so fortunate that I grew up when I did. I'm sure this all sounds very corny to those who didn't. Kids today are so advanced, compared to the goofy kids that I called friends. But I wouldn't trade those years, those friends, those times, those memories, for anything in the world.

The Wife Years

I've written plenty about The Hubs, the man who has made me laugh for forty-eight years. We've hit a few bumps, thru the years, but we always emerge the better for it- mainly because of humor. He's my rock and I'm his pillow. He has propped me up plenty and I've softened his edges a bit through the years.

Forbidden Love

I want to tell you a story of forbidden love- a love story that would probably not take place today, but should serve as a lesson of not being too judgmental of others.

You see, I married my schoolteacher. Well, I didn't actually have him as a teacher, but he was a teacher at the school where I was a student. GASP!

Now, remember, this was forty-eight years ago-a different time, for sure. I hadn't planned on it happening, but it did. He was a friend of my oldest sister and, in that role, I didn't much care for him. But then something changed. And so it began-stolen looks, passed notes, sneaking around...

My parents were aware. They knew my future husband because of his friendship with my oldest sister and thought he was a good guy. Now, remember this was a different time. I always admired the way my folks handled all of this. I also was grateful for the way the high school principal handled everything when our secret was finally out, one month short of my graduation. The priest/principal ended up being the celebrant at our wedding and was probably very relieved that his decision to handle it the way he did, resulted in a forty-eight year (so far) marriage.

Like I said earlier, ours is a love story that probably wouldn't happen today. And we joke that hubby would be getting out of jail, right about now, had it happened in another time. But I sure am glad no one interfered because we've had a terrific life. We have three sons, two daughters-in-law, and grandkids who bring us so much happiness. And I can't help but think how different their life stories would be if that teacher and this gal had never taken a gigantic leap of faith and that chance on "forbidden love."

In Sickness and In Health

Funny, how when you're first starting out in a new marriage, you seem to be more focused on "the "health" part....as it should be... and if you're lucky. You have time for the "sickness" part later...much later...as it should be...and if you're lucky.

Funny how, for us, "much later" is here already! Not sure how it snuck up on us so fast, but here we are. As it does for everyone, eventually, we've hit a bit of a rough patch - the hubs required some serious surgery. Years of football, years of carrying me, years of living...who knows? But some repairs had to be made.

Happy to say, because of a terrific doctor, awesome technology, and sheer will on the hubs' part, he came through everything like a champ. But the ordeal had me counting our blessings... that "the sickness" part has taken this long to get here, that what we have, truly, is a partnership, and that our kids will be there, "in sickness and in health", too.

Anyone who knows my hubs, knows that he's a tough guy when he needs to be. I've always appreciated the fact that he has my back, (no pun intended) but as kind of my protectorate. Our roles will be reversed for awhile (only TEMPORARILY, if he has a voice in the matter) as I've taken on my new role as Nurse Ratchett, that witchy character in *One Flew Over the Cuckoo's Nest*. It isn't a role I relish, but one I'll happily assume, to get him back to full strength.

Loading up my Dad's old walker into the car for the trip to bring the hubs home was an unkind nudge that the years have indeed flown by. Oh, don't get me wrong. He's not ready to fold up the tent yet. "I'm in my prime, good as new," and "I'm just getting started" have been his mantras here of late. And no one should doubt him.

But this latest "wobble in the wheel" (another of his favorite terms) has me even MORE aware that life is tenuous-that life is fragile-and that family and friends' prayers, thoughts, concern and acts of kindness make the "in sickness" part of marriage, doable. Thanks for that.

That Ship Has Sailed

That's a term that's being used more and more around our house-and I don't like it-not even a little bit.

It was used recently by hubby, when he decided (after looking at a particular item) that he was questioning his need for it. "That ship has sailed," he said. I heard it and took it as an age thing-that we've given up and that it's not worth pursuing anymore.

But I guess, instead of looking at "that ship has sailed" as a term of resignation, I should look at it as a sign of acceptance-that we've had things so good for so long and that we can change things up-or not-and still be alright.

So what if I can't wear stilettos anymore? It was fun when I could. "That ship has sailed." Partying until the wee hours? Not appealing anymore. "That ship has sailed." And if our so-called "toys" are enough, why want for more? "That ship has sailed," too.

I'd like to think that we're both – the hubs and I - in charge, making decisions, planning and doing things on our own terms. There may be a whole lot of "ships sailing" around here, but we're still the captains of those ships, and that is alright!

Feeling Powerless

A recent power outage at our place brought it all home again – how dependent we are on things were so used to. It's a case of "You don't appreciate what you've got till you don't have it."

It was a fluky event - a falling tree took down a powerline in our neighborhood. It only affected about ten houses. So there we sat in a dark house on a Friday night with nothing to do. I'm not sure how our forefathers did it! Here we were- no TV, no Wi-Fi, no air conditioning, no fans. Typically, as a sleep aid, these two insomniacs have the place sounding like an airport, with all the fans running! Oh, I know we could've gotten in the car and gone out – if disconnecting an electric garage door didn't require a feat of strength that neither of us were up to, or if a nonworking hair dryer or a mirror in the dark bathroom could help me look presentable. Nope, we just sat here, wallowing in self-pity. This was a wasted evening.

Not so fast! The night had to have humor in it, right? Well, it didn't take long! For starters, when the power went out, the hubs was stranded in his electric recliner in the lay-back position like a bug on his back. He was stuck. When I finally stop laughing, it hit me that I'd be waiting on him all night if this wasn't a short-term thing. "May I get you anything, dear?" isn't my usual Friday night repertoire. Well, eventually, the hubs snaked out of the elevated chair that was holding him captive, with me being of no help. Aside from laughing at his odd moves, I also stupidly reminded him not to break the chair. "How is that being sweet and darling working out for ya?" said the hubs. We laughed it his being stuck, we laughed at his escape, we laughed at my lack of compassion.

Well, in addition to not being "sweet and darling," I'm obviously not the sharpest knife in the drawer, either. The hubs suggested I call the city to report the outage. Anxious to redeem myself for not being "sweet," I whipped out my new smart phone-the only thing with power in the house. "What do you mean? You don't provide service to Elizabeth Drive? Oh, you're in Hamilton, Montana?" Oh, for gawd sake! Well, after laughing at my error, I finally called the correct "Hamilton" to report our troubles (a smart phone apparently has to have a smart person using it to be effective) and after the hubs' initial eye roll at me, we laughed at how dumb the evening was going.

The outage wasn't going to be a brief one, so the hubs, tired and bored, decided to make good use of the darkness. He headed to bed, leaving me, alone with my dog and my own thoughts. As I sat there, in our dark family room, all by myself...no more laughing... no more joking around about our plight, I realized, it IS true. You don't truly appreciate something until you no longer have it....whether it's electricity...or a husband, who, after forty-eight years, can still make you laugh.

And tonight, I have a greater appreciation for both.

A Vintage Cookbook...a Vintage Woman

The things we learn online! I happened upon a vintage cookbook for sale, and after seeing the date of publication, I realized, right then and there, I'm "vintage!" (I know... sometimes, you have to hit me over the head with a hammer.) 1974. Finally, able to put into practice my home ec lessons. 1974. Two years after I took on my wifely duties and became the meal provider for this family. 1974. Years before microwaves simplified things. 1974. When McDonald's was still a treat. Yep, when I look at the young families who have upgraded from McD's to places like Applebee's and Chili's, I, indeed, feel "vintage."

I remember, first starting out in the kitchen, as a young bride, completely clueless, in spite of Ms. Hoffman, my home ec teacher's, finest efforts. I also remember being so anxious to use all of the new and shiny kitchen gifts we'd received at showers and for our wedding. I dove right in.

Anxious to please that first year of marriage (oh, I'm still anxious to please...just not so much...) I asked the hubs what some of his favorite things to eat were. He gave me quite a few ideas, so I was on my way!

I remembered him mentioning liver and onions. (I've never been a fan, but it was one of those "what we do for love" things) so I got out the dependable Betty Crocker cookbook (now "vintage") and prepared a delicious meal of liver and onions. And I prepared it the next week and the next week... After the third week, the hubs finally got up enough nerve to tell this young bride that, perhaps, liver and onions should be enjoyed maybe two or three times a YEAR, not weekly. I remember being kind of hurt - I'd mastered a recipe and now it had to go to the back of the recipe box. I don't think I've fixed liver and onions five times in forty-eight more years either. (That'll show him...criticize MY cookin'. Ha!)

I did the same thing with green beans. He said he liked 'em so that's what we had every other night. He finally put the brakes on, in a kind way, of course, letting me know that one can truly overdose on canned green beans. I wasn't sure what I was going to fix in their place.

Another bone of contention in the early years (and maybe the later years, too) was my failure to make meatloaf like his mom used to make. I could follow her hand-written recipe, to a tee, and "it still doesn't taste like my

Mom's." I miss my mother-in-law terribly - she was such a good person and a terrific cook - but I'm as good as he's gonna get now, so eat up, fella!

Don't even get me started with my early baking experiences! Those who know me, know that I don't bake! I'm creative, which works in cooking, but baking is scientific and mathematical, and I suck at science and math.

My first pie was a blueberry one....baked, not in a pie pan, but a baking dish! How was I supposed to know that a pie pan has a rim that flares out and you "crimp" the crust? And the baking dish I used had my crust standing totally upright! Last pie I ever made. Or the school bus cake I made to celebrate the start of school. Thought I'd get all cutesy, ice a sheet cake with "school-bus yellow" icing and put photos of the schoolboy and his brothers in the windows of the bus. Well, do you know how damaging on the psyche it is to have six-year-old, a four-year-old and a one-year-old, horse-laugh, uncontrollably, making fun of your efforts? I still hear mention of it, once in a while, and they're forty-five, forty-two, and forty now! Haven't baked a cake since!

Now, don't feel too sorry for the hubs and sons. We've all eaten plenty well through the years. And, after all, good food is good food; it doesn't matter the decade or the era. Kinda the same with the women who cook. A good woman is a good woman, "vintage" or otherwise... Yep, I'm going with that!

Liver and onions, anyone?

On the Road

I spent a week this summer on the road with the Hubs, and I realized, more than ever before, how much the times are changing....some for the good, some, maybe not.

The first tip-off... At a stop to get gas, naturally, I used their facilities. (At my age, I never pass THAT up!) There, on the wall, was a machine that dispensed condoms! I checked the door and yep! It said WOMEN. It's good that women are arming themselves these days, but wow! I guess they want to be ready for spontaneity. They've expanded their inventory at public rest rooms, for sure, because I remember when It was just cheap cologne, hairspray, and sanitary napkins - maybe I'm living too long.

As usual, I'm getting ahead of myself... Anyway, we were headed south for some relatives' weekend anniversary celebration, and my mate wanted to make sales calls along the way. I was ready for a little escape, so we packed up the car and took off...four days before the celebration. This was going to be great! Hope the spouse can handle me for four straight days in a car!

In getting ready for this trip, I realized pretty quickly one thing that HASN'T changed, through the years, is how easy it is for men to pack. Some golf shirts, a couple pairs of shorts, some clothes for his business calls and out the door. I think I packed everything I own. Sure, we had the anniversary celebration to dress up for. But who did I think we'd see, in four southern states, who would care what I was wearing? Not too bright, am I? Not bright, maybe, but I looked mighty fine, indeed! Ha!

There was the cooler to pack, the dog to board, the mail to stop - all my tasks, I guess, because he'll be doing the bulk of the driving. Who am I kidding? I'll not be driving at all. We'd be on the road for ten days or in an intensive care ward in the Carolina mountains! Come on! I know my role.

Used to be "me (or us) and the wind and the wheel." That's all changed! Now, with all the electronics, WIFI, tablets, and cell phones, we're never truly "away from it all," are we? But the hubs WAS doing business and those ARE the tools of the trade. The fact that I could keep up with the kids and grands was a bonus (don't want to get away from ALL of "it"!). But we need to get one of those universal adapters for all those gadgets. We had four or five different adapters that we wrestled over all week.

I'm happy to say that the trip was fun. Staying in different Smalltown, USA cities every night was interesting. I got to see how hard the Hubs works on the road, the anniversary party was wonderful, and our marriage is still intact after spending a LOT of time together-but, when we returned home, maybe we both needed a little getaway from our getaway....maybe just a little bit.

What
Are You
Waiting
For?

My husband was a teacher many years ago- and he was a good one. Deciding to leave the profession was probably one of the hardest decisions he ever had to make. Continuing to coach football for thiry some years made it less painful, but I know he missed teaching-and probably misses it, still.

In our house, we have tremendous respect for teachers. We raised two of them. And even though education has changed immensely through the years, the bottom line is still that those who are with our kids, day in and day out, in the classroom, have a huge impact on their lives.

This was driven home recently when the hubs and I were at a community function and what was a fun afternoon provided us with a very profound moment. We had the good fortune of running into a student and football player from hubby's past. (That's one of the nicest things about living in a community like ours. You run into folks you know, all the time...especially if you were involved in their lives or their kids' lives over a thirty-five year span.). This particular guy approached us, shook his old coach's hand and said (in front of those we were with,) "You know, Coach, you're one of four people who have made me the man I am. When others didn't think I'd amount to much, back in high school, and were writing me off, you challenged me to be more."

I don't think I ever said " 'Thanks.' So thanks." And then he was gone. Wow! Who knew?

So, I guess the message is this. If you're a teacher and you think for one minute that you aren't making a difference, you're wrong! You are! It may not be realized immediately, but somewhere down the road, you may find out, as my husband did, that you made a real difference to someone. And the second layer to this message is, if you feel a certain way about someone who has touched your life, in the classroom, in the workplace, or just in your everyday life, tell them! What are you waiting for? Feelings and words are powerful. They can make someone's day or change someone's life. You never know.

For one sunny day in July, I know that someone sure made an old teacher/coach feel good about his efforts those many years ago. Thank you for that.

A Wedding Do-Over?

I get a kick out of weddings-always have. The beautiful brides, the fabulous attire, the promise of a future together, the partying.... always been a fan. And this time of year, I think back to the hottest day of the summer of 1972...yep, our forty-eighth anniversary is coming up.

My own wedding was nice, but by today's standards? Oh, my...

Getting hitched in August was dictated by the fact that hubby was a teacher/football coach and the timing was right. The fact that it would be hotter than hell in the church and at the reception never entered our minds.

It may seem odd, but I never tried on a wedding dress. My Mom, who was a great seamstress, made my dress. I guess we knew what style would look good on me and went with that. (How's that for confidence in your Mom?) Maybe that's why I watch TV shows like, "Say Yes To The Dress." Those girls go on and on about finding the perfect gown. They parade around in several and choose the one that will "make their fairytale come true." (Well, ladies, it won't... Your "fairy tale" will take more work than picking out a wedding gown.) And maybe someone should tell the one bride on that show that the huge tattoo on her back kinda ruins the demure look she's going for!

Our wedding took place in a Catholic church, and the bridal party, made up of family members and friends, looked great. Missing was a sister who was seven months pregnant...she had to sit it out, as pregnancy wasn't a good condition for a bridesmaid back in the 70's. Seems silly now, doesn't it? She was and is my best friend - she was instead a "hostess" at the reception.

The girls in the wedding all wore white and carried a single red carnation. Simple but classy. The fellas looked a little hungover because the bachelor party took place the night before. There were no destination bachelor party weekends like there are today -unless you count the notorious (in the 70's) Newport, Kentucky a destination, where they bar-hopped to.

I wasn't kidding when I said it was the hottest day of the summer. And none of the places we'd be in were air conditioned. Having my hair done in the morning was a total waste of money. After the hair appointment, several of us decorated our reception site -a high school cafeteria! I looked like a drowned rat by noon and the wedding was at 1:30. Great!

The wedding turned out to be lovely...the reception, a fun affair, with people we loved, beer and pop, a band, the traditional cake, dancing - in that sweltering cafeteria!

And when the wedding was over, our old local paper, every Sunday, had write-ups of the weddings that took place the day before. Giving a detailed description of the bride's gown, the bridesmaids' dresses, even the mothers of the bride and groom's attire... It told the whole world where the couple was going on their honeymoon and what the bride would wear – (called the trousseau-a fancy word for the bride's going- away outfits.) Ha! (What was THAT about? And who cared?)

That day in August, in my hand-made wedding gown, with sweaty wet hair, was the beginning of forty-eight years of a terrific marriage- and I wouldn't change one moment of it. And I know my folks did the best they could in making our day special. But if I didn't think I'd look totally ridiculous in a white frilly dress and veil, I'm thinking I should have a wedding do-over. Whatcha think?

Electric
Knives
and
Fondue
Pots...

Funny how I get so nostalgic around the time of our wedding anniversary. I get to thinking back, how, as a young couple, we were so naive about so many things. At the top of that list was setting up our home. I was so clueless when it came to homemaking. Good thing they had such a thing as bridal registries!

I remember being guided thru the different departments at Wilmers/ Elder Beerman,

pen and papers in hand, checking off the wants and needs that were going to transform me into a domestic diva. Yeah, fat chance!

I was digging around, looking for nothing in particular, recently, and came across the booklet, that had listed in it, all the gifts we received for our wedding. It was truly a step back in time! And a lesson for future brides who are in the bridal registry phase of their wedding planning.

I think that my formal china pattern is beautiful and it's wonderful when I bring it out for the holidays, but really? One would think I had plans to entertain royalty when you see the serving pieces, the crystal, the chafing dishes that I accumulated! Nothing but the best for THIS bride! Whateverrr!

At the opposite end of the spectrum was my everyday tableware. I accumulated THAT at my local Liberal Supermarket. If my Mom spent a certain amount of money, she received a stamp. Once the card was full of stamps, we cashed it in for plates, cups, saucers, etc. So that's what we had....Liberal Supermarket ironstone... the pattern was orange and yellow sunflowers. It served us well for years.

We received three electric knives (I thought the reason for registering was to avoid duplication?) We were married twenty years before I cooked a turkey - we were blessed to enjoy family Thanksgiving dinners elsewhere - so that gift was unused for years. It did, however, come in handy when I had to cut foam for a kid's Halloween costume.

Fondue pots were all the rage back in the early 70's. I registered for one and received two to match the Harvest Gold kitchen appliances we had on order. Nothing like making your guests work for their appetizers! Between moves, I must have lost the long forks that came with the pot - that, or maybe our guests just got lazy and I actually had to start serving them...either way, no more fondue parties at the Wright Place!

Popcorn poppers must have been new and cutting edge back then, as we received three of them, as well. (Hey, someone went off the registry and bought one at K-Mart! THAT's why we got more than one!) Well, it sure beat "Jiffy Pop" popcorn- and microwaves weren't invented yet.

Add to all that an iron, an ironing board, tons of towels, sheets, picture frames, blankets, a multitude of other gadgets, gifts and cash, and we were on our way to domestic bliss.

My advice to young brides is this. Take it easy on the bridal registry. You'll develop your own style and tastes, they'll change thru the years and you'll have a lifetime to accumulate things that fit. And if you have a need for an electric knife, a popcorn popper or a fondue pot, don't register for it. Call me instead!

Our First Nest

I was perusing the real estate ads and, of course, that took me back to a simpler (and less expensive) time. Forty-eight years ago to be exact. That was when the hubs and I were getting ready for our wedding and our life together. That, naturally, would require a place to live-and since our folks weren't begging us to stay with them...(no kidding?) we needed to get busy. Buying a house was out of the question; what were we going to do?

Fate was smiling on us, as my sister and her husband were getting ready to buy a house. Talk about luck! The place they had rented was going to be available! They had lived in a charming farmhouse in a farming community that was on the cusp of tremendous growth. And it was going to be OURS!

Not so fast. We had to meet the landlords and they had to give their approval. They were an elderly couple who lived in a farmhouse adjacent to the one we hoped to live in. I wasn't sure how they were going to feel about us. They loved my sister and her husband, but that was "them" and this was "us."

The meeting time was set, we introduced ourselves, and we were welcomed into their home. Very sternly, the woman said, "It will be $100.00 a month, no children, and no pets." Now, this was for a four bedroom house sitting on a beautiful piece of land! Are you kidding me? Kids and pets weren't in our immediate future so YES! YES! YES!

Our wedding took place and we settled into life, as newlyweds, in our homey little nest. We became better acquainted with the landlords and they warmed up to the young couple who was fortunate to be their tenants. Pearl, who never had children of her own, was so kind to a young gal who couldn't cook. She shared her know-how in the kitchen, kept us in produce, and provided us with an occasional chicken that first year of married life. We would sit on their porch swing and listen to their stories about farm life from an earlier time, take them to an occasional appointment, pick up groceries for them when we went to the store-things neighbors and friends do. They were terrific people and we loved them.

Which is why telling Pearl and Bill the wonderful news that we were going to be parents presented us with a dilemma. "No kids allowed." We'd have to leave our dear, sweet neighbors. And where were we going to go?

We mustered up the nerve to go knock on their door. Pearl invited us in. She always had something sweet in the kitchen so we sat down...and before even taking a bite, I blurted out, almost crying "I'm pregnant... we wanted to tell you we'll be moving out. I'm so sorry." (I was apologizing for leaving them, tenant-less, not for being pregnant with my first son.) Anyway, we walked back to our place, not knowing where we would end up.

The next day, Pearl was outside, weeding, and when she saw me, invited us for dessert again that evening. We went over and certainly weren't prepared for what she said next. "Bill and I discussed your situation last night and made a decision. We'd like you to stay."

"Are you kidding us? Thank you! Thank you!"

"We also decided", she said, "that you'll be needing money for the baby, so we want you to pay $90.00 a month for rent. You put that $10.00 to good use, now, hear? " Now, who DOES that? We were overwhelmed by their kindness, mumbled our thanks, and went home to our place.

We had our first son, managed to save up a small down payment for a starter home in Lindenwald, and eventually left that cozy farmhouse in Fairfield. Pearl and Bill are gone now, so is their farm and our first "home." It's funny-people come into your life and, with an act of kindness, become indelible in your memory. That's how it is with Pearl and Bill. They impacted our lives in a way they probably never even realized. Not just the monetary thing, but they showed a young couple, just starting out, how far-reaching an act of kindness can go. Forty-eight years... And I'm STILL grateful for their example.

Couches and Sofas...

The hubs and I purchased a new sofa recently and you're thinking, "So what? Why write about it?" Well, I guess the reason is because I've taken some flack for the substantial number of sofas and couches that have found their way into our home. I get it! There have been plenty in our forty-eight year marriage, but there has always been a reason or a story.

As a newlywed, I chose, for our first home, a beautiful sofa with a cream background and big blue flowers. Of course, my Mom advised against it ("it'll show dirt") but, of course, I knew everything back then and ignored her advice. Turns out, Mom was right - baby spit-up stains and the sweat of the hubs' basketball-playing friends were hard to mask on a cream-colored background. Next up, we were blessed to receive a couch from my sister's mother in law. Nothing I'd have chosen, but glad to have it back in the early days of parenthood. That was the sofa that had the happy memories of fort-building and cushion fights, by the boys, attached to it. Next up was when a Lady Sylvia Furniture truck pulled up to our house and delivered a couch that my Mom surprised us with. Total shock, but much appreciated as we had three boys, under five, and a sofa would've been a frivolous purchase for these cash-strapped parents.

Then, came a new house, so, of course, we needed a new sofa. And when we moved yet again, I really thought we'd arrived when a sofa AND loveseat entered our home. And then another. (The hubs has never forgiven me for allowing THAT one to take its place in a son's home - "Most comfortable damn sofa we ever had!") And then a couch, that seated friends and family for happy and sad occasions with a sleeper sofa, that all three grandkids fit in for sleepovers- and another couch, and another... I've lost track. Truthfully, life was a blur back then. High school kids, reentering the workforce, sports seasons, the boys' college years (Oh, yeah - one of our sofas made it to college! The dorm room of a friend of a son.) So, who's countin'?

What I've neglected to mention is that many of these purchases were because of a need to replace, not some goofy housewife's need to redecorate. Not sure if this is true in your house, but I have come to the realization that boys tend to "plop" when sitting down. No easing onto a seat around here. No sir! And the wrestling and horseplay took its toll on furniture around here, too. Sorry, boys - I needed a scapegoat here because it IS ridiculous, my history with sofa-buying!

This is the last one we'll be purchasing. I promise. It's comfortable -for those nice naps I love. It's practical and durable - I welcome the spit-up stains of grandkids. It's sturdy -because I don't care what they say - they STILL plop! And it will offer us comfort and relaxation in our more sedentary lives now. (Ever hear of "Jeopardy?" Yawn...yeah, we watch it.) This sofa is beautiful and sturdy and comfortable - all the things one looks for in a sofa , but it sure won't have nearly as many fun memories attached to it as the many others that have preceded it.

"Honey, wanna build a fort?"

I Haven't the "Remote-st" Idea!

So, who died and made the male species the main controller of the TV remote? Does that convenient tool always end up in the hands of a guy in your house? I have to say that ours is a 75%- 25% split most of the time... with the hubs maintaining possession the most. And why is that?

Someone once said that "Men are hunters and women are nesters." That's probably true, when applied to our TV remote. Hubby tends to flick through the channels, hoping to find something better than what he just had. I, on the other hand, tend to "nest." I find a show I like and stay there. Maybe it has something to do with attention spans. I don't know...

And I get that HGTV or the Food Network isn't his idea of interesting viewing, but who said football games or countless repeats of movies like

Tombstone or *Gangs of New York* interest ME? Oh, that's right! He has the remote!

Separate rooms with TV's and DVRing -a great service offered by our cable provider - have made our living together a bit more peaceful, but I refuse to give up my custody battle for the main remote! One day, maybe I'll get to have it every other weekend.... We'll see.

Bad Decisions Make Good Stories

"Bad decisions make good stories." Suffice it to say, I have some good stories.

Some of my bad decisions weren't life-changers, (although I was sure our marriage was in jeopardy a few times) but make for some good stories. Let's share.

A bad decision was thinking, early on, that I was qualified to tackle home projects beyond my talents. I usually waited until the hubby was out of town on business to try my hand at home improvements. Seemed easier to "seek forgiveness than ask permission."

There was the time I tried to "pop" a ceiling, which entailed applying a heavy mud-type plaster and using a special brush, creating a design in the ceiling. It was supposed to hide cracks and imperfections, not end up looking like Mammoth Cave, complete with stalagmites, seeming to drip from the ceiling. Our room dimensions changed, too, it seemed, going from nine foot ceilings to eight and a half. That project was pretty hard to hide!

Or the time I painted bathroom tiles...I failed to mention to the paint store guy that the tile was plastic, not ceramic, so he sold me acetone to "rough up the surface so the paint would adhere." How was I to know that acetone melted plastic? I had a vase of flowers, placed very strategically, that hid that mess for three years!

Or the spring I decided we needed a pond in our yard... I purchased the heavy plastic, had large stones loaded into the trunk (who knew a car had a suspension system?) bought a pump that would create a beautiful spray or trickle down like a waterfall. I was all set to start! Would somebody tell that crazy woman how much dirt has to be dug for a pond the size she has planned? Or that there are different sizes of pumps and the one she bought was going to shoot water all over the front porch? I knew I was in over my head on this one and my dear Dad came to the rescue.

There was a time, I think, that my sweet husband was afraid to leave home. And keep in mind this was before the days of HGTV, a TV network that encourages my kind of behavior. I haven't learned my lesson yet, 0but my projects aren't as frequent as they used to be. Aging and physical limitations are one reason... or maybe I have more common sense now. Nah, it's because hubby doesn't go out of town as much as he used to. "Can I pack your bag, honey?"

48 and Counting

Not sure where the years have gone, but I'm happy to say, the hubs and I have made it to our forty-eighth wedding anniversary! There was never a doubt in my mind that we would, as long as the good Lord kept us around that long. We've been a good team. We each have our strengths and weaknesses and the peaks and valleys that everyone experiences in marriage always seemed to level out for us.

We come from the days of punch bowl bridal showers, church-basement receptions, ham sandwiches and beer... and car trip honeymoons. Yes, weddings are certainly different now. But I think of our wedding back in 1972 and just smile

Because...

Who else got yelled at by their dad for staying out too late at her bachelorette party? Not some trip to Nashville...nope, just some gals, meeting at Waldo's Supper Club for drinks, the night before the wedding. Woo hoo! (In defense of my dad, I DID have mono the two weeks before the wedding and he thought I needed more rest than I thought I did.)

Who else has a wedding album of 4 x 6 photos, taken by a friendly fella who took wedding pictures only as a side gig? Nothing staged...or romantic. Just pics of folks having a good time. Nothin' wrong with that!

Who else had their wedding reception in August, in an un-air-conditioned school cafeteria? The bride's hair was plastered to her sweaty head... not some wind-blown long-haired beauty in a bridal magazine. No siree! We're talking drowned rat!

Who else spent their wedding night in Middletown, Ohio, with their hubs' college buddies? The newly formed Bengals had such a following back then, that hotel rooms from Cincy to Dayton were scarce. The hubs, being the accommodating gent that he is, suggested our hotel to his friends. Our honeymoon next door neighbors were the fraternity brothers of Theta Xi. Top THAT for romance!! Ha!

Who else had a one-night honeymoon? Because of the aforementioned mono, I had to be back at work on Monday, after the Saturday wedding. Bummer...

I'm not capping on the way things are these days. We've had some terrific weddings in our family and among our friends in recent years. It's just the way things are done now are vastly different than the way they were done forty-eight years ago. All were celebrations of love, and the current ways are just a normal progression of things, I suppose. And I'm not criticizing my folks. God knows, they had four daughters to get married off, in a span of about seven years. It's just that, forty-eight years ago, more emphasis was on our marriage than the wedding-obviously! And I'm more than okay with that! Forty-eight years with someone I actually like AND truly love is perfect-even if our wedding weekend wasn't.

2020 and Life Is Still Good...

I suppose it's a milestone-maybe a sign of someone getting older, I don't know- because it's so foreign to me. (Not the "getting older" part- I'm very familiar with that! The following is foreign to me.

For the first time in forty-seven years, New Year's Eve found me at home with my husband, alone. No disco balls, no fancy menu, no loud energetic crowd. Just the two of us. And I surprised myself with being happy with that. We have always gone out for the notorious party night, but this year, we were content to stay in.

For so many years, we worked on dance committees that had us having as much fun getting ready for the big night, as we did for the night itself. The school cafeteria would be transformed into a beautiful venue. Bands or DJs kept us moving (and the alcohol made us less inhibited, of course.)

There was a year when we prepared dinner for another couple. It was when we had wee, little ones and it was easier to just let the kids have at it, instead of the adults. But other than that night, we were out. There were a few New Year's Eves that had us going a bit more upscale and landed us at reception halls. The same group of friends, enjoying each other, delicious food and again, the alcohol. Some years, the food and drink were provided by friends in their basements, for a more intimate, less rowdy night. A few years, we even rented our own hall and partied on.

Those days of partying had us lining up babysitters months in advance, finding the perfect outfit to wear, taking longer than usual to get ready. (I remember one year, I even donned fake eyelashes! What was THAT about?) I don't remember even one year when we didn't have the best time!

Those were great nights...wonderful memories. But you know what? Being with the most important person in my life, alone, was alright, too. The clock still struck midnight, the new year still began, and life is still good. Happy New Year, everyone!

P.S. And am I feeling better (less hung-over, less tired) than 80% of you partiers? Yep, life is good.

Another Cockeyed Blessing...

For as long as I can remember, we've had a snoring problem in this house and as we're getting older, it's getting worse! Some nights, it's subtle and occasional; other nights, it's loud and constant. The noises sometime cause me to head to the couch with my pillow and blanket in tow. Now I'm not saying that the hubs is the only culprit. I may be guilty, too. I can't say for sure, because if I'm snoring, I'm sleeping - no way of knowing...

It's gotten to the point that I decided to look into snoring's causes and possible remedies.

I have learned that "snoring is the vibration of respiratory structures and the resulting sound, due to obstructed air movement during breathing while sleeping. In some cases, the sound may be soft, but in other cases, it can be loud and unpleasant." YA THINK? "Snoring is known to cause sleep deprivation to snorers and to those around them, as well as daytime drowsiness, irritability, lack of focus and decreased libido." REALLY?

They offer up all kinds of reasons -none of which sound pleasant or fun -except the part about alcohol consumption being a possible cause. And remedies? Think we'll pass on the machines and surgeries. It's not THAT bad.

I guess if I have no other complaints about life with the hubs, I sure am fortunate. I think the only thing worse than hearing him snore would be NOT hearing him snore. Snoring-another cockeyed blessing. Who knew?

Looking for Love in All The (W)right Places

Those who know me know that, although I'm not resisting this aging thing, I'm not exactly embracing it either. Some days, I still feel like I could kick the world's arse; other days, you'll find me curled up on the couch with the dog and an afghan. But I do feel blessed that I CAN do either. My choice.

I'm blessed, too, for now, with good health and I don't take that for granted for one minute! After a bit of a rough patch with the hubs, we're now counting our blessings for the amazing technology of replacement parts for humans. Yep, we made it to another spring, none the worse for wear.

I guess, when we're younger, we take so much for granted. Not anymore! I'm trying to concentrate on savoring every day. Hanging onto whatever goodness there is. Some days, it's harder to find the positives- more than it used to be, anyway. But luckily, the years have blessed me with a quirky way of looking at things...and it's turning out to be a handy coping mechanism when it comes to all things "aging."

For instance.....

It's kind of romantic when I'm sorting laundry from the clothes dryer, and a hint of static electricity has my unmentionables entwined with the hubs' undies. Okay, maybe not romantic to you - but you have to grab what you can, right? Plus, it reminds me of the time the hubs removed his shirt at the doctor's office, only to have a pair of my static-y undies stuck to his back. He was plenty steamed when he got home - then we laughed....

I've found that the diminishing vision that comes with getting older also comes with some benefit. It's harder for the hubs to see my wrinkles or an occasional stray chin hair (I like to think that's why God gave me sisters and women friends… to point them out..) It's also harder for us to see dust balls roll across the floor, so cleaning can be postponed for one more day. And sometimes, we wave to folks we're sure we know only to find out that we DON'T. Just makin' the world a friendlier place, I guess. And we laugh...

Although the hubs now has "hearing assistance" and I expect I won't be far behind, as I sometimes don't hear like I used to. The hubs always called it "selective hearing." For me, it's more a lack of focus. But I won't allow it to get so bad that an "I'll turn the overhead fan on" is misunderstood and gets an "I love you, too" in response. (True story) - and we laughed.

DVRing has come at the perfect time in history for us baby boomers, don›t you think? Too tired to stay up to watch Dateline? Need an afternoon nap and don›t want to miss the noon news? No worries...we just record it! We can watch programs in half the time as before, by zipping through all the annoying commercials about toilet paper and medical plans. (Not sure why we're "zipping" through anything! It's not like we have THAT much to do at bedtime....) But we laugh...

I hope the hubs and I always have a sense of humor about our lives and our love. In fact, I hope the way I depart this world is either cuddled up with him or laughing with him about something dumb, like we so often do. Others may not get it - how after forth-eight years we still laugh and enjoy each other. But for me, it's easy. I'm just looking for love in all the (W)right places...and laughing.

Choot 'Em"?

For gawd sake! I swear, I don't know what the hubs sees in "Swamp People." It's that reality (?) TV show about a bunch of Cajun dudes out looking for alligators! I guess we have to get alligators somewhere for restaurant menus and shoe closets everywhere. But seriously, these guys with their grimy clothes, smelly looks, and their orders to "choot 'em" (Shoot 'em, in English) is enough to drive me wild!

I truly believe anyone who wants a reality show on TV these days can have one! Had I known we could've lived out our lives in front of a camera and made money off of it, it would've been "ACTION! Take 1!" But since I never had that knowledge, I guess I'm destined to watch the dumb things, instead.

Another one of the dumber shows that finds its way into our home is "Pawn Stars," a show about fellas who run a pawn shop in Vegas. I go nuts when one of the customers comes up to the counter, and says, "I'd like $500 for this rare item."

"I'll give you $50", says the proprietor.

"Oh, okay! I'll take it! Turns out Chumlee isn't the only asshat in that place! - A side note - I cringe when they mention "pristine condition" or "original box." We could've funded our retirement with Star Wars action figures and vehicles, had we kept them in that kind of shape. But ours were chewed up by whichever dog we had then, or pitched by old Mom, who was tired of picking the damn things up!

Speaking of pitching - I'm finding I'm not as anxious to pitch my OWN stuff these days - my collections of shoes, clothes, or chalk paint projects. Not sure if it's the desire to hang onto the past or if it's laziness at having to tackle the closets and basement. Luckily, "Hoarders" or "Buried Alive" aren't on the hubs' list of must-see TV or he may just be kicking me to the curb.

Another show you won't find us watching is HGTV's "Tiny House," the show that features folks looking to downsize to 200 square feet homes. I'm pretty sure the hubs and I would kill each other if we were in such close quarters. (But the place sure would be easy to keep clean!)

"The Alaskan Bush People" isn't a fave around here, but perhaps SHOULD be, as we're heading out on an Alaskan cruise in June and getting some background on that beautiful state would be good. I'm starting to question our sanity - like we didn't get enough snow and cold temps in the longest winter/spring in the history of weather? Maybe a Caribbean cruise would make more sense?

Oh well, now that the weather's nice around here, I can work in the yard, away from these dumb shows. I have this fear that if I'm inside and I hear "Choot 'em" one more time, I will say, "The heck with Troy and his gators! The HUBS might be MY target!"

I've better go clean a closet. See ya!

A Treasured Stradivarius?"

I've been grousing about yet another birthday and grumbling about how quickly time is going; we've become too set in our ways. Almost TOO comfortable. How it doesn't seem that long ago that we were a young couple, busy with raising kids, squeezing in time for ourselves whenever we could, and savoring our alone time. And then here we are! With an overabundance of "alone time."

I don't get so nostalgic, in a negative way, about my life very often, but this time, I was in a real funk. A dried-up old prune, destined to watch old episodes of sitcoms, taking meds, giving the dog an occasional pat on the head.

And that's when I remembered something the Hubs said a few months ago, when I was commenting about how it would be a fun time, in history, to be a young woman. He said, "Nah, the older the violin, the sweeter the music."

I was caught off guard by that because, I'm quite certain, that any fella with a pulse, takes notice when a younger, attractive gal is within view....and my husband, indeed, has a pulse.

I think, from now on, when I look in the mirror, and see a pouchy tummy, arm-wings where toned arms may have once been (Who am I kidding? I've NEVER had toned arms) and lines and wrinkles on my face, I'll remember that sweet thought..."The older the violin, the sweeter the music." And on my birthday, I can maybe even be a Stradivarius- the most treasured violin of all - at least, to the one who matters the most.

I'm No Expert...

"I always let him have my way."... That was the answer of a woman, married to the same man for eighty-one years, when asked the secret to having such a long marriage. I like the way that old gal thinks! Not that it works that way for me, (all of the time) but that woman may be onto something!

First of all, think about that! Eighty-one years! Geawd! They've probably started to look alike! That's twice as long as the hubs and me. I can't imagine! Now, don't get me wrong. I love the hubs of forty-eight years, but really? EIGHT-ONE? Holy moly!

This got me to thinking how all couples have their secrets as to why they're still married. And for anyone who cares about my take on things, here are mine:

1. Have a sense of humor...about EVERYTHING! It gets you through the tough times and makes the good times even better. We laugh a lot in our marriage. The hubs sometimes thinks he's funnier than he is, but it's better than being with an old grump, right? Another benefit of humor in a marriage, when you're falling apart and you don't look or move quite the same as you did years ago, it's not such a shock when he chuckles (or horse-laughs) at how you look and move NOW---and vice-versa.

2. Have two televisions. That way, you don't have to be subjected to his football games, "Walking Dead" marathons, or the thirty-seventh airing of "Tombstone." And he doesn't have to endure your chick flicks, cooking programs, or "House Hunters."

3. If kids are part of the equation, always present a united front...an "us vs them" attitude. Because, if I know anything, it's that kids can be little manipulators (so I've been told, Sons) and if they see a crack in the front, they'll pit one against the other, for sure. I love my sons, but the hubs was Numero Uno in our house-and I think I was, in his world, too. I've found, as everyone does, the kids leave and there you are. You don't want to live the rest of your life with a stranger.

4. Always make time for a date night. With the constant demands of jobs, running a household, and running kids all over, taking time out with your love is important. It gives you a chance to connect - and no talking about the kids, either. Your date should be about the two of you!

5. Make saying "Thank you" a big part of your marital conversation...both sides. An attitude of gratitude makes married life a lot more pleasant. And who doesn't want to feel appreciated?

6. The old adage, "Never go to bed mad" has merit. Now, you may get mad after you go to bed because of his snoring or her blanket-hogging, but don't start off your slumber being aggravated.

7. As you become an old(er) married couple, it's important to maintain outside interests, hobbies, friends. Staying engaged with people and staying current makes for better conversation with your spouse. It's nicer than just talking about the kids and grandkids and your aches and pains (of which, you'll find, there are many.)

This is just my non-expert perspective on the topic. If you were to ask "my rock" what HIS take on a lengthy marriage is, he'd probably say "honesty, candor, and a fear of alimony." (See what I mean about humor?) .

Now, I'm no marriage expert, that's for sure. Everyone has what works for them and you figure it out as you go. But for eighty-one years? That won't happen here, I'm pretty sure, and if it doesn't - what kind of alimony are we talking about?

Senior Madness

March Madness, that crazy time of year when collegiate basketball crowns its champion. And I can't help but think how big a role basketball has played in our family's lives.

Three sons played different levels from grade school to high school. Seems like Saturdays and Sundays, afternoons and nights, were spent sitting on bleachers and cheering on whoever was playing. Weeknights were for carpooling to sooo many practices. And it's not over yet - we still have one active in the sport, as a collegiate coach for a successful women's program. And the grandkids play basketball for their high school and junior high. We follow them when we can make the trek to Columbus and Zanesville. We've always been more of a football family, but that hasn't kept us from enjoying basketball a lot.

So much so that, back in the 80's, the hubs hosted The Seniors' Classic, a backyard basketball tourney that pitted two-men teams against one another. Made up of friends who had to be over thirty (yeah, can you imagine? We considered anyone over thirty "senior?") Guys who didn't play manned the grill. The wives cheered and performed drill team routines (ha!) and the kids ran around and played hoops, during halftime of the seniors' games. It went from morning until night-intense competition between friends, bruises, pulled muscles, broken eyeglasses-hardly worth the tee-shirt each fella had received at the start of the games.

I'd forgotten how much craziness went into the Seniors' Classic. We had a Walk of Fame, which one year had our dear old neighbor, Al Hinkel Sr, an annual spectator, being "inducted." An MVP was named every year - one year, the refrigerator repairman, a.k.a. the "Norge Man," who had to come and fix our fridge in the middle of the tourney, got the nod (probably because he insured that we'd have cold beer all day!) and "The Horse's Ass" award went to someone who was particularly obnoxious that day- or to an occasional referee.

The tournament ran five years; some guys played all five years. A few of the older ones bowed out to make room for younger "seniors." Some of those "seniors" are gone now - way too soon... most of us ladies couldn't do a kick line to save our lives these days, and the kids who ran around the yard back then are "seniors" now.

March Madness, in a Lindenwald backyard- too much beer, a lot of laughs, a few minor injuries, and so many memories...

What A Crock!"

Having just celebrated our forty-eighth wedding anniversary last month, I've been thinking of the many ways my husband has been my support system...my biggest fan and booster. No matter what I've wanted to do, he's always been behind me, cheering me on. Well, almost always...

We've had a joke around our house for a few years about him being a "Dream Squasher" about one of my ideas. And I owe him an apology. I can admit it now... "It" never would have worked.

I thought about this idea with my usual early enthusiasm. But the husband pointed out the errors in my thinking that would, probably, have had a profound impact on our marriage, our bank account, and my sanity (which is questionable to start with!)

Let's begin at the beginning, okay? I'm a soup maker; every weekend, you'll find a pot of soup, simmering on our stove. I don't think there's anything that says "warm and cozy" better. Doesn't matter if it's summer either. "Cozy's" good year-round. And I've been doing it for many years. Some have said I make good soup. All kinds. Veggie, Chicken Noodle, and White Chicken Chili are favorite, but Beer Cheese Soup, Buffalo Chicken Soup, and Taco Soup are gaining on them.

Well, several years ago, I thought it would be fun to open a soup kiosk in our downtown and call it "What a Crock!" The Hubs couldn't argue with the cleverness of the name, but he was quick to point out the holes in my business plan.

Number 1. I have no experience in the food biz and, from what I've been told, it's tough. You have to be there or have folks you trust there, in your absence.

Number 2. I lack "stick-to-it-tiveness." If I love what I'm doing, I'm good, but when it would become work? I don't know.

Number 3. The hours I wanted to operate. 11:00 to 1:00 weekdays. Pretty tough to make money if you're not open.

Okay, okay, I get it! The Hubs was right. (this time...) Lugging around and stocking a soup cart doesn't sound so great when I think of Ohio winters, the prime season for soup. Heck, my love for soup-making might even have been lost forever. And I certainly don't want that! But you gotta admit, "What a Crock" would've been a winner...at least, in the name department!

(Anyone interested in franchising opportunities, call someone else. But that name is MINE!)

Drinking the Kool Aid (It's Not What You Think...)

As happens in our house, when things get boring, the hubs and I will have dumb conversations that seldom lead to anything. Case in point...

He has a new addition to his drinking repertoire...It's called G2, a low calorie over-priced (I think) flavored water. I tease him that he must not have gotten his fill of grape Kool Aid, as a kid, because that's exactly what it smells like to me. And believe me, as a kid, I had my share of Kool Aid!

Kool Aid really was quite a novel invention, I found out online. (Many times, to prove my point in these dumb conversations, I search online and voila! There it is!). Anyway, turns out some fellow grew tired of paying the shipping costs of his liquid refreshment. This led the gentleman to develop a process that removed the liquid from his product and there you are! Kool Aid, that fruity powder that transformed a pitcher of water and a cup of sugar into cold summer refreshment for the entire family!

An envelope cost a nickel or a dime, in the early days of Kool Aid, and my Mom was a fan. There was no bottled water back then - if you drank water, it came from the faucet! Coca Cola or Pepsi was reserved for Saturday nights for the Bruner kids, unless we were at one of the Grandma's houses. She had an open fridge-door policy; if it was in there, we could have it! (Maybe that's where my Coke addiction-the cola kind-got its start.)

But I digress... As a kid, Kool Aid, in flavors of grape, cherry, lime, and orange, was a treat when we took a break from playing outside. It was also a potential money-maker when we'd set up a stand in front of the house. I'm pretty sure we never even recouped the expense of the Kool Aid and sugar because of slow sales (not much foot traffic on Allen Avenue..) and the free-bies we drank ourselves. But it kept us out of Mom's hair for a while, so she probably considered it money well-spent.

It was money, well-spent, for me, as a young Mom, too. Our boys were too active to man a Kool Aid stand for long, but it was a pantry staple in our house because of the price and the sheer number of boys who hung around the Wright Place. And even back then, Kool Aid was a topic of conversation - the boys (the hubs included) all claimed that my Kool Aid never tasted the same way twice (there's my failure to follow directions again!). "Then drink some water from the faucet," this outnumbered female would say.

It amuses me that something as simple as an over-priced flavored water can evoke such memories and discussions in our house. And about something as obscure as a childhood treat like Kool Aid. Go figure! I suppose I should be happy that a grape Kool Aid wannabe keeps the hubs home, happy and available for these silly discussions. I don't miss the Kool Aid days, but I'd sure miss HIM! So, what next? A discussion on the value of watching "The Wizard of Oz" over 100 times? That'll be a good one! Stay tuned!

Fall Means Football

Ah, the crisp air of Fall is almost upon us! And at the Wright Place, that means it's football season! Now, if someone had told me I'd be a football coach's wife and a football widow at the age of sixty-seven, I'd tell them they're crazy, but here I am, nailing it!

Being part of a great program for almost fifty years is something the hubs enjoys; I'm happy he's engaged in something that makes him happy. And high school football has done that for years.

Before coaching, he was a player in that same program (back in the days when football, basketball, and baseball were the major high school sports.) Saturday nights in the fall (or Friday night for the public-school kids,) the athletic field was the place to be! Half the town was there! Cheering...chatting... the smell of popcorn and hot dogs from the concession stand (you didn't really think I wouldn't have food memories thrown in there, did ya?) I never had the pleasure of seeing the hubs play in high school or in college, (there's that pesky age difference) but from what I've heard, he was good. And I do know he forged terrific friendships because of football. Some of his very best friends, then and now, were teammates or fellow coaches.

His playing days behind him, the sweet football memories continued for a young coach and his girl, (not so sweet was the night he stood her up for a date because of an unacceptable loss. He was always a fierce competitor, but he did THAT only one time....) Usually, after the game, we'd join friends at the local watering hole, recounting, it seems, every play of the game. And when the babies started arriving, no problem. They'd go to the games with me and I'd scoop up a high school kid to babysit afterwards so we didn't miss a beat with the post-game socializing. Good times...

When the boys were old enough to play, making football memories continued. Friendships began because the boys played football together. Getting to know the other football moms, team breakfasts, team dinners, and football banquets- all good times and memories. (Well, most of them were good.) Could've done without the distinctive smell of mud on football pants for me to wash or the clumps of dirt from football cleats, left by the back door.)

Now, after all these years, I STILL don't understand all the nuances of football; I never donned a helmet. I don't have an athletic or competitive bone in my body. But it's not hard at all for me to see how a sport can impact folks, friendships, and memories for years... and I'm grateful.

P.S. I'll see you at the game, where this old coach's wife, who's a little (or a lot) "broader in the beam" for those bleachers will still be cheering!

It Just SEEMS That Way...

My husband's gone tonight - on the road, doing what he does well and likes doing. He travels for his job sometimes and seems to enjoy it. He quips that he's "not working a day past age eighty" and as long as his health holds out and he's needed, that'll happen, I'm sure of it! His absence tonight got me to thinking of the past and the memories of his being gone, albeit briefly, through the years.

When the kids were young (three under age five!) I remember the feeling, in the pit of my stomach, as hubby packed his bag. How was I going to ride herd on this crew alone? I remember standing at the front door, with two boys in front of me and holding one, crying, like a baby. (ME, not the one I was holding!) The hubs was never gone for long -it just SEEMED that way!

As the boys got older, it seemed that, if crazy things were going to happen, it would be when Dad was on the road. We laugh about it now, but emergency room visits, speeding tickets, and lackluster grades at school all seemed to be more likely to happen with Dad gone. Luckily, I had family close and leaned on them plenty. And again, the hubs was never gone long... it just SEEMED that way.

It wasn't all bad, being a part-time single parent, back then. Mealtime was easier (How hard is pizza?) and I used to do my big projects when the hubs was gone. (There's that "easier to ask forgiveness than to seek permission" thing, again. Ha!) I have a greater respect, now, for the real single parents, who don't get that relief that comes when Dad walks through the door.

I'll be glad when the hubs gets home from this trip. I DO miss the comfortable routine we have, but I don't stand at the door, crying, these days, when he pulls out of the driveway. With the boys grown up and gone, there's little drama when Dad's not here. Just me and the dog. Yep - I'm always happy when he gets home...he's never gone long...it just SEEMS that way.

48 Valentine Days

When you're riding along on yet another interstate road on a very long trip, there's little to do. Oh sure, I had my phone to play with and magazines to glance at (although my aging eyes make it harder to read in the car these days.) I could also stare out the window at this nation's awesome beauty.

But that day, our forty-eighth Valentine's Day, had me paying intense attention to the man who's been my travel-mate all those years. I thought back to our many trips when we weren't the only ones in the car- the boys, our friends, our folks-but on that day, it was just us.

Sirius Radio on Valentine's Day was probably contributing to my sappiness, with 60's love music playing, and the hubs humming or singing along (when he remembered the words!) Looking over at his profile, I realized the differences from those trips of the old days: a hearing aid, grey hair, and a grey beard, when "Unchained Melody" by the Righteous Brothers meant a dance and not just a glance. Instead of the noise of kids in the back seat or conversation in the car with friends, there was silence. And that was okay.

Riding along (he STILL won't let me drive!) and knowing we're closer to our love story's last chapters than to our love story's starting point, I can't imagine taking this road trip or this life trip with anyone else. It was one of our nicest "Hallmark Days" (the hubs' sentiment about the day.) Blessed, for sure.

The Mom Years

My favorite role in the whole world! I LOVE being a Mom! That, and being a wife, was my career of choice. We had three sons, in pretty quick succession, and although at times it was tough, it assured they'd be best buds forever. The next chapter is ramblings of some of the happenings I experienced as a mom. Can you relate?

Moms Then or Moms Now?

You know, I was thinking the other day, as I peeked at Facebook and saw the many sports pics and activity posts that the moms offer up on social media. There's lot of running around going on...dropping off kids, picking them up. It made me tired just imagining these moms' schedules!

Of course, as I always do, this had me looking back to my childhood and how things were then... how they were for MY Mom. Vastly different, for sure.

I tried to think back to what my mom's day was like. Now, those were the days when most moms were stay at home moms. This was the case for many kids. Oh, there were teachers and nurses who went to work...some office workers, but for most of us, our moms were home. We were a pretty normal 1950's - 1960's family, living a pretty idyllic life.

I remember Mom, seeing Dad off to work every morning after breakfast. Most families had only one car, and that meant Mom was socked in for the day, with the kids. "Captain Kangeroo" and "Uncle Al" on TV entertained us, as Mom straightened up the house and readied the school kids for school.

These were the days before dishwashers...unless you had kids, whose chore THAT was. (And it was in OUR house!) Laundry was another task that was time consuming for Mom. No clothes dryer for us, so it was either hanging clothes outside on the clothesline or down the basement, when the weather wasn't sunny or breezy. And then the ironing. No permanent press back then so ironing the white oxford-cloth shirts that my Dad's job required, took a chunk of Mom's time, I'm sure. Afternoon programs on the one TV in the house made the ironing less tedious, I guess, for Mom.

We all think "Click List" at Kroger, where you let them know your grocery list and it's ready for you to pick up, and Amazon Prime, where everything comes to your door, are new. Not so! My Mom would call a fella by the name of Bill Baumann, who had a store on Central Avenue, and he would jot down the groceries Mom needed and deliver them to our door. Other neighborhood Mom and Pop stores offered the same service. And one or two mornings a week, fresh milk, cottage cheese, and butter would be delivered by the milkman. The Omar Bread man would often bring bread to our doorstep. Having one car meant limited trips to the store. All those services solved that problem. Dr. Zettler made house calls when we were sick, and when THAT ended, had evening hours to accommodate the "car-less during the day" moms. The drugstores made deliveries when a prescription was needed.

Now, these weren't frivolous luxuries. With three, then four, then five kids and no car, these services were necessities. We had after-school activities, but the neighborhood schools made possible a fun walk home with school friends, afterward. No need to bother Mom or Dad for that. There weren't all of the sports activities available now - maybe CYO football and basketball cheerleading - but those were usually on a weekend, when Dad and the car were available.

I can't decide which "days" I favor...the ones my mom lived or the ones today's moms do. It seems the busy-ness of the moms of 2020 would be so tiring. Running here, running there, getting homework done, meals served plus, most, working fulltime. Again, I'm exhausted, just thinking about it. But the extra workload and lack of conveniences for my mom and her mom-friends were tiring, too. Plus, maybe being at home with the kids, day in and day out, would have today's moms going crazy, too. Perhaps?

So, which is it? I guess it's what you know...what YOUR life is....and none of us would trade it for anything in the world. Just don't forget to unplug once in a while, savor what you've been given, and enjoy the life you have.

Boy
Times
Three

I'm a Mom of boys and, as a girl from a family made up predominately of girls, (three sisters and one brother) I didn't know what I was in for. I popped out three boys in five years, so I was going to find out in a hurry, wasn't I? I'm no expert, but I offer up these tidbits-things I've learned through the years-to young moms in the same spot.

1. Forget about grass. I'm pretty sure the backyard lawn of our old houses on Benninghofen, Tiffin, and Freeman, STILL have bald spots where first base, second base, third base and home plate were.

2. Boys don't sit...they plop. I've lost count of the number of sofas and recliners we've gone through! And I'm not sure they ever outgrow that habit.

3. Boys cannot whisper or walk softly. I don't think they're genetically capable of doing either.

4. Brothers, walking towards each other in a hallway, can't resist tapping or shoving each other.

5. Boys have terrible aim when using the john. It should be so easy-I have never understood that!

6. There is nothing quite as distinctive or disgusting a smell as a sweaty, muddy football uniform.

7. There will be times when you go to the fridge or the pantry and, despite your trip to the grocery store yesterday, will find nothing to eat.

I'm not grumblin'; raising boys was a challenge - the chatter, teasing, and wrestling all made our home a lively one....and I loved that! And as an old mom, I can tell you, at some point, you'll have your lawn, your bathroom will be spotless, and there will be lunch meat in the fridge. The chaos will be gone---and you'll miss it.

The Lean Years - But Richer Than We Knew...

I was recently in the grocery store line, with my usual buys - fruits, veggies, milk-nothing exciting. I found myself in line with several young moms with their carts filled to the top with items they needed (or thought they needed) for the week ahead.

That took me back years, to when we, as a young couple, were just getting started. Sure, there were grocery store chains that we frequented, but the neighborhood Mom and Pop stores were the ones that have the fondest place in my memory.

It was at one of those that we were greeted warmly by the proprietors, Fran and Shug, and although their place was small, it had everything one needed. Their store was within walking distance of our first place, so, pushing a stroller, I could take care of our grocery shopping, without the need for a car.

I will never forget these kind folks because these were the days before credit cards and before I was very skilled at budgeting (something I sometimes STILL struggle with.) Shug would be behind the meat counter, ready to provide what this young mom would need - ground beef, bacon, hot dogs-and he usually had a story or a joke to brighten the day. Fran, who, I'm pretty sure, was "the straw that stirred the drink" in their business, would be behind the cashier's counter, ready to ring up what looked like very frugal purchases.

I mentioned, earlier, credit cards- or the lack of, because these kind souls would let us run a tab for those days when the money ran out right after the food did-never judging (sometimes it was for cigarettes and Coca Cola - I know -shame on me!) Fran would just take the cash register tape, write our name on it and slip it into the cash drawer, knowing that on payday, we would come in and pay off our debt. And bless them - I know we weren't the only customers they afforded this kindness to.

How different things are now! With the swipe of a card, young moms can fill their carts up and be on their way. Good for them! They'll reconcile, at the end of the month, with whatever company that credit or debit card represents, but they won't get the kind smile that we got from Fran or the funny story that Shug offered up when we went into that small corner store of our younger years. And although those were our lean years, because of gems like Fran and Shug, we were really richer than we knew.

School Days - Hurray!

I must have been the most awful mom! I can say that, now, because our boys have turned out quite well...and I've stepped it up a bit, as a grandma. But looking at all the cute back-to-school photos on social media and reading the sweet sentiments about the return to school makes me realize what a slug I truly was. I'm not judging the moms who are tearful this time of year-please know that. Just as I would hope you don't judge those of us who seldom shed a tear over the inevitable.

Nope, no tears around here when September rolled around. (Yep, that's right! School started after Labor Day!) Heck, I got excited at the prospect of buying the boys' new school supplies, like binders, new pencils, and fresh notebook paper. (I think I bought 'em in June! How's THAT for excitement?) But even THAT paled in comparison to the excitement I had when school was actually back in session. I'm pretty sure folks could hear the shouts of joy (and luckily, not witness my cheer jumps) when the boys were safely in their desks for another school year. Oh, sure, I was never a fan of the home-work we'd face and there were twinges of sadness for "the firsts," (I'm not a TOTAL witch!) but once they were established as students, it was "let's get this show on the road!"

Summers were fun around here and I loved those days, too. It seems there were always kids at the house, playing some kind of ball, fussin' and fightin', and eating everything in sight. Moms, back then, weren't the pro-viders of fun that they are today, it seems. If that's good or bad, I don't know, but my role was more of a referee/food service worker. And our grocery bills proved it! Ah, September! Time to get those boys back into a structured environment!

As the boys got older and college was on the horizon, I changed my tune a bit. Their leaving the nest was daunting. I will never forget when, once, I had a down day when we'd taken one of the boys back to college. I was mop-ing around on a visit to my folks' home. When I told my Dad how I wasn't a fan of school starting and those departures, he, very matter of factly, said, "You don't want him living in your basement for the rest of his life, do you?"

I learned early on, that kids need schedules and kids want to be with their circle of friends. So, what better place than school? The fact that they actually learned things was a bonus. Yeah, that's it! I was just very big on education!

Well, maybe I wasn't so awful after all. Last time I checked, there's nobody living in the basement...

P.S. Thanks to all the terrific teachers who made the boys' transition to school so smooth through the years...and my autumns so pleasant.

Scientifically Speaking...

I saw online recently, a post about science fairs - those necessary evils that all school kids have to endure.

That particular post was a humorous one about a girl who used the actual science fair as her topic. Her materials were: a kid, parents, procrastination, and a-half-baked idea. Her results were, "75% of kids cried, 90% of parents yelled, and fifteen hours of family time were sacrificed." Her findings were that, "Everyone hates the science fair!"

In addition to my getting a kick out of that girl's project, it also brought back memories of the Wright Place during the science fair days. I truly think that you either have the science gene or you don't. The hubs and I do not. And it must be generational because our boys seemed to have missed out on that, too.

The first science fair project I oversaw was the effects of cigarette smoke on plant life. That one consisted of me blowing smoke on a plant that we bought. (These projects really are a joint effort, aren't they?) and what did my son theorize would happen? The plant looked awful after thirty days, so mission accomplished! I felt evil for smoking, as a young mom, and our son had a "finding" for his science fair project. "Smoking's bad for you." I think the surgeon general was onto that before my son was, but he (and I) got a decent grade anyway.

The other projects that the boys did, after that one, aren't as memorable, although I'm sure there was wailing and gnashing of teeth over them (by the boys and by me) as well. The ideas were harder to come by, the deadlines, more daunting. And by the time son #3 had a science fair in his future, my tolerance and patience, I'm sure, were really waning! We got thru all of the science fairs, unscathed, our relationships still intact, but failed to produce a scientist out of the whole lot.

I really enjoyed the aforementioned girl's science fair project, and although, saying "Everyone hates the science fair" may be unfair, I certainly hope she got a blue ribbon for her efforts because, in my judgement, she's a genius!

Black
Frames
and
Black
and
White
Photos

Christmas is a week past now and I'm still basking in the afterglow of a very nice one. It truly was! Oh, they're all nice, really, but this one? I'm not usually one to be struck by a gift. I like giving much better than receiving. Truly. But THIS one gift produced a reaction in my heart I don't usually get from gifts.

Christmas Day, as we were gathered with our kids and their kids, the hubs and I were given, by the sons and their families, identical boxes to open. In each, was a frame. I thought, "Perhaps portraits of the family?" That would've been great, but instead the hubs and I held framed prints of the homes we've owned in our soon-to-be forty-eight years of marriage! Nothing fancy or elaborate. Black and white photos in simple black frames. But I've got to tell you, I shed a tear. Turns out, the eldest son had driven around and taken the pics the last time he was home. And this collaborative gift held so many memories of our family's eras that I cried.

The first frame included our first purchased home-the home we'd saved so hard for that sometimes it seemed unattainable. It was the home that cost what a lower-priced car costs today- the home when a family with one son became a family with two, the home of walks, with strollers, the home of stripping wallpaper and of testing my home decorating skills (and failing at the first of many...) These were our first-time attempts at lawncare and of walking to the neighborhood store for groceries with kids in tow.

That frame also included our second family home. The home when a family with two sons would become a family of three sons. It was the home that became walks with strollers AND Big Wheels, the home when date night had us paying fifty cents to a dollar for babysitters for the young 'uns, the home of the finished basement project, so the rascals could spread out and give mom some peace, the home of the first dog (after we were sure we'd never have one...)

The second frame pictured the third home. The home of the boys' paper routes, the poured backyard basketball court that provided the hubs and friends with an annual tournament, and had mom, refereeing tiffs the rest of the year. It was the home of boys' bikes and crossing streets, of me, letting go, a little bit more. It was the home of little grass, because of baseball games, wrestling around in the yard, and the aforementioned dog...

Our next move, and the final pictured home, took us closer to the school where I would work and the boys would attend high school. That home became the home of the high school and college years. The home of drivers' licenses, of first dates, of football and basketball practices, of having high school friends hanging at the house (Living close to a high school? The benefit - we always knew who the boys were with. The downside? The grocery bills!) Graduations and departures - as the boys headed off to out-of-town colleges-and our first taste of grandparenthood.

There were two homes not included in our gift. The first -a rental, now demolished - hence, no photo - that would find a young couple getting used to being married - the cooking mishaps of a new cook and the arrival of our firstborn. The other-the home we now occupy. Don't need a photo, as we're living it. The Empty Nest home. The home, where new family members have been added, more grands have entered the fray-the home, where I have plenty of time to think of memories of old homes, and the home, we swear, we'll be carried out of, feet first. Beginnings and Endings. Kinda.

Yep. This gift of two simple frames, with four simple black and white photos that would mean little to anyone else, made me tear up. I don't know if the tears on my cheeks were from the memories of a pretty terrific life which has passed so quickly or was it the fact that we've raised thoughtful sons? Both...and blessed.

Christmas Nostalgia

When it comes to nostalgia, is there anything that evokes more memories than the Christmas season? To me, reminiscing is the best part. Whether it goes all the way back to my childhood, thinking about Christmases when our boys were younger, or just thinking back to last year with the grandkids, there's nothing better!

I remember the excitement as a kid, leading up to Christmas. Taking rides to see the lights in Lindenwald, visiting a live Nativity scene at the First Church of God on Pleasant Avenue, finding a tree at the town tree lot by Frisch's, shopping for gifts at Roemer's Hardware, and holding my Dad's hand, as we paid a visit to Santa uptown. I'm pretty sure I had an extensive list for Santa, but when the magical night arrived, I forgot that list and loved everything under the tree. Our house on Allen Avenue was always the hub for the extended family's celebration and sharing the holidays then, with those who are now no longer with us. That makes those memories even sweeter.

As a mom, Christmas brought the big responsibility of making it as special for the boys as it had been for me. Some years, we nailed it, sometimes not so much. The boys may tell you their Christmas memories always involved dorky sweaters, (and judging from the pictures, they may be right!) but my memories are different. I remember trying to keep them calm, during Mass at St Ann's, before the chaos started. I remember the year one son got a drum set from my folks (not sure what I did to deserve THAT!) or another year, when an uncle thought outer space guns that made twelve different sounds were a good gift idea for all three boys (Payback the following year was his three too-young daughters who received make-up kits, complete with nail polish and lipstick!) We had our share of football, basketball, and baseball stuff, GI Joes (or the cheaper version, GI Jim) and building blocks. Back then, what I wouldn't have done for a baby doll!

Having grandkids has added another layer of enjoyment for us at Christmas. They make the trek here, and their joy and excitement brings back so many memories of when our boys were that age. They make new memories for Grandpa and me with their joy and innocence.

I've always been a traditionalist, but I've learned that when you have a family of your own, you'd best be flexible. There were years when sick kids kept us from making the rounds-years, because of work or the kids sharing the holiday with in-laws- when everyone isn't in the same place at the same time. But you make it work-because it's family and it's Christmas.

I Miss the Wish Book....

Does anyone else miss the catalogs that used to come in the mail from Sear's and Penney's? I remember, first, as a kid, and then, as a young mom, excitedly opening their colorful pages. There were so many wonderful things to look at and, hopefully, purchase.

I know that "paperless" and "going green" is the way to go now, but looking at pictures in a catalog and marking the pages of things we wished for, seemed a lot more fun than looking at merchandise online. Call me old-fashioned, I guess.

I especially remember the excitement that came with the special Christmas edition of the catalogs! It was then that the ideas for our Christmas lists were formed. I loved the dolls, the board games, the stuffed animals, and the special holiday dresses. (I'm pretty sure my early love for red velvet began because of a dress, modeled on the cover of one of the wish books!) I don't know if "Santa" paid attention to all the dog-earred pages, but I can't remember one Christmas when I was disappointed with what I received.

As a young mom, my excitement over catalogs didn't wane. Being able to order the boys' school uniforms and getting ideas for their gifts, now that the hubs and I were "Santa," was great! It was wonderful being able to see so many beautiful items all in one place and all without leaving the comfort of home.

That was until our order came to the store. It was then I would get the call and would head to Penney's or Sear's store catalog counter to get our merchandise. I'd tell the clerk my name and she would then go to the files, pull our order, go to the back of the store, and come out with our purchases.

I know that today's online shopping is very similar. We can find everything we could possibly want online, from many different vendors, all with the click of a mouse and all delivered to our doors. But there was something magical about poring over the catalogs of those major retailers, turning those pages - outfitting our kids, decorating our home, or making Christmas wishes come true with the many treasures we'd find in the wish book....and I, for one, "wish" they were back.

Santa, St Nick, and Snitch the Elf

Is there a busier time of year than Christmas? With the holiday preparations, the shopping, the baking, and cooking? And is there a time of year when youngsters get as excited as they do during the holiday season?

I'm not ashamed to admit that, as a young mom, I had an arsenal to deal with bad behavior this time of year and I bet you did, too. Whether it was caused by a lack of sleep, too much sugar, or just the fact that kids can be buttheads sometimes, it didn't matter. During those trying episodes, I wasn't afraid to call on The Christmas Trinity - Santa, St. Nick and Snitch the Elf.

"Santa won't come if you don't behave," was a frequent comment in our house this time of year. I couldn't have been the first mom to use that tactic, I'm pretty sure. A song with the lyric, "He knows when you are sleeping; he knows when you're awake," was around long before I became a mom. (And isn't it kind of creepy that we encouraged the belief that some kind of stalker was checking out our kids at night?)

St. Nick was the more dignified character (he's a saint, after all!) who was the midterm gauge on how the boys were behaving. If the boys got an orange, a few pieces of candy, and maybe a small toy, (like a Match Box car or a Star War's figure) they knew they were in pretty good stead with the main dude of the season, at least in early December. St. Nick was kind of an assistant Santa. You didn't want to tick him off, but come on! An orange?

If that didn't keep the guys in line, our house had another go-to guy named Snitch the Elf. We told the boys that Snitch the Elf was looking in the window and if they behaved that day, a piece of candy could be found on the windowsill at night. It was pretty amusing to see the boys try to figure out who messed up that day when there were only two pieces of candy on the windowsill and we had three boys. In the end, THEY knew. THEY knew.

It's not like our boys were juvenile delinquents-just normal kids, caught up in the excitement of the season. But it sure was nice to know that those three Christmas characters had our backs during the most hectic time of year.

And young moms-feel free to borrow any of the ideas. I mean, after all, what says Christmas, like a stalker, an orange peddler, and a peeping Tom elf?

Dog Kisses
and
Baby Books

Our youngest son turned forty recently... and I gotta tell you - I think it bothers me a little bit more than when I hit those milestones myself! And why is that? I guess it's because the years have gone by at breakneck speed and there's not a thing that I can do about it, is there? I just wish it would slow down a bit.

Having three sons, in pretty quick succession, their early years were kind of a blur. Oh, I remember the big moments. I just wish I could remember more of the little ones-more of the days-and not just the years.

When the boys were young, I had some plaques on our wall-one for each. The one for the firstborn said something about how he was the one who got the new parents and the new clothes.

The one for the middle child said that he was the one who got the formula-stained burp rags and the parents' realization that dog kisses wouldn't kill him.

And the plaque for the youngest of the family spoke of how he had broken-in parents, had a baby book that probably had more recipes stuck in it than photos, and that no matter how old he got, he would always be our baby.

I don't know how that all figures for bigger or smaller families, but it's pretty accurate for ours. You love them all, but birth order, your station in life when they were born, and your experience with raising kids, really does make a difference with each one, as they grow, doesn't it?

The hubs was fond of telling folks that when we took the first son to college, I cried all the way home. With the second son, I cried only halfway home, and with our youngest, we barely stopped the car to drop him off. That's not true, of course, but it DID get easier. I'm not sure seeing my kids hit these age milestones ever will.

I suppose I should feel very blessed that, despite some bumps in the road and a few hiccups along the way, they DID grow up and I've been able to witness that growth. And I'm proud of the way they've turned out. I love them all, but nowhere is it written that I have to LIKE being the parent of middle-aged kids. Like I said earlier, I just wish it would slow down a bit!

People Plan;
God Laughs

Saw that yesterday and realized how true it is. Just four words. You can plan and plan and then whammo! God has a different idea. I'm not sure I can picture God actually laughing at our having to change our plans, but I guess it's a nice visual when life takes a turn that is not to our liking.

There were plenty of times, I'm sure, when God was laughing at the Wrights, in the course of our married lives. It started out with the bride having mononucleosis right before our wedding and having to take two weeks off work to heal, beforehand, which meant no honeymoon. God got a kick out of that, I bet!

I'm pretty sure the good Lord thought he'd be getting a chuckle out of our planned vacation to Myrtle Beach that was almost halted by three boys with chicken pox. But God would have to wait for his laughs that time. After fretting and polling the ten other families making the trip to make sure they were okay with us going (they were,) we loaded up the old station wagon and headed south. Turns out the salt water was great for chicken pox. Who knew? And not one kid from our group came down with the rash, after being with our kids for a week. However, we have no way of knowing if a worldwide epidemic didn't start with kids NOT in our group, like the ones who happened to be in the hotel game room, which emptied when our boys entered. (Ah, unlimited Pac-Man!) Maybe God got his giggles out of THOSE kids' parents' wrecked plans.

When some of our plans-serious life ones- never came to fruition, it wasn't as funny. Plans that involved money, serious health issues, real estate challenges, job changes, the kids being disappointed over something -all were unavoidable, as they are for everyone. But while God was smiling (maybe even laughing) at these times, He was also helping us get through 'em.

Yes, life has a way of moving along. We can plan and plan and it just doesn't work out the way we want it to all of the time. I guess we should just try to roll with the punches-smiling, maybe even laughing- when our plans don't work out. Because I'm pretty sure God is.

Finally Vindicated!

I think that people who nap have long been looked down upon, considered lazy, and not very driven. Well, I am a firm believer in naps and am downright giddy right now! And why? Because the science community finally backs me up and says that naps are good for you! The vindication I've been waiting for!

The experts say, "a ten or twenty-minute power nap provides a boost in alertness and energy" and "a sixty minute nap has been proven to improve remembering facts, faces and names." And who doesn't need help with that? The experts "caution that too long of naps can lead to sleep problems at night." Minor details! I love naps!

When the boys were younger, they knew it behooved everyone in the house to let mom nap. I'd turn on the box fan to drown out the noise and catch a few winks. Amazingly, the law was never summoned, and Children's Services weren't called in. I'm just sure the boys were well-behaved while mom napped in the other room....yeah, right!

About that box fan...if I have any apologies to my sons and the hubs, it's for causing them to also become addicted to the hum of a fan while they sleep. There were a few years, in our house, with all the fans going that it sounded like an airport and the entire house was going to take off! When the boys all went off to school and left the nest, not only did the food bills get smaller, but there was also a noticeable reduction in our electric bill.

When you're young, it's funny - running after kids, so busy with your lives, the opportunities to nap are fewer. And when you're old(er) and have all the time in the world, naps aren't as needed. Oh, who am I kidding? I STILL love naps, and I highly recommend them!

They Turn Out ---In Spite of Us

Do you remember the pressure you put on yourself as a young mom? I certainly do!

Back in the 70's, one big dilemma was deciding whether to be a working mom or a stay-at -home mom. For the working moms, it was, "How will the kids fare in daycare?"

For the stay-at-home Moms, it was, "Is one salary gonna do it for the family?" No matter if it's at home or in the workplace, mothers "work" and no matter where you were, your heart was where your kids were, most of the time.

Breastfeeding was another topic that ignited the passion on opposing sides. It wasn't for everyone and those who thought it was were vocal. I remember the La Leche League, a group dedicated to educating women on the benefits of breastfeeding, had meetings advertised in our newspaper. I was invited, but said, "No thanks." I don't need a meeting for THAT; that's something I'll handle myself."

Whether to start a preschooler at an early age or hold one back from kindergarten was another dilemma that many moms had -and have -to face. "Are they ready? Am I ready?" or "Should my son play football?" or "Should my daughter take dance lessons?" Those kinds of decisions seemed so big at the time and they were. As new moms, we had a lot to learn and to decide.

As long as there are moms, there are going to be decisions to be made about what's best for our kids, our families, and ourselves. Things that are just assumed now were real stumpers back in the day. And there will be new stumpers for moms that we old moms can't even imagine.

I'm proud to say that, after all the soul-searching, decision-making, and wringing of hands through the years, I have three reasonably normal sons. And I maintained my sanity (most would say.) I guess the message here, is ... Relax, moms, don't overthink things, and enjoy your kids. They turn out --- in spite of us.

Body
Found
on I 75

Get your attention with that? I'll explain in a bit.

The hubs and I decided to go on a road trip. Oh, why not?! We're usually all about the destination. Fly somewhere, get unpacked, and enjoy. Well, we decided to slow things down a bit and make it about the journey. So our meandering through the south would begin.

Now I should probably preface this with letting you know, in case you weren't aware, that I can be a talker. Sometimes an unfiltered talker. And this is also the same woman who had to stop for a bathroom break on a recent two-and-a-half-hour car ride. When I got back into the car, the hubs said, "This doesn't bode well for the Florida trip, does it?" Ha! So, it isn't without some concern, that planning to go by car is a big decision. Sure hope it's the right one!

Well, we'll have Sirius radio for the hubs to listen to and I'll have my phone to play with. There'll be limited liquid intake for me and a pillow for my naps. Yep, those things will hopefully keep us on speaking terms and prevent the hubs from tossing me out of the car and onto the interstate.

I know there will be plenty of time, sitting in the car, to think back to other road trips we've taken, to the times when air fare wasn't in the budget for a family of five.

Like the trip to Myrtle Beach with three chicken pox- ridden sons. Oh, don't judge! Our doctor said the salt water would dry things right up. He failed to mention that we were probably going to be ground-zero for a world-wide chicken pox epidemic! (The upside to all this was the boys never had to wait in line to play Pac Man in the hotel game room. The place would clear out when the scabby Wright boys entered. Ha!)

Or the trip that had a caravan of fourteen families' cars being waved on to keep going, when we had to pull over at a hospital in Kentucky for a son's asthma attack. (The hospital emergency room had a screen door - I kid you not - and a young red-haired, pony-tailed doctor, in sandals, who entered with a, "Hey, dude, what's happenin'? " (I'm entrusting my baby to THIS guy?)

Or the road trips that had us leaving in the middle of the night so the boys would sleep through most of our drive. Those were the days of non-existent seat belts - we'd throw the boys in the back of the station wagon, with pillows and blankets. We'd never get away with that now, would we?

Or the long trip when, in addition to the boys, we had the elderly in-laws piled into a minivan. (The one time we were grateful that they were hard of hearing so they couldn't hear the tussling with the boys that was going on in the cramped back seat.) Or the trip with my folks that was plagued with car trouble and my worry-wart Dad, showing his true colors. "He knows what he's doing, Dad."

Someday, perhaps, we can take our time, go off the beaten path, stay in charming bed and breakfast. But baby steps for now, right? First, we'll have to see if THIS trip is about the journey and not the destination. And I'm gonna try my hardest to be a good traveling companion. I promise. But if a body IS found on Interstate 75, I'll be wearing jeans, a cream-colored top, gym shoes, and I'll have a small tattoo and my own teeth. And please tell my kids and grands that I love 'em.

An Act of Kindness...

I want to recount an act of kindness that happened to me recently. And I do so, not because I think I did anything to deserve it, but more as a lesson to others.

As you know, we raised three boys. I still call them boys, but truth of the matter, they've been grown men for years. Anyway, when they were boys in high school, we moved to a home that was near the high school that they all attended. That made it mighty handy for their friends to gather there...before practices, after school, and after games.

I always loved the fact that their friends felt comfortable enough to make themselves at home. It wasn't unheard of for me to come home from work and a group of them would be watching TV (and none of our sons were even in the mix!) Some days, I wasn't even sure whose laundry I was doing. If a particular shirt would go missing, I would say, "Ask Mark if he has it." These guys were tight, and I liked the fact, too, that we knew who our kids were hanging with-and they were all terrific kids (on most days.)

Some weekends, they wouldn't leave. Seems that sleepovers were constant. One particular spell of cold and snowy weather had them socked in at our place for four days! And I had the grocery bills to prove it! But that was okay. They brought a lot of fun and enjoyment into our lives. All these different personalities, getting along, cutting up, laughing...it was great! I'm sure there was plenty of things that we weren't aware of (nothing mean, illegal, or destructive, of course) and for me, sometimes "Ignorance is bliss."

But then, graduations happened and kids moved on, as they always do- on to college, on to jobs, and some started families.

We have a few out of town sons now. It's different for us-fewer drop-in visits than most of you enjoy. I've never said I like it, but I've said before, kids have to be happy where they are, and mine are happy. I guess that's what makes it so special when one of the boys' (there I go again with "the boys") friends take time out of their day to stop in to pay a visit to some old timers from their past. And that happened here the other day. One of the boys, whom we probably could've claimed as a dependent with the IRS back in the day, stopped in to see us on a visit from Tennessee to see his own family. Catching up, finding out how things have turned out, and seeing pictures of his young family-gosh, I loved those guys then and I love 'em now.

Why am I even telling you this? It's not because I think we're special or deserve any kind of plaudits. Not at all. It's because I hope some who are reading this, realize that making an effort to visit someone from your long ago past can truly touch a heart. It doesn't have to be a long stop, just a brief hello will do. It sure can make an old timer feel special. And blessed. And I do.

And the Grandma Years

Someone once said they should've skipped the kid part and gone straight to the grandkids. Granted, being a grandma is easier than being a mom, but I'd have missed too many great memories, and I DID enjoy being a Mom. But these grandkids have my heart!

I Want to Tell Them That....

Grandkids...Is there anything better? The joy of having youngsters around without the constant need to keep an eye on them. That's their parents' job. Sure, there's a lot of love and concern for them, but the ultimate way they turn out rests on someone else's shoulders...our kids'.

I don't have the luxury of having all my grandkids here in the same town that we live in. I don't have the weekly or daily drop ins with them like I had as a kid and as a young(er) mom, but I learned a long time ago that our kids have to be happy where they are-and I'm glad to say, my kids are happy.

My biggest concern for having out-of-town grandkids is that I don't want them to forget me. Their visits are a couple times a year for the holidays and they each stay with us for several days in the summer, for one-on-one time. And the younger, in-town grands? Will they remember me?

Just in case:

- I want to tell them that, even though we're not at all their games, shows and all their other activities, they're always in our hearts and on our minds.

- I want to tell them that they don't need anyone's affection or approval to be good enough.

- I want to tell them that if they're kind and pleasant to others and "they" don't reciprocate, that's a "them" problem and not a "you" problem. Keep being kind and pleasant.

- I want to tell them (and this is from someone far wiser than me) that one smile can start a friendship, one word can end a fight, and one person can change a life. Have that smile, say that word, and be that person.

- I'd tell them to get along with their siblings. Hard to imagine sometimes, but they'll be their lifelong friends. They'll be a true gift, with a shared history when they're older. I promise.

- I want to tell them not to sweat the small stuff...and it's all small stuff.

- I want to tell them how truly blessed they are and to always be grateful for what they have.

- I want to tell them to keep God in their lives; they're going to need Him.

- I want to tell them that they should take time to appreciate the little things.

- I want to tell them how much they're loved by their parents and the rest of their family -no matter what.

- I want to tell them that laughter is the best therapy in the world.

There are so many things going on in kids' lives today that we never had to deal with when we were raising kids. It's tough, I know. And just in case my kids read this, I want to tell them, too, that laughter is the best therapy in the world, for parents, as well. So, keep laughin', kids, and thanks for sharing your "blessings" with us....

Time Moves On

You know you're getting to be an old(er) grandma when the visiting granddaughters choose to sleep in on Easter Sunday instead of scampering up the steps to see what the Easter Bunny brought them. Time moves on...

The two granddaughters and I went to the Candlelight Vigil Mass at St. Ann's and I'm so happy we did! Aside from avoiding the fight for the showers and the frantic activity that was sure to take place Easter morning, it was a lovely Mass. And it came at the request of one of the granddaughters. She WANTED to go to what is usually a rather long, drawn out affair. (It wasn't drawn out this year). Time moves on...

It used to be that, seeing my grandkids anywhere NEAR fire, scared the heck out of me, but here were two beautiful young ladies, holding candles beside me, basking in their glow and looking far more mature than I want them to. Time moves on.

There was a time when keeping enough food in the house for three growing boys and their dad was tough. But then, we hit a bit of a slow down on food consumption; little ones don't eat that much, and the grownups were more conscious of what they consumed. (Well, MOST of us, anyway!). Now, we're back, full throttle, with the grandkids' (especially grandson's) appetites rivaling the adults. Time moves on...

I can remember buying cute little dresses, strappy shoes, and sweet purses for the girls, and now they have their own tastes and styles and it's harder to guess what will please them. They've grown to the point that, if need be, I could borrow THEIR shoes. Buying boys' clothes isn't nearly as fun (some things never change). Time moves on....

They've all returned to their lives picking up where they left off before the holiday weekend. Papaw and I will return to our lives, which aren't nearly as exciting and busy as theirs, I'm sure. And that's okay. After the dishes are all put away, the overloaded recycling bin is pushed to the curb, the last of the bath towels washed, and the scant leftovers consumed, we'll realize how blessed we are that they all can - and do - make it home for such special family times. And we'll savor these precious moments.... because time moves on.

Life with Lola - The Things I've Learned

Who says you can't teach an old(er) dog new tricks? It's been awhile since I was a grandma to a little one. Our four grandkids are soon to be eighteen, seventeen, fourteen, and three. That's quite a span there.

I love being a grandma. It's way more fun than being a mom. Not that I didn't absolutely love THAT role. It's just easier to be a grandma. We get the fun and not so much of the work. Seeing our first three grands growing up has been such a blessing. But, you know, when kids hit a certain age, they have their own lives; that's the way it's supposed to be. Oh, they still need us, but growing up is a good thing. And that's what they're doing. And then along came Lola at a great time in our lives. It's funny how you forget things. Lola, our fourth grandchild, has been kind of a refresher course in grandma-hood for me. I recently had the good fortune of having a sleepover with Miss Lola. You wouldn't think I'd be so out of touch with babies, but..

- I'd kind of forgotten that no matter how many toys a child has, they'll go for the box and papers, laying around first.

- I'd kind of forgotten that *Toy Story* is a fine movie, no matter the age. In fact, I noticed, again, that there are a lot of jokes in the movie that would go right over a kid's head...and I laughed again.

- I'd kind of forgotten that...there's not a better scent in the world than a baby-shampooed head.

- I'd kind of forgotten that..."Smart" phones are intriguing to kids - and Lola seems smarter about technology than her grandma already!

- I'd kind of forgotten... that hearing a baby's jibber-jabber, right outside their bedroom door, is the very best way to start a morning.

- I'd kind of forgotten that...When you're counting in months, the time sure goes quickly...slow it down there, Lola!

- I'd kind of forgotten that...TV has a mesmerizing effect on babies. Lola is as entertained by Chip and Joanna Gaines on HGTV as her Grandma is.

- I'd kind of forgotten that...chunky cheeks and squishy thighs are just so irresistible.

- I'd kind of forgotten that...There are many different ways of parenting. Not better- just different.

- I'd kind of forgotten that...Kids are way smarter than we give them credit for. The expressions and mannerisms of our young grand tells me that she's always thinkin'...always plannin' on her next move.

- I'd kind of forgotten that...Stamina and strength are less evident in a sixty-seven-year-old, compared to a fifty-five year old, when carrying around or playing on the floor with a little one.

Our grandkids have my heart, for sure. It's fun to see how they're all turning out...makes me proud of the job the kids are doing with their kids. I wouldn't want to be starting over with child-rearing, but it sure is fun to watch our babies with their babies, isn't it? And sharing in their lives is one of the nicest things, I've found, about growing old(er).

Now where is that damn heating pad?!?!

An addendum – we've been blessed with another sweet little grand-daughter – Avett Harper will be part of our continuing ed, I suppose, reminding us of how wonderful little ones are!

The Daughter Years

My mom has suffered from dementia and been in a nursing care facility for over five years. Writing my thoughts seemed to help me deal with, first, my dad's passing and then my mom's slow decline. Many times, I found that laughing, instead of crying was my best defense. And writing....

My Dad's Gloves

The husband has been on me this summer about this-and I admit-I have become a lawncare hoarder in my later years. Our garage has become the disorganized collection of all the things I need (or think I need) to keep the yard, the garden, and the flower beds healthy and attractive (kind of like how my make-up drawer is for my face.)

Anyway, it's gotten to the point that we've been shopping sheds to handle the overflow of stuff- things too useful to throw out just yet, but certainly a mess that needs to be improved upon. I think the garage is adequate for the two of us, so I took it upon myself to try to get in there and pitch the unwanted, hoping to fend off the need for a shed.

Now mind you, it's been 15 years since we purchased this place from my folks, and things have accumulated. In digging around out in the garage, I came across a pair of Dad's old work gloves. Nothing special about them-heavy leather gloves used for outdoor chores that have seen better days. And although the trash can is calling their name, I cannot part with them.

Those old, ugly, and rugged gloves represent the hard worker my dad was. He had a white-collar job his whole life, but his entire persona changed when he got home. Off came the tie and the man toiled, tirelessly, in the yard, in the woods, and around the house.

If I sit on our deck, I can almost see him, pushing yet another wheelbarrow full of dirt for a flower bed. I can hear his saw, cutting back the honeysuckle that I've grown to hate! I can almost see him, in his old-man undershirt, sitting under the shade of one of the trees he had planted, years before, taking a short break and sipping on a glass of water.

This place holds so many memories - that's what happens when you live in your folks' house - and it's a privilege in a way; I've continued what they'd started. But the downside? I know I'll never measure up to the work ethic my Dad had when it comes to this property, but maybe-just maybe-his gloves will wield a power, in memories, that will have me trying to. I'm keeping them.

Those Greeks Were onto Something!

"A society grows great when old men plant trees whose shade they know they shall never sit in." — *Greek Proverb*

Guess we're going to find out how smart those Greeks were!

That saying caught my eye recently, probably because we're facing the removal of twenty-seven trees in our yard. And I LOVE trees! Some darn bug, an ash borer by name, is practically decimating our beloved woods. Sure, I'll miss the shade these beauties have provided, but it goes deeper than that. I'm taking this personally because we purchased this home from my folks fifteen years ago. The house has had its share of problems, but it's our home now. It just seems the very things my late dad had a hand in are being chipped away, needing to be replaced or repaired, and that makes me sad.

I remember Dad, taking a break from his yardwork, sitting on the deck, enjoying the shade of these trees. The lot was wooded when they built the house-he didn't do the actual planting - but he tended to them to make sure they thrived.

It's probably good that Dad's not here to see these trees come down. Would've been hard on him; he loved the woods even more than I do. We'll probably plant something hardier than the ones we're losing. We have no idea how long we'll be here to enjoy them-you know how life goes. Maybe those Greeks were onto something...

A Sentimental Find

I've taken on a summer project of refinishing some furniture - kind of refreshing some things and repurposing some others. Things always have a way of snowballin' around here, so it's been a bigger task than I'd planned. In going through some of the drawers I was working on, I happened upon a personal treasure that I didn't even know I had- Dad's tie tacks, lapel pins, and his old rosary. Now this would mean nothing to anyone, except those he loved and those who loved him. I know that. But to me, it was a very sentimental find and made my summer project even MORE rewarding.

So here is this collection of things that are pretty much obsolete now. Rosaries get used, I know, (though probably not enough) but men don't wear ties like they used to and I doubt if anyone wears a tie tack anymore. But my dad did and, in examining what I'd found, one would get a real understand-ing of the man he was. And, although he's been gone for a while, it's been a reminder of what I still miss.

Among my treasures, there was a tie tack from the Republican National Committee, probably a thank you for a donation he made when he switched parties. And then there's the Hamilton, Ohio one. Dad was a proud ambassador of his hometown, so no surprise there. The Ohio Casualty diamond pin represented his achievements in the workplace. The Ohio Life one represented his being named vice president of that company. The Elks clip represented camaraderie and an opportunity to take his family to a place for summer swims and nice dinners out. The golf club tie clip was a fun nod to his favorite pastime. And the black rosary (back then, men's rosaries were usually black or brown and the ladies' were pearl or gemstones) was a symbol of his faith.

I don't recall noticing the tie clips Dad wore when I was growing up, nor did I see the rosary in his hands, (his was a quiet faith...) but looking at them now as a collection, these trinkets ARE him. The things he did, the things he loved, and the things he represented.

Oh, my dad was more complex than a little box of things, in a long-forgotten drawer. I'm sure of that. I know, even after all these years since his passing, that he's still teaching me lessons. And the lesson here is: "What will I leave behind that will have others recalling what I did? What I loved? What I represented?" wasn't lost on this old-er broad. Thanks for that lesson, Dad.

80 Years of Friendship...

Recently, I had the good fortune of taking my elderly Mom to visit an old friend who was in failing health. To see these old gals who had been best friends for eighty years holding hands, like a couple of schoolgirls, touched my heart.

To say I had the good fortune of doing this sounds odd, I know, but it really was an honor to witness. Eighty years! What a tribute to friendship!

When I pondered the visit later on in the day, I tried to imagine what all had gone on in those two old gals' lives...eighty years! They met in grade school and probably shared stories of secret crushes. They went through high school together and met their future husbands. They saw those young men off to war, each carrying on their own love affairs over years and miles. They were witnesses in each other's weddings and began their families, coincidentally, both having five kids each. I imagine they shared recipes, child-rearing ideas, fashion, and fads-all the things moms do.

They were part of a card club with other lady friends -although I don't remember ever seeing a deck of cards. I DO remember the food that was served when it was Mom's turn. There would be leftovers the next day-appetizer and dessert treats we got to sample, if there were leftovers. I remember, too, sitting on the top stair, out of view, listening to the chatting and giggling-something that we didn't hear too often. Our moms, cackling and carrying on!

My mom and her dear friend's social lives intertwined through the years, and their husbands were best friends, too, all because of their friendship. Dances, trips, and dinners out, all the fun things couples do. The years took their toll and their fun times started to dwindle. Health problems entered the picture and my dad passed away. Although the couples' fun ended, the two old gals' friendship never waned.

Mom wasn't sure she wanted to visit her friend in those last days. "I don't think I can stand to see her that way." I realize now that my mom was saying good-bye, not only to her dear friend, but also to such a large and fun part of her own life. It was hard.

Mom has said since, that the hardest part of growing old is losing your friends and being left behind. Life, good health, and friendships are precious. Thanks, Mom and Dorth, for that reminder...

The
Gift

Recently, I had the nicest, most unexpected thing happen. And who says, "You can't go home again?"

Let me start at the beginning. My folks were always so hard to buy for at Christmas. "We don't need a thing; spend it on your own family." Well, one year, we had the idea to have a talented friend draw prints of all the homes my folks owned in their nearly sixty-year marriage. Those framed prints hung, proudly, in their last home for years.

When Mom entered the nursing home, we decided to divvy the prints up, according to all the kids' life timelines. I took the print of the home we reside in now, the one we bought from my folks. All the other prints were claimed by my siblings except for one. Seems everybody's timeline kind of crisscrossed on that one, and so it sat in my laundry room for months.

That is, until I got an idea - a kind of crazy one - that would take some courage. "I'm gonna do it!" I went, framed print in hand, to the address of that home and rang the doorbell. Didn't know what I was going to find, but, it turns out, the woman who had bought the home from my parents nearly fifty years ago answered the door. I introduced myself and she recognized my maiden name. I managed to fumble out the words that, "Yes, I had lived there," and showed her the print, explained its history, and handed it to her. She got misty-eyed and told me her husband had passed away a few years earlier, and although it was a lot of work, she could never leave that home.

Then, surprisingly, she invited me in and proudly gave me a tour of the place my family called home for ten years. Talk about surreal! The memories came flooding back! Here, was the beautiful living room where I received the engagement ring from my husband so long ago. And how did seven of us ever fit into that kitchen/dinette? It was also the site of my getting smacked for saying "crap" at the dinner table! (I didn't say ALL the memories were pleasant.) The TV room was still a TV room and then there was the one bathroom-only one - for four girls, one boy, and two parents to wrangle over. It's lost its mauvish tile, but still had the mirror that reflected my teenage face. I couldn't believe that two of my sisters and I shared that bedroom - the place of many giggles and a few tussles. It seemed small. The patio, where we sunbathed is gone, but other than that, it was as if time had stood still. And I'm glad it did.

As I left, the kind woman gave me a hug and thanked me for the gift. But really, it was she, who gave the gift-one, that a woman - a stranger, really - gave me, by inviting me in for a beautiful walk down memory lane. Who says, "You can't go home again?"

Driving Miss Daisy

Someone lost her independence today. You won't see it on the news; no one will be staging a protest. There was no drama, no tug of war-it was just another senior giving up her license to drive. It happens every day, all over the world, but this time, it's personal.

It was my mom who surrendered her car keys and shiny red car to us-nothing dramatic- more of a resignation that her eyes, memory, and reflexes aren't what they used to be. And giving up that license is a good thing. Her safety, and that of those on the road around her, is too important. Except why do I hear, in my head, the soundtrack of Driving *Miss Daisy* starring me, in the Morgan Freeman role, and my mom, playing the Jessica Tandy one?

My mom was a late bloomer when it came to drive. Maybe it was that way for many women back then. There was no getting your license when you were in high school, like now. I'm pretty sure of that. When my mom started to drive, she was a young wife and mother. Having groceries, bread, and milk delivered to our doorstep sounds wonderful to me, now, but I bet my mom had had enough of that and was anxious to get out and do things for herself.

I remember my mom's driving lessons. I was only about six years old, but I recall it very clearly. I seldom question my late dad's wisdom, but piling three kids into the backseat of a car and heading out to old Ford Blvd to teach his very pregnant wife how to drive wasn't his most shining moment. It must have gone okay because no one was injured, and Mom eventually got her license.

It's funny how so much is attached to that piece of plastic (although a license was just paper back then.) The freedom to pick up and take off, to do your own thing, or to assist others in doing their own thing. My own mom spent twenty years chauffeuring her non-driving mother around to appointments, to stores, and to lunches. So, I guess it really is true that everything in life is cyclical. What goes around... I know my folks took their turns, carting five kids around from place to place, and now it's our turn to return the favor.

Yep, a woman lost her independence today - my mom did - and maybe I'm losing a little bit of mine, too, but that's okay. I'm "taking one for the team" so that you can go to sleep tonight, knowing that the streets are a wee bit safer.

There's that damn music again! "Where to now, Miss Daisy?"

Hope
Springs
Eternal

As I just mentioned, my mom gave up her license recently and one of the duties that has fallen to me is taking her for her Friday beauty shop appointment. It's no problem - pick her up, drop her off, go to the grocery store for her while she's in the salon chair, pick her up, do lunch, and take her home. Glad to do it, as I'm sure she ran me all over the place when I was license-less.

Little did I know that I would be on the learning end of a very important lesson because of my new duties. And that is that hope springs eternal.

Now, the beauty shop my mom frequents has been around awhile. It's built up a fine reputation among its clientele. The hairdressers are very competent and friendly, as are the customers. But I don't think it's the kind of place that caters to younger ladies; you'd not see a gal getting purple streaks put into her hair or having a side of her head shaved, at this place. In fact, I think it'd be safe to say when I walk in, the median age drops down to seventy. (I'm am sixty-seven.) Fine old ladies are the primary clientele.

Believe me, I don't mean any disrespect here, but most of these women shouldn't even be buying green bananas! But here they are, week after week, getting their hair done. A few have walkers to get them to their chair and many are dropped off my husbands or kids. Perms, dye jobs, wash, and style- that all-important beauty appointment must be kept!

When I asked one gal how she was doing, her reply was, "I don't feel very good today, but I'll feel better after I get my hair done." And there lies the lesson.

It doesn't matter how old we are. We have to get up every day, put our best foot forward and plow ahead. At an age when I would, perhaps, be throwing in the towel, here are these women, at their age, putting forth the effort to look good for those around them. And it makes them feel good.

Yes, "hope springs eternal," and these Friday beauty shop ladies I've come to know, prove it. Thanks, ladies!

A Necessary Evil?

My mom will be going into a nursing home this weekend-kind of a necessary evil type of thing. I know that it's for the best; it's for her safety and for her mental and physical health. But it sure is harder than I thought it would be.

A once vibrant woman, she can't remember things now. She repeats herself a lot, she's unable to do the simple tasks she once did and has that "deer in the headlights" look that comes with dementia.

They say many of us regress as we age. It applies to kids putting their folks into nursing homes, I'm finding, too. I have the same feelings of trepidation I felt, as a young mom, when the boys entered kindergarten. "Will she be safe? Will she make friends? Will she know her way around? Will she behave?"

Nursing homes have come a long way. I know that. Maybe they were once a place to tuck away those who have outlived their supposed usefulness, but not anymore. There are activities to engage the residents and they have attention paid to their needs; perhaps this will enhance and maybe even prolong their lives.

Mom's handling it (for now) with the same grace she had when she surrendered her car keys-knowing it's best for her and that it is the right time. Worrying about the kids who have helped her live her life lately has been a consideration, too. We've gathered some of the precious mementos of a life well-lived, with which to decorate her new "home" and hopefully, she'll live out the rest of her life content with this decision. I really pray so.

I know I should feel blessed to even be in this position-to have had my mom for so long. At age sixty-seven, how many can even say that? But I guess with this milestone, if you want to call it that, comes the realization that we're becoming the oldest generation. And I'm not really prepared for that yet.

Aging's a funny thing. The years fly by and there you are. But I would like it to be noted, by my three sons, that their dad and I aren't "there" yet, contrary to what they may think some days. So, don't be getting any ideas, guys! I may not handle it as gracefully as my mom has.

It's Just Stuff...

We've been going through things at my mom's house as she's downsized and entered an assisted living facility. Now my folks lived well, not extravagantly, but they had a good life. My mom never was a hoarder to start with and she began "editing" long before that word became a common term in home organization. In fact, after Dad passed, we had to put the brakes on her pitching too many mementos from their past.

Thinking back, I see that my parents really were the antithesis of accumulating stuff....something that seems so common in our culture. My folks could have afforded it all, but it wasn't important to them. The biggest house filled with high-end décor, the nicest car. the latest phone or electronics-none of that mattered. They lived well...just not show-offy well.

What was important to them was how people were treated. It was about the values they tried to instill in their kids. It was the memories they shared with us and their encouragement for us to make memories of our own. It was about the good that comes from sharing your talents and treasures with others-of giving back.

On a grey day in November, as I sat at my mom's place sifting through photos- some framed, some not. It struck me how many memories and how many relationships they had accumulated in their lifetime. I'd love to emulate my folks, but know that many times I fall short, getting caught up, caving in, buying stuff, when it really IS about having people in my life, not things.

Maybe I'll work on that. Simplify, treat people better, make more memories...and share my talents.

Because in the end, it's all just "stuff".

I Can Remember.....

As I'm sitting here, our Christmas tree aglow and the first snow of the season falling outside, I'm reminded of past Christmases, all more precious because of events of the past few days. My mom is in the hospital, having fallen at the nursing home. The woman must be pretty darn flexible because she came out of it with no broken bones-pretty remarkable for ninety-five years, right? As she's in, yet, another foreign environment, her dementia is taking her further and further away from us. In a strange way, I kinda feel like I've lost my beautiful mother already. And during this season of love, peace, and joy, the joy's kind of hard to muster.

Christmas has always been a favorite time of year for mom, who was the hostess for most of our Christmas Eve celebrations with our families. She could decorate the house beautifully, but frugally, long before dollar stores came along. And I truly can't remember ever being disappointed in a single gift she and Dad put under the tree, all for Santa to take credit for.

Never one to crank out Christmas cookies, (I must get that non-baking gene from her!) I remember we always had plenty for the holidays. Not sure where the cookies came from, but she WAS big on making appetizers that she'd seen in magazines, I suppose. And the table always looked festive for both her family, Dad's family, and in later years, all of ours.

Christmases.... One, when there were new bikes at the end of a string we had to follow. One, when there was the Barbie Doll House, after I'd been told it was probably too expensive for Santa to bring. One, when we awakened to a neighbor lady in our living room, because Mom and Dad were at the hospital, getting the first son of the family. (Yep, born on Christmas, after having four girls - you think Dad wasn't over the moon?) One, when an engagement ring was retrieved from the pocket of a new suede coat from my future hubs. One, when Dad was in the hospital, but Mom carried on because it was the first Christmas with a grandchild in the family. One, when our young boys received bedspreads from their grandparents (epic fail, Grandma, THAT year!) One, after Dad had passed away and Mom was adamant that the tradition of the reading of Christ's birth be continued, this time by the aforementioned "Christmas son."

Christmas will be different this year, as it has been, since Mom, the Christmas hostess, is no longer in charge. We've all begun our own traditions, while carrying on the ones started by our folks, too. As I sit here, savoring the seasons of the past and pondering what THIS Christmas has in store for us, (and for Mom) the memories come flooding back. Beautiful memories...

My mom can no longer remember, but I can. Thanks, Mom.

The Plant Thief...

It isn't too often that I am surprised, maybe even overwhelmed, by a friendly gesture. I'm blessed with many wonderful people in my life and it's not really an expectation of goodness, but when you're surrounded by good and kind people, good and kind is what you have in life. So, this recent occurrence took place and caught me totally off guard...well, let me explain.

My mom resides in a nursing facility. Physically, she may well outlive me, but mentally, dementia has taken its toll and takes her further from us daily. She's still smiling, friendly, and kind, but every once in a while, her state of mind brings out quirky traits she never had before. Case in point. Mom has become a "Plant Thief." (Never thought those words would be attached to a description of my mom. And I'm only saying it, at all, to explain my story.). Recently, she's been collecting plants from throughout the facility and taking them to her room. The nursing staff lovingly retrieves them and returns them to their rightful places, until the plant thief strikes again.

I relayed this story to a friend who has a nursing background, is familiar with the elderly and with dementia. It felt good to be able to get her insight into Mom's most recent fixation, to just unload this "if you don't laugh, you'd cry" story, onto someone who understands.

So today, I went in to visit mom and the desk gal was carrying three plants. I jokingly said (and not really meaning it) "Has Mom been busy?"

She said "Yes, and she left this new one down here in the lobby... it's really hers. She took the tag off so I'm not sure who it's from. But the name began with an S." Remembering that the friend I had told the plant thief story to, had asked for Mom's address "so I can send a card," I knew who it was immediately.

Now, mind you, this friend lives a thousand miles away. We correspond, but I've seen her only once in thirty-five years. I was so touched by her kindness, a sweet gesture that could've been totally missed, had it not been for an astute employee who was looking out for my mom, and incredible timing. Mom and I sat in the lobby, talking about that friend, recounting some of the mischief we got into so many years ago, and Mom smiled. I went to my car, after that visit and cried.

I'm writing this, not to elicit sympathy. My mom's doing great and we're all handling it. And it's not to belittle or make fun of the elderly or dementia (although my mom was never a hoarder or even a big plant lover, so I smile at all this.) But it's to share a reminder that, in a world that seems to have so much divisiveness and hatefulness in it, if we have friends who listen, empathize, and touch our hearts with kindness, we're blessed beyond measure. I know I am.

The Eternal Cruise

Recently, my family was faced with the inevitable. Mom, whom I've written about plenty, is getting bumped up a couple of floors at the nursing home for more intense care. Her dementia has brought more challenges for her, for us, and for the nursing staff. We knew it was coming, but still it's rough.

Aside from the emotional impact, there's the financial impact, as well. My dad worked hard his whole life, socking away money to provide a safe and comfortable life for the two of them in their golden years. I'm sure he never fathomed that the ritziest neighborhood my mom would ever live in would be this - elder care - and she's not even aware of it.

After discussing with the hubs how this necessary care will nearly double the monthly costs, I've hatched a plan for us. And who knows? Maybe some of you would like to join us.

The hubs and I are looking into buying tickets for an Eternal Cruise (Hmmmm...Not an original idea, but maybe I'll patent that name.) When it comes time for us to require a nursing home, instead, we're going to buy tickets for a cruise and we'll never get off the ship! We think that for the same amount of money as a nursing home, perhaps, we can live the good life, afloat.

We figure the staff HAS to clean our room (or cabin) every day, no matter how messy we are! Meals, better than anything a nursing home could provide, would be available any hour of the day. Tropical drinks, gambling, swimming, bingo, and ballroom dancing, all right outside our door. Bathing suits and pj's would be our only wardrobe needs. If the spirit (and legs) move us, we can explore various ports of call, or just sit in a deck chair if that's what we want to do. If we get to the point where we forget where we are, no worries! Folks on cruises, out in the middle of the sea, never REALLY know where they are, do they? There's a doctor on board who, I'm sure, would like to have familiar and friendly patients who will stay with his practice. (Ha - we'd HAVE to!) We can send the kids postcards, allowing them to live their lives, without worry - letting them know we're doing just fine. And when really miss them, they, the grandkids and (maybe by that time) the great grandkids - well, they can join us for a big family vacation onboard.

When the end comes, we'll save even more money. Just slip the captain (who we'll be on a first-name basis with, by now) a few bucks, for a burial at sea. The perfect plan, right?

So, the conundrum? Blow it all now? Spend it down for you Medicaid purists. Or book that cruise?

I'm being flippant, I know. But the cost of taking care of folks as they age is concerning! I know the nursing staffs works hard for their money - believe me, I KNOW that! But it truly is sad that such a large chunk of our estates will be spent for the least amount of enjoyment at the end of our lives. "The Eternal Cruise" will change all that!

So, I'm just throwing another option out there. Anyone wishing to join us in about ten years (good Lord willing) let me know. We could probably get a terrific group rate with Royal Caribbean! Bon Voyage!

I Want My "Old Mom" Back...

What is it about older women and dementia? Do they have a monopoly on it, as opposed to men? And why is that? I am no expert on it, but I'm learning more about it than I ever thought I would. And on this topic, I just wish my mom wasn't such a good mentor.

My theory is that women keep track of everybody's schedules for years. Most men have to only keep track of their own. The women have so much going on in their heads that, as they get older, do they just short-circuit? Blow a fuse? Or are we just living too long?

I HAVE learned, through this journey with my mom, that if you don't laugh or at least smile at some of the antics, you'll cry....and I've done enough of that.

A few years ago, we noticed her repetition of things. With five kids to relay things to, it was understandable. She thought she had told all of us something and she was really just telling that one kid the same thing over and over. NOW, it may be the same remark, three times in a five minute conversation.

My mom has always been a proud woman and she still is. But that woman of old would never have done an impromptu hula in a lobby full of her peers. (No alcohol involved, either.) She would never have pouted because someone took her seat in the cafeteria. ("There ARE no assigned seats, mom. You take HER seat and you'll just have a different view today.") In her past life, Mom would never have obsessed over silly things. My "old Mom" would never have called me on the phone three times before 8:00 a.m. for no reason. The "old Mom" wouldn't welcome my sister back from her trip to Florida, every time she sees her - and my sister has been back home here for months. The "old Mom" would never have hoarded orange juice and bananas in her nursing home room fridge, like World War food-rationing was going into effect tomorrow. My "old Mom" wouldn't tell fibs, like the one that she was crowned queen of the home's senior prom. The photographs of Betty, with the glittery crown atop her head, in the nursing home photo gallery proved otherwise. (Busted, Mom!) The "old Mom" wouldn't always introduce me as, "My third daughter, who gave me this grey hair...SHE was somethin' to raise!"

("Not ALWAYS true, Mom.")

It'd almost be funny, if it wasn't so sad, that things are, indeed, going in a backward direction. My mom USED to be the one to solve our immature and petty arguments. She's the one who would call US out when we fibbed, she's the one who would be doing OUR laundry, or coaxing US to eat. The roles have definitely reversed.

I didn't write this to evoke sympathy or make light of something at the expense of my Mom. I wrote it because, I'm finding, that if we're blessed enough to have elderly parents, many of us will have these same struggles with that blessing.

And I also wrote it because I love my mom. She played a big role in the woman I've become and that's a good thing, I think-on most days. I even grew up wanting to be like Mom. But not anymore.... Now, I just want my "old Mom" back.

Perhaps...

I visited my sweet mom this morning at the nursing home. God, I hate that place! I hate ALL of them! And I hate the need for them! I know the employees there, thankfully, perform services and provide care to folks in my mom's condition that I couldn't provide, but I still hate them!

Perhaps, it's her attire. My "old" mom was a bit of a fashionista and she would be appalled at the sweatpants and sweatshirts she now wears..."It makes her care easier," they say. No wonder she gets combative when they dress her! Maybe she remembers the former wardrobe she stylishly wore.

Perhaps, it's the gibberish and disjointed thoughts she now tries to voice. My "old" Mom used to converse. She'd ask about the kids, talk about her love for my dad... In the early stages of her mental descent, she used to attach my name, instead of the real culprit's name, to any story from long ago that had anything bad connected to it. Nothing awful, just irritating, because of my innocence. But I'd give anything to hear Mom say, "Marysue used to....." again.

Perhaps, it's her hair now. White, straight, flat, and mannish-looking.... she used to be a weekly customer at a local beauty shop, where she'd emerge, proud and well-coiffed. I bitched and moaned plenty when it was my turn to take her to her appointment, but I'd give anything to be able to take her there now.

Perhaps, it's the wheelchair. Seeing her walk unaided would be such a gift. Taking her anywhere now is such an undertaking, with lifting her, comfortably - for both of us - and it almost makes her a hostage at the nursing home.

Perhaps, it's the blank stares. Her eyes used to show an interest in others... show a love for me. When I look into her eyes now, into that blankness, I just wish I could see what she's thinking-or where my "old" Mom went?"

Perhaps it's that, when I look at my Mom, I see me. I hate nursing homes and I pray that my kids never have to visit me in one-unless I'm still aware of my surroundings, care about the way I look, am able to communicate my love to them, and able to dance a jig, if I feel like it.

I guess I'm writing this to make myself feel better, (writing is therapeutic for me and I hope you don't mind) but probably more, to remind others to love your mom while she can still feel it. Talk to her, while she can still enjoy your conversations, walk with her while she still can, and take her places, while she is still aware of her surroundings.

God is keeping this shell of my mom on this good earth for a reason. Perhaps to teach me the lessons of patience-of giving back to someone who gave me life-of unconditional love. And it's all on HIS time. I know that. I also know that when Mom is gone, I'll wish that I could visit her in the nursing home, one more time. But the visits there now cause an ache in my heart for what used to be-and for what I wish, still was.

Yes, I hate nursing homes. But I hate dementia even more.

Things I Want to Say to My Mom Before She's Gone...

Those of you around my age will get this...For you younger readers, my message is this: Don't wait to tell your moms what you want them to know NOW. You may think they feel your gratitude, but you can't be sure. Say it now, while they're here and "here."

My Mom will never read, nor would any of the following words be remembered by her, but it sure would be great if she knew that I wanted to say...

- Thanks for loving Dad.
- Thanks for not quitting after you gave birth to two daughters.
- Thanks for listening, after school, to my stories of how my day went.
- Thanks for allowing me to make mistakes; I learned many lessons from them.
- Thanks for being such a great example of womanhood and femininity.
- Thanks for seeing to it that we went to church when we were kids.
- Thanks for not always taking my side, when I was involved in a disagreement with someone because I wasn't always right.
- Thanks for insisting I get summer jobs when I was in high school.
- Thanks for understanding, even when you didn't.
- Thanks for not being too vocal about my makeup, hair, or clothing choices growing up.
- Thanks for providing sound advice after we were married.
- Thanks for waiting to be asked for that advice.
- Thanks for the occasional purchases, when you knew I didn't have the money to treat myself.

- Thanks for supporting us, even when you and Dad weren't convinced we were right.
- Thanks for loving my kids and their kids; we can never have too much of THAT!
- Thanks for establishing traditions that will, hopefully, continue after we're gone.
- Thanks for giving me siblings. We're five very unique individuals, with a rich and fun shared history.
- Thanks for your example in love, family, and faith...

Thanks for being my mom.

Love ya, Mom...
Marysue

Prettiest Girl in The Second Grade

Age has shown me that our lives have many phases, chapters, and stages- whatever you want to call them. Sometimes, as the years go by, those chapters change in our minds. What once terrified or saddened us, becomes humorous, after enough years go by. And many things become even more precious as time passes.

Case in point? My mom.

Now, please don't think I'm a one-trick-pony. "Oh, there she goes again – Debbie Downer and her woes about dementia and nursing homes again." There IS a bittersweet tilt to this so please read on.

Those who know me, know I'm not a fan of nursing homes. I know they serve a valuable purpose, but I don't have to LIKE them. Going to see my mom, who has been a resident at a local one going on five years, is always on my list of things to do. It's not dread when I have to visit her, but it's not a bright spot in my days either.

All of the things I do, on my visits, I do for myself. I KNOW that. My mom is seldom aware of me even being there. But I go, in the hopes that my one-sided conversation -the photos I show her- will spark a memory...a smile. I occasionally take her flowers, bought at the local farmers' market. She never acknowledges them, but maybe, just maybe, a glance at the bouquet, will have her thinking they're pretty or knowing that she's loved.

On a recent visit, I decided to get mom away from the wing that imprisons her every day. I know an old, old friend is also a resident in another part of the nursing home. "Want to pay him a visit, Mom?" Nothing. I brush Mom's hair, put a touch of my lipstick on her lips, (she never left home without lipstick) and off we went.

Now, when I say "old, old friend," I'm not kidding! My mom and this gentleman go back almost ninety years- grade school friends - and they are now both ninety-five! He's more lucid than mom, but he, too, has entered the muddled world of dementia. I wasn't sure what we were in for, on this visit.

I needn't have worried. When we entered the common area, a smile came across the face of Mom's friend and I SWEAR there was a glimmer of recognition from my mom. Fumbling at conversation to bring these two together, I asked how far back these two friends went. Without hesitation, Mom's friend said, "Your Mom was the prettiest girl in the second grade at Saint Pete's." (In Mom's past life, she would've blushed and sat up a little straighter at the compliment.) Prompted by more questions from me, Mom's friend told me he "lived on North E. St. and she lived on Ridgelawn Avenue when they were kids," and added, "Jeannie's nineteen days older than me." I delighted in his clarity with the details, until he commented that his wife had brought him the snazzy new gym shoes he sported. (His wife has been gone for quite a few years.) I HATE dementia!

I knew that, years ago, Mom's friend went on to become Dad's best friend in grade school and high school. And his future wife was Mom's best childhood and high school friend, too. They were in each others' weddings. They shared their child-raising years with each other, experienced the empty-nest years together, and went on dinner dances (before wheelchairs and walkers.) They had parties (when smiles and laughter were the norm and they went on trips that my folks said were some of their best times. They continued to be lifelong friends, until life ended for two of them.

So, my mom and her gentleman friend remain. Mom told me, years ago, before her mind began to fade that the worst part of living so long is the family and friends who leave you. And many have left these two old friends, for sure! (Mom, the oldest of eight, lost her last remaining sibling recently.) When we were set to leave, ready to return to her room, Mom gave a gentle pat to her old friend's hand, (something I haven't been on the receiving end from her for years) but I didn't leave the place in my usual melancholy. It was a sweet visit.

Who even knows what went through those two old friends' minds? Two old friends who won't, most assuredly, even remember their brief encounter. But I will. Yep, it was a good day.

"The Pioneer Diva"

My beautiful mom is gone. She had a terrific run- ninety-five years of a great life and the love of a wonderful family and many friends. But with her passing, the world just got a little less pretty-a little less proud.

You see, my mom was a "pioneer diva." She was a "diva" long before "diva" became such a big word in our vocabularies. And I mean "diva" in the best way.

You'd never expect that-from a girl who was the oldest of eight kids and the mother of five-but she was. The epitome of femininity. I never heard her raise her voice with us kids and she was always dressed well, even on a budget that having five kids would demand. Her hair, always well-coiffed, even in her later years. And I don't remember my mom ever leaving the house without her lipstick. Always lady-like, she expected nothing less from her daughters.

A big reason for my mom's behavior was the way my dad worshipped her. No one could ever question that man's love for her-and it showed. She was proud of what she and Dad had accomplished and proud of the kids they had-and that showed, too.

When Dad passed away fourteen years ago, we weren't sure how things would go. They had been such a team for almost sixty years. We're pretty sure Dad was the one who called the shots in their relationship. But we're also quite certain that it was usually to appease the woman he loved. After Dad's death, Mom proved, in addition to being a proud and pretty woman, that she was also resilient. And, although she was never the same after Dad died, she retained that proud demeanor.

Those of you who know me also know that my ninety-five-year-old mom suffered from dementia the last five years of her life. She was getting further and further away from us toward the end. And although I began missing my "real" Mom a few years ago, it's now I realize how much I'll miss that beautiful face-the one that, when I was a kid, had a smile for me when I came home from school. I'll miss those hands that brushed a young girl's hair and sewed handmade clothes that I probably should have appreciated more. I'll miss that voice that offered advice to a dumb teenager or talked a young mom through a baby's first fever. I hope you don't think ill of me and that you understand, but towards the end, she wasn't the mom I want to remember. My beautiful mom, the one I DO want to remember, is gone.

Yes, the Pioneer Diva is in my heart and in my memory now-and the world just got a little less pretty-a little less proud.

"There's My Mom"

"Those we love and lose are no longer where they were before.
They are now wherever we are."
— Author: St John Chrystostom

Those words sustained me, after my mom left this earth recently. This was a woman who had a very long run-a good life. Someone who knew she was only renting space here, and lived her life, accordingly. She was a mom who, towards the end, was so mentally distant from those she loved and those who loved her. I hurt now, because her once beautiful face, body, heart, and mind are truly gone from this earth. But I also believe she's with my dad, her mind and memory restored, continuing their beautiful love story. This is all a new normal for me, as, at the age of sixty-seven, I've become an orphan. When I awaken every morning from now on, I'm the oldest generation of my family.

Yes, I've been thinking, a lot lately, "Those we love and lose are no longer where they were before. They are now wherever we are."

When I'm at the grocery store, there's my mom-choosing her favorite wine or picking up the ingredients for her vegetable soup recipe.

When I'm at Mass, there's my mom-telling me to stop leaning back on my fanny and to kneel properly.

When I'm holding my husband's hand, there's my mom- holding my Dad's.

When I'm fixing my breakfast, there's my mom-fixing cinnamon toast and chocolate milk for some impatient little girl.

When I'm shopping for cologne, there's my mom- sampling the fragrances at the counter at the local department store.

When I'm loving on my kids and grandkids, there's my mom-loving on hers.

I was blessed with a wonderful mom, for many years. Many aren't as fortunate as I've been-having her with us for so long. Oh, she wasn't perfect, and neither am I. But my mom set a great example of love, living her faith, being a lady, and valuing her family. And although she's gone now, I'll carry her lessons in my mind and her love in my heart forever. Because, although she's "no longer where she was before, she's now, wherever I am." And I consider myself blessed.

The Woman Years

It's a great time to be an old(er) Broad! That's what I'm finding out anyway.

The Old Girl Out Front

"When you came into the world, crying, everyone around you was smiling. Live a life that when you leave this world, you'll be smiling and everyone around you is crying." That is a neat thing to strive for, don't you think?

Nobody knows what their legacy will be. Is being nice to folks, putting on a positive face, and leaving the space we've occupied in better shape going to get it done? Leave folks misting up when we go?

I was thinking about this while I was raking leaves today. We have this huge oak tree in our front yard. I don't know if my dad planted it when he and Mom lived here or if they built the house around this tree. Either way, she's old and she's big-so much so, that her leaves make a mess in the front yard, then some blow over the house and mess up the back yard, as well. Every fall, I grumble about the ten million leaves I have to rake. In the spring, all is forgotten, and I love the shade and the coolness the old girl provides.

Maybe things will go that way for me. So, folks won't be wailing at my wake, but if they're ticked off at me, half the time, and love and appreciate me the rest of the time, like the old oak tree out front, I'm okay with that.

The Squirrel Lady

If one were to peruse my page on social media, they would see an ongoing barrage of squirrel jokes and pictures. Okay, I get it! I have become the unofficial "Squirrel Lady" of Facebook and it's all been a lot of fun, taking the teasing and all. But some don't know the back story and may just think

I'm some kind of goof. So, to set the record straight, several years ago, I wrote a blog about squirrels in our attic, a dilemma that has cost us a lot of money through the years. They're destructive to electrical wiring, they dig up bulbs, and feast on my tomatoes. They are truly rats with bushy tails, and I hate the critters!

In thinking back, I've never been a true lover of nature's creatures- at least of them being where they don't belong, like in my house or in my garden.

An early memory, that may have set the tone on this matter, has me sitting in St. Ann's Church, leaning on my beautiful mom. She was all decked out in her fox stole - you know what I'm talking about? Yep, fashionable women used to wear a dead animal around their necks, with the mouth of the animal forming a clasp onto the tail. (And we think today's fashions are out of whack?) Anyway, I must have been bored with Mass and decided to make Mom's fox, talk- you know, like a puppet. I got smacked for that. Was my resentment at being disciplined over that damn fox the start of it all?

Or was it when our beloved bunny, Bunzo, decided to eat her babies in our presence. No Mother of the Year award for Bunzo! Wow! Talk about being traumatized! Could that have been when the seeds were planted for my disdain for animals?

Or was it the parakeet that I purchased as a newlywed? We couldn't have a dog because we were renters at our first home. (Who wouldn't think a bird would be a good substitute for a dog? What a young idiot I must have been!) The hubs was at a football clinic (and you may remember -I seek forgiveness rather than ask permission) so why not? But I had to agree with him THIS time-it WAS a dumb purchase. I named him Pecker (I SAID I was a newlywed. Ha!) and had him for about three weeks when he started losing feathers. My Grandma B., a lover of birds, offered to take him and nurse him back to health. Before handing him over, we renamed him Petey, because no one wants to hear a seventy-five-year-old woman saying, "Pecker, want a cracker?" And we never reclaimed him. Could my dislike for the animal kingdom have gone back to then?

There have been countless episodes with creatures throughout my life that I could pinpoint to my "me vs them" mentality about animals. A fruit bat in a new home that could've been killed with a tap of a toe-steeled boot, but the hubs was so PO'd at it, that he pounded it to smithereens - on new carpet, no less. Or the mouse that had only its tail caught in the trap and dragged the trap around in the basement (I could hear it through the registers!) for two days before "giving up the ghost." Could that have been when I became a curmudgeon about Mother Nature?

Fast forward to now. At the present time, squirrels and deer are my nemeses. I know they're all God's creatures; they were here on His green earth first, too. But I see no reason why I can't have my tomatoes to myself. Or that I can't enjoy a night of sleep without hearing some damn squirrel, starring in his version of American Bandstand, dancing all over the attic!

So sure! I'll take on the persona of The Squirrel Lady. But now that you know my history with these critters, maybe you'll understand why a normally pleasant person takes on a hateful demeanor when she sees cute pictures and memes of them on Facebook. And if you don't get it? Be careful. I know where you live and I'd be happy to share God's natural bounty with you - and I'm not talking about tomatoes! (Told you I get hateful about it!)

A Hand Model? Nope.....

One can tell a lot about a person by looking at their hands. But you would be wrong, in MY case. I haven't worked in a mine, haven't spent a lifetime washing dishes, and I'm not a carpenter. I just have unattractive old hands. They're disproportionately small for the rest of my body, with short, stubby fingers, and they have not been very pampered-unless you count the fake nails that have graced them, off and on, through the years. (Looking back, that was kind of "like putting earrings on a pig.") So, you get it. My hands would never make it as a hand model.

I remember, as a kid, how firmly my Dad would hold my hand when we were crossing streets. He had a strong grip and made me feel safe. I remember Mom's hand on my forehead when I wasn't feeling well. Her touch made me feel loved. I remember getting bopped by one of their hands when I used the word "crap" - a grievous sin back then (but, boy! They should hear me NOW!). I used to tease my mom about her hands not being really pretty.

Shame on me; mine have surpassed hers, in the looking-old category, and she's ninety-five!

I shouldn't complain. My hands have held precious babies, caressed the same face for almost forty-eight years, and been shook by some wonderful folks. They've lovingly prepared countless meals, created some beautiful crafts and have patted the backs of some remarkable people. They've allowed me to type my memories for several years and they've done some acts of kindness for others. And they've been folded in prayer for small miracles and big ones.

Yep, my hands have served me well so far. They're far from pretty, but I hope they have many more prayers in 'em.

Cruisin'

I'm not a big car person; as long as it gets me where I need to go, I'm good. It's funny how the memories come flooding back though, over just seeing a picture of an old car you once owned or drove.

I learned to drive in a stick-shift Mercury, a hand me down from Grandpa. It was a good car, if you didn't mind the cigar smell. And when I graduated to a pea-green Chevy Nova, I thought I was ALL that! After our boys started arriving, an old blue Chevy station wagon got us where we needed to go. Back then, throwing a bunch of boys in the back end of a wagon, sans seat belts, was legal, and we did plenty of hauling boys that way! Then, we went through the van phase... The days of helping with paper routes and long-distance vacations when we drove through the night while the kids all slept.

I'm pretty sure every car in my past has a special place in my memory-most good, some bad. The rides to ballgames and the drive-thru windows of fast food places, the launching of three new drivers, licenses in hand-those memories are much fonder than the fender benders and speeding tickets that followed...and not just the boys'! (I've mentioned I'm not very good at driving...)

But one car that I drove, seemed to span more stages in my life and, as dorky as it was, I'll always have a special place in my heart for my old red Cruiser....

That car was the one that I drove when racing to the hospital to greet our first grandchild, the one that took Dad to appointments and treatments in his final years, the one I packed up numerous times when we moved one block over from our last home, the one that took me to our sons' homes when they moved out of town and interstates weren't really in my regular repertoire yet, the one I drove from a school parking lot, after my career there was over, the one that elicited honks and waves, just because folks were familiar with "her." (She'd been around awhile....)

I was surprised at the sadness that came at turning my old red Cruiser in several years ago. After all, I was getting a nice, new SUV. The old Cruiser didn't have air conditioning anymore, she practically limped onto the lot when we traded her in. She wasn't as shiny as she used to be. She and I had a lot in common. Maybe that's why that now-obsolete car has a special place in my memory and in my heart. I hope she's still on the road, like I am, making someone happy and getting them where they need to go. Who knows? And I hope, too, that we both have a lot more miles and smiles left in us! That would be just fine.

Lovely, Lovely Lindenwald...

Oh, I was grumbling, as I usually do when something messes up my schedule of doing things. This time, it was running unexpected errands that found me back in the place of my early years -Lindenwald. It was a beautiful, unseasonably warm day in December, nothing that would put one in the Christmas mood, but I'll take fifty-two degrees in December anytime!

I had my dog in the car- she assumes she's a welcome travel companion whenever I walk out the door- and her leash was on the floor of the car. So once my errands were taken care of, I figured, "Why not walk the dog here rather than when I get home?" The fact that it's a flat route, rather than the hilly one I usually walk (and dread) had nothing to do with that decision. Okay, maybe just a little bit.

Anyway, I parked the car on one of Lindenwald's many tree-lined streets and we began our walk, or, as it turns out, our trip down memory lane. You see, I'm a native of Lindenwald. I was born there, went to school there, and after a brief stay in a neighboring town, returned there to raise a family. I no longer live in Lindenwald (we moved to the west side when I began my job at a nearby school and our three sons began their high school years there.) But that unique part of town has never really left my heart.

In my journey that day, I passed the places I passed years ago. The drugstore, when penny candy was still around and prescriptions and healthcare were foreign topics, the corner groceries, before credit cards and fuel points, St. Ann's Church, where I made my First Communion-and our sons made theirs. The voices on St. Ann's playground I heard that day, could've been the voices of our boys and their friends forty years ago. On my walk through Lindenwald that morning, I recognized the homes of folks from my past - the kids I grew up with, the boys we had crushes on, and the ones we thought had cooties. I saw the homes of neighbors who were so kind to a young mom in the 80's. (I even stopped briefly to give some of those said neighbors a holiday hug!) I walked past the same parks and green space that I played in as a child-and where had I pushed my sons in the swings. What a fine place to be as a kid in the 60's, a young mom in the 80's, and that morning in 2019!

Sure, Lindenwald has its issues and problems; there isn't a city or town in this great nation of ours which doesn't. Some of the homes aren't in the pristine condition I recall as a child. And I swear, some of the cracks and bumps in the sidewalks are the same ones I used to traverse, pushing a baby stroller. But Lindenwald has a distinctive old charm to it that I know the old timers, who've never left, feel every day. (That's probably why they've never left!) I hope the newcomers feel it, as well. There's a renewed sense of pride in the air, in Lindenwald, too. Improvements being made-a sense of community being felt. I hope all those blessed to live there appreciate it.

Lindenwald was a terrific place to be a kid and Lindenwald was a great place to raise 'em. I'm grateful that Lindenwald played such a cherished part in my life. And I'm also grateful the good Lord gave me a fifty-two-degree day in December so I could go back and appreciate it all over again.

The
Address
Book

I'm always a bit slow, latching on to all things digital. I know so many new things are better and make things easier or more efficient. Case in point - the ability to enter and store the phone numbers and addresses, in my phone, of those who are close to me. But I'm struggling with my latest possible transition to the digital world.

I have an address book, as most of you probably do...or did. Mine is nothing special. Just a small, hardbound book I keep in a drawer, always at the ready, to provide me with the information I need to make a call or to send a card or a letter. This book has been around awhile and if I had the energy, I should probably replace it. Its pages are smudged, scratched, and scribbled on, but, in paging through it, I can see that, in a sweet way, it's a written history of friendships and family connections that are too important to just toss.

My book tells me who has been in my life for years. There are some newer entries, too. All family and friends who have gone through a lot with me. The scribbles show who has changed their addresses (one son, four times and one sister, three times) or who just moved on from being in touch like they used to be. With light lines drawn through their names, my book reminds me of who is no longer with us. It seems hitting a delete button on my phone would be so final, kinda, like erasing them forever from my memory. And I don't like that.

Texting and emails may very well replace phone calls, cards, and letters. That's progress, I suppose. I'm probably not very "with it," holding onto an old address book. But, to me, it's a testament to the family, friends, memories, and the many changes in my life that I've enjoyed and endured-almost as many as my address book.

Yep. I think I'll hang onto it -to serve as a reminder to stay in touch - by phone or by mail, and to give me a nudge, every once in a while, to say a prayer for loved ones no longer with us-the ones with the light line drawn through their names. Call me slow...old fashioned... I don't care.

I'm keeping it!

Picture Perfect-NOT!

I've been working on an ongoing project for about three years now and I can finally celebrate its completion!

Now it's my fault that I allowed things to get to this state in the first place - I'm talking about family photos! I've been throwing them into boxes for forty years-talk about overwhelming! Wow! I've been the photographer all those years -turns out I just didn't want to be the family archivist!

There are pictures of the boys, pictures of friends, pictures of the boys' friends, pictures of my folks, my siblings, the in-laws, my co-workers, hubby and me. There are family vacations, holidays, and trips with friends. I took a lot of photos! As a first-time mom, I couldn't get enough photos of our new addition. When the second son arrived, the photos were fewer and by the time the third son came, I was lucky to be able to even find the camera, let alone, take pictures! We joke now that if we can't identify a picture of one of the boys, we put it in the youngest one's stack, because he got so short-changed! (Just kiddin', "youngest one"...)

So, my plan was to make an album for each of the boys. Now I'm not talking a cute, elaborate scrapbook; this is a basic album with different stages in their lives noted. The remainder of the photos are going into a manila envelope for them to do what they want with them. Mission accomplished! My project is complete!

Oh, not so fast! What, at this stage of my life, am I going to do with the rest of the pictures? To put them in albums at this late date, seems silly. When I'm gone, who's going to even want them?

Remember when the drugstores that developed our photos offered free doubles? How hard would it have been for me to send them to those special people who were in the photos -or to even just pitch them? Nope, into the box they went. I guess I thought the relationships were too precious to throw away any evidence of them. And those cameras in the 90's that produced those long landscape photos? Even if I DID keep up with albums, those pictures wouldn't have fit! And why, oh why, didn't I mark the backs of the photos with names, or dates, or places? I struggle to identify some of those faces now and those who inherit the photos after I'm gone certainly won't know who they are!

I think today, there should be concern for a dilemma the opposite of mine. In this world of camera phones and selfies, is anyone developing their photos anymore? If not, I have a few hundred you can have. In forty years, you probably won't be able to identify yours, either!

Photos, Cameras, Fotomats

These are the days of selfies, Instagram, Snapchat, and phones that have pretty much replaced cameras. And as an old(er) broad, that saddens me. And the question begs to be asked, "Is anyone saving their precious photos? I mean saving to something other than Facebook or just on that phone?"

I know I'm from a long-ago era and photo albums are viewed about as outdated as I am. But for me, looking through one of those albums is comforting-seeing faces, places, and memories from my past is much more desirable than scrolling through a phone. Am I alone in this?

I come from the time when having a camera was a big deal. A time of the little Brownie or the Kodak Instamatic. Sure, buying film, loading it, tracking down those cube-like light bulbs for those cameras, was a pain. So was dropping off the film to be developed, whether it was at a camera shop or at the drugstore. I remember the excitement, when Fotomats, those little kiosks in shopping center parking lots across the country, promised quicker turn-around time for getting your pictures-from maybe five days to two! And the Polaroid camera that offered a picture "in seconds!" The quality suffered a bit, but you saw your pictures in quick fashion and you didn't have to go through the development process with drugstores.

But I'm afraid that now, with the way things are, we're sacrificing permanence for immediate satisfaction. We see our pictures as soon as we take them and that's terrific! But are we saving them for future generations to see? Or to jog our own memories, when our memories are fading? I hope so!

This may be another case of my living too long. But, for me, capturing those moments and preserving them for the future was worth the effort. Oh, our boys, when the hubs and I are gone, will probably back a dump truck up to the house and pitch the boxes and albums of photos I've treasured all these years. And that's okay. Just so they know that I held those shiny pieces of photo paper in my hands and savored the memories they represented. And they may, one day, be sorry if they don't do the same.

Now That's A Tall Order!

Where was the fashion industry forty years ago when I needed them?

I'm a tall gal. I was always ahead of the curve in terms of height. In grade school, I could pass for the mom of some of the boys in my class. In high school, I'd have had a basketball career-if I'd also had an athletic bone in my body. So, you get it-I'm tall.

It's not that uncommon anymore. There are tall women all over the place! And the fashion world is taking notice! Finally!

That wasn't always the case. Back in the 70's, when jeans were popular, my dear mother, a talented seamstress, sewed strips of patriotic fabric along the bottom legs of my jeans so I would fit in. Luckily, the hippie movement was in full force, so I only looked like half a dork and not a full-blown one.

Then there was the stirrup pants era. Stirrup pants were stretch pants with a band of fabric that went under your foot, causing your slacks to maintain a smooth line and keep them in place when wearing boots. Remember? They seemed like a great solution for a tall girl-that little band, tugging the slacks closer to the ankle...NOT SO! For about two years of my life, I walked around, tugging my slacks up, so the crotch wasn't down to my knees. Maybe suspenders would've helped. Nah, that could've been painful...

Thank you, fashion industry, for recognizing tall girls-finally! We appreciate it!

P.S. And I would kiss the lips of the person who came up with the idea of capris, where height doesn't matter at all. You, sir (or madam) are a genius!

Things I Learned on A Cruise

I was fortunate to take an Alaskan Cruise recently with the hubs and some dear friends. We had a terrific time, saw beautiful sights, laughed a lot, and were all still getting along when the voyage ended.

In addition to the geological and historical facts one absorbs when traveling, I picked up some additional tidbits, too.

I learned that...

the lines at the bottom portion of your face have a name- marionette lines. It took getting a facial to find out I'm looking more and more like Howdy Doody every day. Oh, great!

I learned that…

sometimes, the term "ugly American" is deserved. Many Americans are just spoiled, impatient, and rude. Be nice, asshats. You're representing a nation; the cruise staff- they're just hard- working folks, doing their jobs and that kind of behavior is totally unnecessary.

I learned that...

one can hear "Iceberg ahead!" and other Titanic references way too much in one week (fellas!)

I learned that...

by booking the room at the very back of the ship, (I never got that fore and aft business) you needn't go to the gym while on vacation. That's because the bars, dining rooms, and shops that we frequented (frequently!) were at the other end of the ship. Great view, nice walk!

I learned that...

The sounds of the sea outside one's open door, would eliminate the need for a bedroom fan at night at home. I'm SURE of it!

I learned that...

the world is a big place and that we're all just tiny, tiny, blips in the big picture. And we need to take care of the beautiful backdrop of nature we've been given. (Except for squirrels... I STILL hate squirrels!)

I learned that...

portions of food from other cultures are smaller than Americans' portions. (Which explains the obesity in our country - present company included.)

I learned that...

if I had a mirror on our ceiling, like the one at the spa, I would weigh fifty pounds less....no doubt! Ugghh!

I learned that...

the Catholic Church truly IS universal. No matter where you go, our Mass is the same!

I learned that...

there may be no better alcoholic drink than a Lemon Drop unless it's a Jameson and Ginger (no hangovers.) And our bartender was a gem!

I learned that...

if the hubs were in such close quarters with me, for more than seven days very often, I'm not sure we'd be celebrating a forty-eight-year anniversary this summer. And that's on me, not him.

I learned that...

dirty clothes weigh more than clean ones. Or was it the souvenirs we bought that had us sweating it at the airline check-in counter? Weight overages are pricey which probably explains why they don't have scales at the airport before you get up to the counter. As my friend suggested, we wouldn't hold up the line, now would we? Stellar idea, friend!

I learned that...

one must count their blessings every day. I already knew that, but a phenomenal trip with some terrific traveling companions in a beautiful setting, like Alaska, was a great reminder. Feeling blessed, for sure!

Bon Voyage!

A Kid for A Day - Not Hardly!

So, are amusement parks about ten times bigger than the amusement park of my youth or is it that my legs are fifty years older? The answer to both is YES!

I had the pleasure of taking my granddaughter to one on a summer visit here. We were joined by my sister and her granddaughter-this was going to be fun! Now, it's been about thirty years since I'd been to that huge amusement park and I was as excited for myself as I was for my granddaughter. There's just something about an amusement park that brings out the kid in me. Well, it didn't take long for me to grow up that day! One ride on a roller coaster and I was well-aware of my age! Yikes! And that was a mild roller coaster.

It was a great day, once I determined it was wiser to ride more tranquil rides. Congo Falls sounded pleasant enough, until we emerged soaking wet, with raccoon eyes, where eye makeup had once been! Or the Wind Seeker where we flew way above the park and then slowly descended. But, you know, in watching the kids riding all those thrilling rides, I decided that they sure wouldn't be very thrilled with the rides of my youth.

LeSourdesville Lake was a summer destination for us every year. The excitement would build, as we'd talk about which rides we'd ride first. The day would finally arrive! I can still smell the waffles and funnel cakes, their scents wafting through the air as we entered the park. (Always a food memory! Why IS that?) And once inside its gates, the amusement park was, indeed, a magical place!

Kiddie Land was the first stop. How would a ride down a plexiglas Old Lady In The Shoe slide, sit with kids today? Or riding the train to the Wild West, where we'd see pretend gunfights, only to end up at the saloon for some sarsaparilla? Driving the antique cars and the Turnpike cars made me feel so grown up, although it never really helped with my driving later on! The Haunted House was scary back then, but would be pretty lame, I'm thinking, by today's standards. The Dodge Cars were about as daring as I got. Getting slammed into, like that, would pain me now, but back then? That was fun! I was never a fan of the old wooden roller coaster - too rickety - and the ferris wheel was pretty boring, even for me.

For the kids enjoying this place now, the $15 chicken tenders, $4 bottles of water, and the many crazy, extreme rides will be their good old days. Things will get bigger and better (as they always do) and those "kids" will have their own memories of amusement parks far different than THEIR kids. Yes, amusement parks are magical places. And things are bigger, shinier, and better now. I know that. But I don't remember needing a heating pad after taking a ride on the Old Lady in The Shoe slide, either!

The Aromas, the Tastes, the Memories

Anyone who knows me, even barely, knows that I'm a food fan. I love to eat, I love to cook, I love to read about food, and I love to hear about it. It's an obsession I don't want to get rid of! I also love to reminisce about it, thinking back to fine meals, snacks, and treats. Food jolts me into memories - maybe that's why I love food so-because I love to look back.

If I taste a powdered sugar coffee cake, my mind always goes back to Mt. Pleasant Bakery, a little store in the community in which I was blessed to spend my youth, or Ted's Bakery, in another part of town, that brings back memories of sleepovers with my high school friend; those carefree days, of picking something from the glass-enclosed bakery case was the biggest decision we'd have to make that day.

The bar was set so high, back in the 70's, at Isgro's, an Italian restaurant that was a frequent date place for the hubs and me. Their steaks were wonderful and I'm not sure I've had one as good since. Sadly, Isgro's is long gone and gratefully, the hubs is not.

I have my mother-in-law's meat loaf recipe in her handwriting, and even if I follow it to the letter, I can't duplicate it; it was so good! Her tiny kitchen produced some of the best meals I ever ate. I smile when I watch home improvement shows that boast huge kitchens and probably produce nothing, even close, to the meals that came from that little kitchen on Linda Lane.

One of my sisters makes the best lasagna (I sure wish she'd make it for me now!) and that conjures up memories of Sunday night dinners at their house when we were young couples, just starting out. Another sister's specialty of Chicken Tetrazzini reminds me of the countless times she helped me out with that meal, when things weren't going well, as a young Mom with three boys under five.

My grandma and then my mom, gave me their vegetable soup recipe that provides a soothing aroma in our home, even now. And fixing my rendition in a soup pot that Grandma gave me as a bridal shower gift forty-eight years ago, adds to the memories.

My other grandmother was the master apple pie-baker, a talent I greatly appreciate because I don't bake-her apron, dusty with flour, rolling out the dough, on her screened-in back porch. I can't smell an apple-cinnamon candle now and not think of my Grandma Bruner.

The smells, the tastes, the places - yep, food certainly conjures up all kinds of memories for me. I could go on and on. But what are some of yours?

Obsolescence-What's Next?

I was recently reading an article about tech gadgets that have become obsolete in the past decade. Ten years! Things are moving that quickly! Floppy disks are an example. When we started on computers, those were such important parts of the whole idea of computing. We could save everything! Another obsolete tech item? E-Mail service we had to pay for! Remember those AOL disks we received in the mail about every week? Ninety-day free trial and then you started paying?

I like to think back in bigger slots of time. Generations and eras seem to slow things down a bit more for me than decades. With that in mind, I offer to you, items from past eras that, I'm pretty sure, we'll not be seeing anymore.

- *Jiffy Pop* - or just plain popcorn, cooking in oil on the stovetop. Sure, microwaves have changed the way we cook, but there was something about the fragrance of bubbling oil and the "pop, pop, pop" of the kernels hitting the pan lid. I could always count on burning Jiffy Pop! It was more of a novelty than a matter of taste, seeing that foil stretch before your eyes- it was pretty amazing.

- *Dippity Do*- that gooey hair-setting concoction -pink for "regular and green for "hard to hold." Might as well put mesh hair rollers and picks with them. We won't be seeing them anytime soon either - and I say, "good riddance!" I think I STILL have some indentations in my head from those suckers!

- *Foto Mats* - Those cute little kiosks, found in parking lots all over the U.S. Just drive up, drop your film off, and return in a few days -that's right -days!! To get your photo prints. Say so long to film, too. Not needed anymore. Just click and download. The upside to film, in my eyes? We'd be seeing fewer selfies if people had to pay to have them developed!

- *Ash Trays* -I would've been screwed in my ceramic classes in the 70's! Ash trays were the go-to item in my repertoire. Nothing tedious-I could go outside the lines with my painting and still be okay. Just slap that paint on and done! Bundle with the ash trays, candy cigarettes, and bubble gum cigars. You won't be seeing them anymore - at least, not out in public. But I could be a closet smoker with a pack of those Winston candy cigarettes right about now!

- *Electric Football Games* - remember the little plastic players, carrying a tiny cotton ball on a vibrating field? I always had the fella that seldom ran for the right goalpost-he always got turned around. Video games provide more sophisticated fun, I guess, but not the laughs that that goofy electric one did.

- *Diaper Service* - Before the invention of Pampers, we had fresh cloth diapers delivered and soiled ones picked up by a friendly diaper guy in a truck. Whoever thought that was that sanitary of an idea back then would never make it now, but it really was a pretty lucrative and popular business years ago.

Well, there you have it. My short list of things, although obsolete now, were fun, interesting, or handy when we had them. It's funny how our opinions, our needs -heck, life itself - changes so quickly. Don't you wonder what's around now that will meet with the same fate of obsolescence, as Jiffy Pop and Foto-Mat?

Well, hopefully, not us!

Flying the Friendly Skies

Do you remember flying the friendly skies years ago? Recently, the airlines have been portrayed in the news as being far from friendly. So much has changed in air travel since the good old days. And don't you yearn for them again-just a little bit?

I remember my first time on an airplane. I was in the eighth grade and was flying to Washington D.C. with my folks and two of my siblings. Everything was so exciting! It all seemed so grown up and elegant. Taking off from the Cincinnati Airport, we breezed through check-in, with ticket in hand, and walked out onto the tarmac and up the steps to the plane. As we boarded the plane, we were greeted by young and attractive stewardesses. If memory serves me right, the passengers were dressed up like we were going somewhere important. We were seated and told "to fasten our seat belts" (a new concept.) Remember? We didn't have seat belts in our cars in the 60's, so we needed the instructions. We weren't in our seats for long when we were served a meal. It didn't matter the time of the flight, a meal or a substantial snack was served on most flights. How fun! It didn't matter that it wasn't fine cuisine; it was something new and different. We were settled in for what was going to be a great trip.

How things have changed! On a recent trip, as we waited in line for bags to be checked, I thought back to those simpler times. Whoever would've thought that we'd be charged extra for bags? That we would have to go through a security check, where we would be scanned and probed? That we'd be greeted by older women and men, instead of the stewardesses from the *Coffee, Tea, or Me* days? That people would be cramming full-sized luggage into the overhead compartments to avoid paying those baggage fees? That most of my fellow passengers would be in sweats and jeans? That, after using seat belts in our cars for forty years, we'd still be hearing an explanation on how to use them? That we'd have peanuts and pretzels thrown at us, instead of those fun meals?

I know a lot of these changes had to happen, because of circumstances beyond our control, like 9/11. And some of them just because of the way things are. Folks don't get that dressed up anymore. The airlines, facing high oil prices, have to charge more and serve less. I sound like an old-timer, I know, longing for the good old days. Change is good, most of the time, I guess. More people fly than ever before and that's a good thing.

But forgive me if, instead of listening to the seat belt instructions, I just sit there, in my slacks and sweater, anxiously awaiting my peanuts.

What
Price
Beauty?

I know I've touched on this topic before...how far we women go to look good. The hair coloring, the clothes, the working out, the makeup. And I know I've joked about how Mom would cut my bangs, unbelievably short, the night before school pictures or how we all endured those smelly permanents, as kids. All for the sake of looking good.

I had forgotten until I was looking through some old photos, perhaps, the most ridiculous lengths we went to-and that was the use of hair rollers! Whether they were the plastic ones or those mesh, bristly ones, we counted on them to give us gorgeous curls or beautiful waves. Sometimes they worked, sometimes-not so much.

I remember slathering on Dippity-Do, a pink gelatinous product that was supposed to increase the "hold," and rolling my hair almost nightly. That's right! We slept on those tortuous tubes, with picks poking into our scalps, didn't we? That may have been when my sleeping disorder got its start-and no wonder! I remember, too, having rollers in my hair, during the daytime, and throwing on a scarf, before heading to the store. Yeah, that scarf really made it all look better!

In looking at old photos, I can honestly say that my hair never looked good enough to justify having endured the pain and inconvenience of hair rollers.

We all have it so much easier with nicer haircuts, better styling products, hair dryers, and curling irons these days-and never having to put up with those goofy looking curlers again. I'm certain that today's young women wouldn't be caught dead outside in those things. They have too much sense and class. Oh, wait a minute-I just spotted a young lady at the store in flannel sleep pants. I stand corrected!

What's My Shelf Life?

As I've gotten older, I'm seeing that more and more of the things I love are discontinued. My favorite shade of lipstick - the one I've used for ten years - is no longer available. The brand of my make-up? Same deal.

And the colognes of my high school years-Ambush? Emeraude? They've been relegated to *Drugstore.com* and probably wouldn't smell the same as they did those many years ago, anyway.

The days of equating the smell of a shampoo with pleasant memories of our younger days are obviously over, too. Remember Prell, that thick, green shampoo concoction? Or Adorn hairspray? Now, the formulas of everything we use are "new" or "improved" upon so often, who can zoom in on a favorite? Or connect it to a memory?

There's a lot to be said for longevity, so I should probably be grateful that I'm outliving all the products of my past. Maybe I just need to be "new" and keep on "improving", too, but I sure wish they'd let some of those old favorites hang around just little while longer. Don't you?

Bouncin', Behavin' Hair

Okay, so who has "bouncing, behavin' hair?" Whoever did?

Anyone who knows me knows I struggle with my hair. So, it should never surprise anyone if they see me hanging out in the drug store aisle, checking things out. What SHOULD surprise everyone, as it does me, is the sheer number of hair products out there now! Yikes!

I remember the good old days when Breck shampoo promised us that "bouncin', behavin' hair." And it took its place on the drugstore shelf next to the beautiful bottle of Prell shampoo, that thick, luscious, green concoction that smelled so good. Not to be outdone was Halo, which I guess, got its name from the brilliance it was supposed to give our crowns. And V05. I never knew what that name meant, did you? The point I'm making is that the selection wasn't very extensive back then, but the brands were certainly memorable, weren't they?

Same deal with the hairsprays. I can still remember the fragrance of Adorn and Aqua Net because whenever high school girls gathered in a restroom, clouds of the stuff choked us! My grandmother used Adorn and I remember sneaking around to use her hairspray because the cheaper White Rain hairspray my mom used just wasn't doing the trick.

Hair setting gels, like Dippity- Do, were used when "rolling" our hair or using bobby pins to curl it. I remember thinking that the reason my hair wasn't looking great was because I used the pink "regular" and not the green "hard to hold." Yeah, sure! The real reason I had bad, uncooperative hair that was far from "bouncing and behavin" was because I had bad, uncooperative hair!

And like turning to hair coloring was going to help? Who remembers the, "She's not getting older - she's getting better," Clairol campaign? Boy, oh, boy! Did I ever get sucked in by those ads! Ha! "Only her hairdresser knows for sure," was far from true for me, too. EVERYBODY knew that I colored my hair because 1) it was never the same color for long and 2) most of the time, it was a color that our good Lord would never have created! The countless botch jobs!

It has amazed me for years that A) I still have a hair on my head after all the abuse. B) that I didn't spend the majority of my teen years grounded for spending my hard-earned money on such non-sense and C) that my husband has been a real trooper thru my many shades, styles, and mishaps. (It probably helps that the man is clinically color blind.)

There are so many choices nowadays in shampoos, sprays, oils, gels, and colors. A far cry from the days of Prell, Adorn, and Dippity-Do.... It makes me kind of glad I'm an old(er) broad now. I couldn't handle it! Too many tempting choices! But if you should ever hear that I've gone missing, please send the rescuers to the Walgreen's hair care aisle. You know, "Old habits die hard."

They say that it's a thin line between genius and insanity. Sadly, that's probably as close to genius as I'll ever get.

Yes, I'm on the other side of that line, for sure. I have issues -and claustrophobia is one of them. Not sure why or when it started. Did my sister and her best friend lock me in a closet years ago? Was I held under water by some of the bratty boys at the swimming pool? I don't know, but my fear of enclosed spaces is always in the back of my mind and I'm getting tired of it.

Elevators, airplanes, caves-those have been triggers for years. If I HAVE to take an elevator, I have to be right in front of the door. Don't ask me to move to the back of the elevator, cuz I'm not moving! If I am flying, that little overhead fan better keep running, because if that airflow stops, someone's going to get arrested. And caves? At a museum trip, when the boys were little, we were welcomed with a cave entrance. The hubs and the boys took off. I entered, gave it my best shot, and ended up forcing my way back out, pushing little kids and their parents out of my path to fresh air. Kind of like a salmon going the wrong way in the spawning season.

I guess some health events lately have me thinking, more than ever, that I need to seek treatment for my condition. It's probably time to get help when MRI's have me more upset about the procedure than the possible outcome. I was once told that I would be the first person in the history of the hospital to require a sedative for an ankle MRI! Not a fan of that tube! Maybe it goes back to seeing those iron lungs" that were used to treat polio when I was a kid that have me spooked. Who knows?

And movies? If there is a grave, a submarine, or a spaceship featured, hubby can go alone! No thanks! And that's terrible, isn't it?

If anyone has any ideas on how I can conquer my fear of enclosed spaces, I'm open to anything, short of becoming a druggie. The name of a good therapist, maybe?

Or perhaps I should just embrace my condition-after all, I'm almost a genius!

Editing, De-Cluttering, Simplifying

I've decided that if this weather is going to hang around for a while, I'm going to do something productive inside. That way, when the holidays are over and spring follows, I'll be ready to tackle things outside.

My project will be to declutter things around here. "Edit" is a big word used by professional organizers these days, so I'm going to start editing the heck out of the house-starting with closets. There are many terrific organizations that could use the things that I no longer use -or can they? Well, I'm going to de-clutter. Maybe there will be a home for my cast-offs. I hope so, anyway!

Why is it we accumulate so much stuff anyway? I've hung onto my professional clothes, and that ship has sailed for sure! Am I sentimental about having had a career, and it's over now? I miss the good folks I worked with and for, but I love things the way they are now. Time to pitch 'em! (The clothes...not the people I worked with...)

I have three different sizes represented in my closet. Even if some of those clothes ever fit again, they're far from current. Whoever thought shoulder pads in women's clothes were a good idea? I'm sure I thought I was *all that* back then when all I really looked like was an NFL linebacker! But not everything in my collection is so dated. Some of it doesn't fit anymore, never looked good in the first place, or went with anything else in my closet. We just don't get that dressed up anymore! Why am I saving all these dresses and skirts?

And shoes? I used to love high heels! I had some great looking stilettos back in the day. The foot pain that came with wearing them or towering over most of the men in our circle, was no deterrent. I rocked that look and what for? Well, not anymore! Comfort has become too important so out they go, too!

There really is no good reason to have closets, bulging with things that are no longer of use. I certainly hope they can be used by someone. Maybe a kid taking part in an 90's Theme Day at a school somewhere? Maybe someone who's into vintage will think my cast-offs are a hoot to wear. I don't know, but my closets are going to have the hell "edited" out of 'em. It's just stuff and I'm going to simplify.

So, if you see someone walking around in stilettos, looking like a line-backer, just know that she found some terrific bargains at a local thrift store and I've accomplished my task!

We Grow Too Soon Old and Too Late Wise

"We Grow Too Soon Old and Too Late Wise,"-Have truer words ever been written? I know it certainly resonates with me.

In the third grade, I remember thinking that

my teacher was old. Doing some calculations, she was, maybe, forty years old-old to a third grader, but certainly not to me now. Take a look at some old-time photos. Granted, they had harder lives than we have now, but really? "Old" truly is all a matter of perspective.

Many young girls seem to be in such a rush to be older. Years ago, you could count me among them. I remember sneaking into my sister's make-up or begging my mom to let me wear nylons. I get it. I can also tell the young-sters that becoming older comes soon enough and then, there you are-older.

And the "too late wise" part? I should have taken learning more seriously. There's a difference between book smarts and common sense, and if given a choice, I guess I'd rather opt for the commonsense part. But I should have worked harder at having a combination of the two. Maybe it's not too late.

I know age on your face doesn't guarantee wisdom, that's for sure. There are plenty of old-timers who, in spite of making countless mistakes, haven't learned from them yet. And plenty of fresh-faced kids who are wise beyond their years. Perhaps we could form a coalition, learn from one another and change that up a bit to, "grow too soon wise and too late old." I wish!

Any Takers?

I'm not what you'd call a shopper. Oh, I like finding bargains, but I've always been one of those "go find what you're there for and go home" kind of shoppers. No lolly-gaggin' for THIS old(er) broad!

With that being said, you'd think I'd be a natural for online shopping, right? Lounging around in my robe, coffee nearby, picking and choosing (and charging) to my heart's content, and at my leisure.

Some would ask why WOULDN'T you like finding something online, ordering things with ease, and having your merchandise delivered to your door (many times with free shipping?) Oh, sure, I do my fair share of online business, but it seems there's something missing.

And what would THAT be? The lack of memories that come with it, that's what!

If shopping online back in the 50's, 60's, and 70's had it been available, I would've missed:

*   Bus rides uptown to shop with my mom....or my sister...or my friends.

*   Trips to Imfeld Music for the latest single by The Temptations or The Beatles...

*   Trying on bathing suits at Elder Beerman with my sister, who was horse-laughing on the other side of the dressing room door...

*   Perusing the aisles of the specialty dress shops for a new ensemble that I didn't need nor could I afford....

*   Practicing walking in high heels at the shoe store with girlfriends who were just as clumsy as I was....

*   Looking for dress shirts at Shillito's with the teacher-hubs...

*   Handpicking the paint at Sears that would decorate a new son's nursery...

So many memories come from getting out with family and friends and enjoying the brick and mortar stores of my past.

Online is the way to go now - I get it - and young(er) folks won't miss what they never had.

I should probably appreciate online shopping more at this particular time in my life. No driving all over in search of something, no parking the car, no fighting the crowds, and no hauling packages down the street to the car.

Maybe, I'll start to enjoy online shopping more. Who knows?

But I would probably like it even more if some girlfriends would join me on the couch... giggling and making fun of each other-you know, making memories! That would help!

Any takers?

Lost Dog?

So, our dog went missing the other morning for three hours. So unlike her. I let her out to use the john at four a.m. and she just kept on going to gawd knows where. Luckily, the hubs went out in search of her (That's so unlike HIM; he must like her some, too.) Anyway, she's back, now and asleep. I don't have that luxury today.

I haven't been walking her much this week because of a bad case of poison ivy-itches too much when I get hot-so maybe she got fed up and walked herself. Or maybe she has a friend down the street she's been missing. Or maybe she was just feeling independent, or defiant-or tired of me bossing her around. Sure wish she'd been wearing a body-cam. I'd love to know where her adventure took her.

Maybe someone kidnapped her - I've always said they'd bring her back once they saw what a goof she is. Anyway, I'm glad she's back, unless I don't get a nap today. Then we may have to rethink that.

An Addendum to The Lost Dog
Things Ain't Right at the Wright House

After telling the world about our dog's adventure on the road (or avenue) and being gone for hours, I have an addendum to that story.

After playing his round of golf and heading to work, the hubs calls and asks, "Well, did you get your dog back?"

I said, "Well, sure. I texted you. Thanks for finding the dog." (Why does no one read my texts?) He said he drove around the neighborhood, up and down the side streets, on his way to the course, but no dog. I was sure he was pulling my leg.

"No, seriously, I couldn't find her. Is she there?"

Still not convinced that he wasn't teasing, I told him I'd fallen asleep on the couch and when I got up, I went to the door to call her once more. She came up behind me and scared me to death! I figured, "My husband, the hero! He let her in and had let me sleep."

Well, that's not the case. All we can figure now, is the lost dog was never lost; she'd never even left the house! Not sure where she was or why she didn't speak up when I went to the door, calling her name- eleven times! The hubs is convinced either the poison ivy meds have made me a mess or the poison ivy has infiltrated my brain. And the way the dog's been acting today, I'm pretty sure she thinks I've lost my mind, too.

From now on, she will be wearing her jingly-jangly collar throughout the night, even if it costs me sleep, just so I can keep track of her. IN the house!

What's Important?

I had the good fortune, recently, to take a trip with my sisters (ages sixty-two to seventy-two) to a warmer climate. It hadn't really gotten cold back home yet - that would have increased our appreciation for the heat when we got there - but getting away for a bit was our goal and we achieved it. We picked the travel date long before the actual trip. With kids, grands, hubs, and jobs, carving out some time for ourselves wasn't easy, but it was important.

We caught up with what's going on in each of our lives, in our kids' and grandkids' lives. We talked about our late dad, laughing -NOW- at some of the memories. We discussed our still-living mom and her care. (Forgive me for saying this, but one of the nicer benefits of the trip was getting away from that for a bit.) We ate and drank well - probably TOO well! We laughed more than the neighbors probably cared to hear. We laughed in the car (I was the clueless in-town driver, so you can imagine!) We people-watched at the beach and laughed. (Some folks down there must not own mirrors!) Zany mishaps and silly stories, we laughed through it all, but it was important.

This trip, with the women who had the same start in life as I did and who have shared so much with me, reinforced again the notion that we shouldn't wallow over what is no longer- Whether it's youth, our figures, or relationships. Instead celebrate what we still have, whether it's the people in our lives, the good fortune we have, or the good health we enjoy. Because time's moving on and what we have is IT! Friendships, life, time itself. Knowing that is important.

I've been blessed with terrific siblings -not everyone's as blessed - I know that. We have a shared history that has taken different turns-different choices, and different ways of doing things. But when we merge together again, as we did on this trip, with shared memories and future hopes, I realize how fortunate I am. I'm glad we did this and feel blessed beyond measure. A lot of gratitude in my heart today - and THAT, friends, is the MOST important.

The Ever-Elusive Sleep

I joke a lot about my inability to sleep-how on countless nights I awaken, sometimes hourly, to look at the clock, hoping it's later than it is-but it never is. Laying in the dark, thinking of the damnedest things at 4:00 a.m., things I can't do a thing about at that hour-if I could do anything about it EVER!

I was amazed, but not surprised, by the number of women who have since let me know that they, too, suffer from this elusive sleep. Turns out I'm sure not alone! Looks like we could maybe even form an "Insomniacs Anonymous" chapter! And why IS that? In a world of melatonin, Advil P.M. and Ambian, why do women have such a tough time falling asleep and staying asleep, awakening refreshed, and ready to tackle the day? I wish I knew!

It's not like I have the weight of the world on me. Oh, I have some daily struggles, but is it anything so big that I have to lose sleep over it? Can you imagine what a woman CEO who has hundreds of careers depending on her goes through at night? Or a mom, struggling with a chronically ill child?

Or a woman who has lost her means of support, because of a divorce, death of her spouse, or loss of her job? I can't imagine! And if they DO sleep, what's their secret?

No, I think of piddly things like shopping lists-or "Should I have said that?" Or "I wonder if this stiff neck is something more than a stiff neck?" Or "Are my kids okay?"

Oh, I've tried praying, which sets off a whole new set of thoughts, like, "Do I live my faith? Are my grandkids healthy?" I've tried counting sheep-sometimes switching the sheep out for clouds, hoping that that visual will put me in a calm state of mind. Sometimes, I turn the clock around. "If I can't see it, it won't matter." But nothing works!

I know that the "Insomniacs Anonymous" chapter isn't a "women only" club. The hubs has his sleep issues, too. But it really IS interesting to hear how many women aren't getting their proper rest. Is it hormonal? Or are women just bigger worriers by nature? Some who don't suffer my affliction might say, "I'll get plenty of rest when I'm dead." What if all this lack of sleep hastens that process? I KNOW it's aging me. Will it kill me?

I kind of long for the days when I fought off naps, when I resisted going to bed early like it was some kind of punishment, when I woke up ready to begin a new day, all rested and refreshed.

Those days are gone for good, I fear. If anyone has any ideas on how I can recapture my youthful sleep habits, please tell me! I suppose I could dream about all of the wonderful nights of my youth. But in order to dream, you have to be asleep.

I am so screwed!

Freshmen 15
or
Summer 10

You know what I'm talking about? How college freshmen supposedly pack on fifteen pounds that first year of college? They're away from Mom and Dad, eating and drinking stuff that they perhaps didn't indulge in at home?

I didn't have the good fortune of going to college, but I'd be right there with 'em, I'm sure, packing it on!!

My folks would've been happy to finance my education IF I wanted to be a teacher or a nurse. That was in the early 70's and my folks probably weren't the only ones who thought those were the career choices of young women, back in the day. But I wanted to be neither. My folks probably knew, too, that the social side of college would be more to my liking -so it wouldn't have lasted anyway. What I REALLY wanted to be was a wife and mom! Wish granted! Probably too young by today's standards, but after forty-eight years, I think it was the best career choice for me!

I digress... After reading about some college kids bemoaning their weight gain online, I got to wondering, "Is there's such a thing as a "Summer ten?"

No matter how many fruits and veggies I ate this summer, no matter how much water I drank, there's that weight! Oh, who am I kidding!?! Summer's the time for burgers and beers, metts and bratts, corn on the cob, and ice cream, and I enjoyed plenty of all of it! I've got to believe that the summer eating season ranks second only to that time of year between Thanksgiving and New Year's. Ahh! Turkey and the trimmings, appetizers galore, and holiday cookies (that I didn't bake!) I'm getting hungry just writing about it!

And usually an avid walker, the heat and humidity made me sluggish about that, too, this summer. I'm not a big fan of sweating -going out to the garden this summer to harvest those fruits and veggies I was SUPPOSED to be eating, was about all the heat I could stand!

Well, I've got about eight weeks to drop these pounds before the holiday season arrives. I hope I can do it so I can enjoy another season's eatings. Either that, or maybe I'll just say, "It's the Freshman fifteen about fifty years late." Yeah, that's it!

Coming Out of The Dark

Maybe I paid too much attention to the magazines, to the HGTV shows, or to friends. But no more! What used to be a dark decor is getting lightened up around here!

I haven't painted a room for a while-maybe since I went over to "the dark side." The room that was getting refreshed was a dark gold on the top with plaid paper on the bottom, with a golf-themed border. (See the recent blog about wallpaper removal. Ugh!). It was cute at the time - maybe my enthusiasm for golf was stronger then - I don't know. But its time was up.

Sure, I could have paid someone to come in and do it. But I'm frugal and just stubborn enough to think I can still handle projects like this. Anyway, there was no turning back now! I had four half gold and half-nothing walls that needed to be painted.

Well, I had forgotten how hard it was to zoom in on a color choice, how heavy a ladder was, and how much stretching and bending is needed to get to those hard-to-reach areas. Up and down a ladder, this time with a bigger arse than the last time I painted, that ended up with as much paint on it as the walls. I was really questioning my sanity at even starting this.

It took an entire day - I had to take breaks, ya know - but just seeing the room lighten up with the soft blue I'd chosen spurred me on. And it was done!

I'd like to personally thank the genius who came up with the idea of primer and paint in one! This innovation kept me from needing to paint a second coat - something this body couldn't have taken.

I'm not saying this was the last room that's going to get lightened up, but it's going to be awhile. The hot tub beckons...

"Reading, Observing, or Pissing on An Electric Fence"

I got your attention with that title, didn't I? Well, it's a quote from humorist Will Rogers. I got it from a friend, and I've been trying to figure out into which category does it fit.

"There are three kinds of people. The ones who learn by reading and the few who learn by observation, but the rest of them have to piss on the electric fence for themselves."

You, by now know, I'm not much of a reader. Wish I had been because I'd be writing books now instead of blogs. Reading would certainly have expanded my view of the world and grown my vocabulary.

I've learned plenty by observing. Seeing how my folks raised kids certainly gave me ideas on how I wanted to raise mine. Watching my grandma make soup years ago influenced me in the kitchen and gave me my love of cooking. Watching the many football and basketball games our boys played and coached in should have probably taught me more about those sports, but I'm a talker. Sorry, boys, I can't help it if I have a short attention span.

I probably fall into the "have to piss on an electric fence" group more than I should, as most folks would, if they think about it.

We're born into this world with zero knowledge, zero experience, zero sense. I'm one of those who have to practically be hit on the head with a hammer to get some things. But it was probably trying things and failing that has taught me the most.

My list is quite extensive - I had to "piss on quite a few electric fences" before I gained the knowledge and experience or figured out how to overcome some of my deficits. But the neat thing about life is we DO gain that experience, we DO learn, we DO figure out what 's right- what will work and what doesn't. It may take a lifetime, but we, hopefully, get it- eventually.

Sometimes, I wish I could transmit my knowledge and experience to my kids, my grandkids or anyone who's trying to make their way. But I can't. They have to "piss on their own electric fence" and "get it" as we all have. I just hope it doesn't take them as long.

What Would You Tell Your Younger Self?"

I recently saw an online campaign by the name of "Dear Me." It was an exercise to see how folks would do things differently, if given the chance. Here's my take....

Dear Me,

- Don't be in such a hurry to grow up! Or to have your kids grow up. Enjoy every age because time goes by so quickly.

- Just because it pops into your head, doesn't mean it has to come out of your mouth. It's a lifelong problem that I should've nipped in the bud years ago.

- Read more. It expands your horizons and had I been more of a reader, perhaps I'd be a real author by now. They say you have to read if you want to write.

- Let it go. What's the use of hanging onto old resentments, old arguments, old clothes? What purpose does it serve?

- Really listen to the older generation. They offer wisdom and a unique perspective that you may not realize the value of until they're gone.

- Don't give so much importance to what other people think. Sure, their opinions matter sometimes, but I've based plenty of how I did things on how others felt about it -and I shouldn't have.

- Travel to new places whenever you have the opportunity. It enriches your life and broadens your view of the world.

- Move more. Get your body used to it because there'll come a time when it doesn't move like you'd like it to.

- Don't be judgmental. You have no clue what others have been through or how you would've handled what they may have had to.

- Savor what you eat. (Instead of shoveling stuff in, enjoy every bite.)

- Tell people you love them. I've waited too many years to say it to some folks. I just assumed they knew it-and maybe they didn't. Say it!

There it is... Sadly, there are no true do-overs in life, but this exercise really gave me the chance to look back and maybe change things up a bit.

Feel free to add to my list, comment or write a "Dear Me" letter. What would YOU tell your younger self?"

Purses, Handbags, and Pocketbooks

Purse, handbag, pocketbook (okay, nobody carries a pocketbook anymore!) No matter what you call it, they say one can tell a lot by looking inside it. Uh, oh...

It's not so much the contents of my purse that's telling. I have the usual items. My reading glasses-or two pair. A few tubes of lipstick, worn down to various levels, (even though I only use one shade) hand sanitizer, two packs of sugarless gum, some tissues, my wallet with the prerequisite credit cards, my driver's license, (that has the same weight I was twenty-five years ago and a photo that makes me look like a crystal meth user) a little bit of cash and change, sometimes a bottle of water, and, of course, photos of the grandkids. Nothing revealing there. I bet 80% of the women I know have the same items in theirs, some of the time.

What's more telling than the contents of my purse is the condition. One would think I'm a terrible housekeeper if the interior of a purse was the gauge. I carry a purse until it wears out and then I throw it out and get a new one. (Designer purses aren't an option then, are they?) I also use my purse as a receptacle for receipts, gum wrappers, and any other paraphernalia I may accumulate over a period of months. And it stays that way until it gets so heavy that I start walking like Quasimod- or Rumpke Trash Service schedules a special recycling stop just for me.

I envy women who are so organized that their purse is pristine at all times. It must be wonderful -being so organized. But I like my purse the way it is. I never know what I'll find when I empty it. And who doesn't love a treasure hunt?

The Wonderful World of Ceramics!

When one of my granddaughters was here for her summer visit, I knew I had to come up with something for her to do-something with an artistic tilt to it. After checking out different places, we settled on a ceramic studio. I thought it would be perfect for a fun afternoon with Grandma. And it was!

But it wasn't Grandma's first venture into the world of ceramics! Oh, nooo-I'd been there before, in the early 70's. Back then, it was the chance for young moms to get away from the kids and Monday Night Football, as the Dads took care of business at home on the gals' night out.

It was my older sisters and a friend who got me interested in a class that would have us in some woman's basement every week. There, we would pay our weekly fee, choose our piece and paint away. Only problem was that my need to hurry and get things done fast didn't just spring up recently. Uh, uh-it goes back that far!

My sisters and friend would choose things with intricate detail, like gorgeous canister sets and cartoon character lamps. Each week, they would retrieve their handiwork from the shelf and continue with their work. Each week, I'd choose (and pay for) a new piece! The others would, painstakingly, paint the beautiful flowers and the life-like eyes, and take weeks to complete their projects. Meanwhile, I'm over in the corner, cranking out solid colored ashtrays like I was on an assembly line! Do you know how expensive ceramics can get, at that rate?

One of the masterpieces that I particularly liked was the hubcap-sized ash tray. I guess, if we were having a LARGE party in the '70's, it'd get some smokers' use. That or I could use it as a chip bowl! It only took me half of the class time to complete THAT one!

Good thing the conversation was great on those Monday nights in the 70's. I, at least, got THAT out of the class. And the conversation was good on that July day with my granddaughter, too; the laughter wasn't as raucous as it was in the 70's, but we had a terrific time.

And for you smart alecks out there wondering-I didn't paint an ashtray this time. I painted a solid colored tile and my granddaughter thought it was LOVELY!

What's Wrong with Your Foot?
"Oh, I Had A Mammogram."

Every year, I have a mammogram. I know that it's a valuable tool in the fight against that insidious disease -breast cancer. And I know so many women who have fought and won the battle because of that machine. But I don't have to LIKE it.

I don't want to be dismissive of its importance or jokey about its use, but come on! Everyone knows that women had little say in its design. It had to be a sadistic guy. I just know it! Men, consider what putting your "junk" in a vise would feel like... Ouch....

I know I'm a bigger wimp than most, but twice now, during my yearly examines, I've gotten light-headed and slid to the floor. The first time, I'm still not sure how I managed to snap out of the machine on my way down. Most recently, the technician helped me ease down to the floor, but not before I banged the heck out of my foot. She had me lay down until I regained my composure. EMBARRASSING! She was so kind and told me that everyone reacts differently, and it doesn't matter if you're flat as a board or as ample as Dolly Parton. It's an uncomfortable and unnatural position to be in.

Oh, I talk big about not going back, but I'm going to keep getting mammograms. They're too important to discontinue just because I'm a big baby. But I AM going to start wearing steel-toed boots to my appointment from now on!

Somebody Stop Me!

I have a favor to ask -would somebody stop me!!! The holiday magazine covers have just about weakened me into thinking, once again, that I can bake!

Anyone who knows me on Facebook, knows that I have met with failure, time after time, when I have attempted to produce the beautiful Christmas trees, stars, and more that adorn these covers. Whatever makes someone who hates measuring, sucks at math, and has zero patience in just about everything, think that they can recreate these beauties is beyond me!

Those who know me know that I'm a sucker for the fragrance of baked goods, wafting through the house-especially this time of year. After feeling it was a cozy thing to do a few years ago, I attempted to bake, and then posted, a picture of my creations on Facebook. The result was some dear souls, anonymously, leaving boxes and tins of cookies on our porch for my deprived family. Some folks are just so sweet. I tried the same thing the following year, but those sweet folks caught on to my ploy.

I can cook with some of the best of 'em. A dash of this, a splash of that can enhance a dish and truth be told, some of my finest creations have come about because of that kind of experimentation. But try that with cookies? They can puff up, become distorted, look nothing like the magazine covers, make the house smell nothing like the holidays, (burning cookies are the worst!) or just plain taste awful!

Maybe God just made some people to be non-bakers. Why else would he have allowed the good people at Glade to come up with their Apple Cinnamon fragrance for their wall plug-ins? Just somebody-please stop me!

P.S. This is, in no way, a solicitation, for home-baked goods. Those who know me well know that self-control is also a weakness I have this time of year. Merry Christmas and a wonderful holiday season to you!

Size 12 is A Plus Size? Whateverrr..

Recently I saw a segment on TV that said size twelve is now considered a plus size. And judging by the absence of that size on store racks, it's also the most purchased size of women's apparel. I'm a size twelve, so I can attest to that. Obesity is a huge problem in this country and nothing to be taken lightly. But size twelve, a plus size? Come on!

I can go up and down-my son's recent wedding motivated me to lose weight and I'm glad I did it. I felt wonderful! But I'm not a kale, water, yogurt kind of gal. It's all about smart portions of wise food choices, and I try to keep that in mind. But I like to cook and I love to eat, especially this time of year. I make no apologies. And I still feel wonderful.

I've continued to work out because I want to be fit. But if my weight fluctuates, I'm not going to beat myself up over it. I have a closet full of size tens, twelves, and some fourteens so I've got it covered. I've come to the realization that I'm never gonna be a cute little old lady. I'll be more of a handsome old woman and I'm okay with that. As long as I'm fit and it all works, I'm good!

I've Had It All Wrong!

"Eat breakfast like a king, lunch, like a prince and dinner, like a college kid with a maxed-out charge card."

All these years, I've had it wrong! I've been doing it backwards! No wonder my metabolism's been screwed up!

Never one to cook big breakfasts, except on weekends, I've always been content with a piece of fruit, a bowl of cereal, or a donut. Not that I don't love omelets and waffles; I just thought it was best to save the calories for later in the day.

Many times, I flat out skip lunch or grab a piece of fruit (or a sandwich or a bowl of soup, or a donut.)

And dinner? I'm a meat and potatoes girl, and still cook dinner like three college-age sons still live here - and they don't!

I understand the thinking- if you follow this order of eating a big breakfast and lessen your intake throughout the day, you have more time to burn off the calories. Makes sense. But something is also missing from their logic.

They say nothing about snacking. That's the true bane of my existence. A handful of pretzels here, a can of Coke there. Tis the season for Easter candy and I have a weakness for marshmallow Peeps and malted milk eggs, especially at bedtime. It all adds up. I really must change my ways.

I'm going to try this process of eating like a king, a prince and a college kid, in the proper order, because there's a dress that I would like to wear again

- comfortably - if you get my drift. Now, I won't be hitting Denny's every morning for their Grand Slam breakfast. And if you think I'm going to start eating Ramen noodles for dinner, you're crazy. But I'm going to try this, and we'll see how it goes. Now, where are the breakfast Peeps I've been looking for?

Yoga Pants, Leggings, and "It"

Okay...I've held off as long as I can! Yoga Pants! Or leggings! Oh, I know there's a difference, but lately, to me, they're the same- in that they show too much! (The guys might hate this, but I'm not sure how many will even see it anyway...)

I love yoga pants! What's not to like about them? They're comfortable and if you're not heading to the gym, they make folks THINK you are. But please, wear a top or a jacket that's long enough to cover things! We get it! You're proud of the bum you've acquired from your workouts. It takes a lot of sweat and commitment to get that booty, but do we have to see the front as well?

Same deal with leggings. Love the look with boots, leggings, and a long sweater. But if you're not wearing a long sweater, how is that any different than wearing pantyhose (okay, I'm old!) without a skirt?

I compare yoga pants and leggings, without longer tops, to men's Speedo swimming trunks. We know they've got it, but I sure don't care to see it on full display! Save it for someone special-how 'bout it?

And while I'm on my tirade, let's discuss flannel sleep pants. When did they become streetwear? Do me a favor, huh? You keep your sleep pants in your house and bed, and I'll do the same with my night gown! (Oh, that visual! Me, at the dollar store, in my satin number! Some things you just can't unsee! And I apologize for that!) Told you I was old!

Okay, I'm done.

Thanks for the Memories

Last week, I had the opportunity to say goodbye to a dear old friend. She'd been on life support for a while, her demise hastened by neglect. I know I should have visited her more often, but you know how busy life can get and how we get into other routines. The end came in stages, but she's gone for good now and I'm going to miss her.

I said so long to the last of the Elder Beerman stores. It was the store of my youth and the bank of memories from milestones in my life. And it makes me sad.

Her end started a few years ago when the store in my town closed, the new shiny malls drawing folks elsewhere. I went into mourning then, too. I was still able to frequent other locations, when I went out of town to see the grandkids, or when I had the chance to go to another town where the EB brand was still a part of their commercial landscape. But they're now gone, as well.

Some critics would say that she was old-fashioned and didn't keep up with the times. That other factors, like online shopping, were chipping away at her usefulness. But memories aren't made on laptops and cell phones. And now, my memories of that place are all I have now.

Memories:

- of a youngster, shopping with my mom for whatever bargains she could find for her five kids...

- of a young girl, riding the city bus with Mom, anxiously pulling the rope when we reached our destination...

- of a teenager trying on the samples of glorious colognes and make-up, knowing she couldn't afford to purchase any of them...

- of a young lady, trying on formals, not knowing if she'd even be asked to the upcoming prom....

- of scoops of chocolates from their candy counter....

- of lunching in the tearoom and acting way more sophisticated than I was...

- of a young bride, registering for the gifts she hoped would make their first house a home....
- of a gal, getting my first charge card, introducing me to the concept of having something now and paying for it later..
- of visits to the hosiery department, where my mother-in -law worked, after she became a widow...
- of a young mom, hoping to find winter coats on sale, for my three sons....
- of an older mom, buying what those sons would need when they were packed off to college.
- of a Grandma, shopping for pretty party dresses for the out-of-town granddaughters to wear to their uncle's wedding...

While the Amazons, the "click lists" and online shopping of today provide timesaving and convenience, they will never provide the memories that brick and mortar stores have. Particularly, the now-shuttered ones. And for that, I'm both sad and grateful. Sad, that once again, another fragment of my past is gone. And grateful, that I truly enjoyed that era and have these memories.

Rest in peace, Elder Beerman. You were a good friend and I'll miss you.

A Slender Brunette? Sure!

Is there anything more aggravating than going to the DMV to get your license renewed? I was number nine in line. and an hour later walked out with that all-important document. Well, not really. They now mail your license to you - which seems kind of risky in terms of identity theft. But the good news is I passed!

As the years go by and I get older, it gets a little scarier, seeking that paper of independence. One poor elderly lady (hell, she may have been MY age!) failed her eye test. One fella was waiting for a fax that would tell them his driving suspension had been lifted. Another gal, waited in that long line with me, only to be told that she didn't have the correct documentation. She handled herself quite nicely whereas I may have been arrested. She claimed she had called them, asked what was needed, brought what they asked-and then, was told to come back with the right stuff. Grrrrrrr....

It seems to be tougher these days than years ago, when we first acquired proof of our being able to get behind the wheel. I suppose it's because there are so many more drivers on the road and because there are more rules and regulations. Immigration, national security, and identity theft have probably all played a part-or were we just more patient when we were younger? I don't know. One would think it would be a smoother process with computers now than when things were hand-written or typed on a typewriter. Well, it's not.

I know those clerks have a tough job, dealing with countless, clueless folks - all of them, wishing they were anywhere else than at the DMV- many not accustomed to having to wait for anything. There were a steady stream of customers, lined up, out the door-some, just behaving like asshats.

Well, I'm glad I have that behind me for four more years, the good Lord willing. With my vision less than it used to be, and my reflexes being those of a sixty-year-old instead of a sixteen-year-old, it always worries me a bit. Having to take my driver's test over? Yikes! Having the hubs haul me around town because I failed to keep my license? That would suck for both of us! Believe me!

I AM happy to report that my weight hasn't changed in the last thirty years! And I'm still a brunette! The great state of Ohio says so! Perhaps, those clerks should take that vision test, too. Just sayin'. There IS a sign, warning that "Presenting false documentation is fraudulent and prosecutable, by law." I'd sure hate to go to jail over twenty pounds...okay, thirty! Or have my desire to frequently experiment with old Lady Clairol land me in the klink, but still...

All in all, waiting in line for a chunk of my afternoon and enduring a bit of worry and stress, is a small price to pay for the privilege of driving all over the place. And, finding out that I'm still a slender brunette was a bonus. Thanks, DMV! You're aces in MY book!

P.S. A word to the wise: Contributing to whatever fund they ask a dollar for or signing up for organ donation at the DMV, does not induce the clerk to be any more kind when taking your photograph. I signed up for both and STILL look like a crystal meth user!

Tick
Tock

Tick tock, tick tock-time is flying, with almost breakneck speed! I have always heard that the older you get, the faster it goes, and I know others my age would say that is absolutely true! When I'm in a pensive mood, I wonder if I could go back in time, what would I do differently?

I would try to seize the moment more. To quote Erma Bombeck, "Think of all the women on the Titanic who waved off the dessert cart!" I'd have not dwelt on my weight so much. Looking back on old photos, I wish I was as fat now as I thought I was then.

I'd have worn the beautiful earrings my husband bought me more often. I was afraid I'd lose them, so there they sat in my jewelry box!

I wouldn't have worn high heels so often. What was I thinking, as a young mom, wearing them with jeans? And to football games? Good Lord!

I'd have worn, more often, the perfumes, colognes, and nightgowns I'd been saving for special occasions. Shouldn't every day (and night) be considered special?

I'd have spent more time with the old-timers in my life. They had some wisdom, I'm sure, that I could be using right about now. Plus, they would've felt needed- not a bad thing, I'm finding, at this stage.

I'd have heeded my parents' warnings about standing up straight. I was 5'9 and did I really think slouching made me shorter? With the shrinkage that's come with aging, I'm getting my wish, anyway.

I wouldn't be so concerned about what others thought about just about everything.

I would've read more. I've always been a magazine reader, so for current matters, I'm good. But books are where the real knowledge is and my horizons would've been broadened, for sure.

I'd be more open-minded. I've been pretty rigid all these years and, in this world, I'm finding that you have lighten up some.

I don't want anyone to think I'm full of regrets. My life has been a good one --it really has been--- but how would my feet be feeling now if I'd have stuck with flats?

I'm learnin'!

"Party Time, Faux Sure!"

Well, my "What Are You Waiting For?" mantra has become more than just that. I'm putting it into action now. I've done something that, in some minds, may seem silly, crazy, or maybe even dumb. But I'm making a concerted effort to appreciate the life I've been given and some of the things that I possess. And to that end, I've set the dining room table, as if we're having a fancy dinner party - and we aren't. Yep, I got out all my "pretties" - the placemats, my china and silverware, sparkling crystal, napkin rings, candles...the works!

As a young bride, when I registered for the china, I envisioned the kinds of gatherings that we would host and how my gorgeous table would be the star of the show. We were blessed with family gatherings like Thanksgiving dinner, Christmas dinner, occasional dinner parties, when I would drag out the good stuff and my table DID look guest worthy. But today, brides don't even register for pretty china anymore, do they? Or pretty silverware? And I get it! The Fiestaware type tableware many of them favor is beautiful- more casual-and it fits their lifestyle. Yes, the china we received as gifts, as a young couple starting out, is beautiful. But our style is more casual now, too. So, the lovely silver-rimmed china stayed, hidden away, in my dining room hutch. Until now.

I came up with the idea of setting the table for a faux party on a rainy day, when I was cleaning the dining room. So much beauty - locked away. And why? My kids won't want my china when I'm gone, I'm pretty sure. And anyone who peruses the aisles of area antique malls can see that others folks' kids didn't want THEIR china either. So, what am I waiting for?

In my continuing quest to enjoy what I have, I've started putting the good towels out more often now, too. Aren't the hubs and I worth that little bit of nicer- than- usual pampering? And the colognes and perfumes that sat on my dresser, saved for special occasions get daily use now. The special night negligees and lingerie? Yep. Got 'em out. (I'm sixty-seven- I ain't dead - yet!). What am I waiting for?

Yes, my dining room looks like a festive party is ready to erupt-like family or friends are going to be gathering here for food and fun. With the daylight sun shining through the window, that china IS the star of the show, for REAL this time. All sparkly and shiny and bright and I love it! And, for as long as my "what am I waiting for?" mantra remains in effect, it will stay that way. Oh, I know all of this may seem lame to some, maybe even rather shallow, but, to me, for now, it feels good- it makes me happy; it brings back great memories.

Eventually, I'll put all the "pretties" away. We'll use plastic for the next social event we host (easier cleanup makes more sense, right?) but for now, my faux party is going on and I'm going to enjoy what I have - now. And you're invited to join me!

What are you waiting for?

I CAN STILL.....

Someone once said, "Gettin' old - there ain't no future in it..."

Well, I say "The heck there ain't!"

As I say, "so long" to the age that gifted me with Medicare, I will say "hello", gladly, to my sixty-sixth year! And I'm happy about it! I know many would think I'm blowing smoke, but I'm not! I'm truly glad to be celebrating yet another birthday! Sure, there are plenty of things that I'd change, if I could, but I'm here! And that's good enough!

I CAN STILL

Get up in the morning, in a warm home, aside a loving husband (okay, most mornings I wake up in a different bed because of his snoring or my insomnia) but I wake up!

I CAN STILL

Enjoy the company of my sons and their wives. And I really enjoy them. It's fun to see the stages in their lives they're all going through (and, by the way, are nailing!)

I CAN STILL

See the sweet faces of my grandkids - not often enough, to my liking - but whether it's the one who's going to soon be starting her college search or the newest one who's just beginning to show her emerging personality, or the three in between, I am, thankfully, a presence in their lives.

I CAN STILL

Enjoy the company of my siblings; we remember childhood memories and our shared histories and, although the memories are a bit fuzzier now, they still bring a smile to my heart.

I CAN STILL

Laugh with friends-and although, many times, we're comparing notes on our ills and aches - we still laugh.

I CAN STILL

Contribute - whether it's to a conversation, or time to a committee, I hope I'm always needed.

I CAN STILL

Play with hair stuff and make up - it takes more time, more products and sometimes a whole village, but I can still make the effort to look present-able - and some days, I succeed.

I CAN STILL

Walk with my walking buddy and go to the gym - for fitness' sake. So many can't.

I CAN STILL

Enjoy getting on Facebook. And although I was kinda late joining the party, I'm so glad I came- whether it's been reconnecting with folks, making new friends, stirring the pot, or lightening things up, I've had fun.

I CAN STILL

Travel and see more of God's beautiful gift to us-whether it's around the block or across the ocean. The world's not perfect, but it's what we have, and I still want to see it!

I CAN STILL

Count my many blessings - one, of which, is reaching sixty-six.

Yep, I'm glad I'm here for another birthday. And I sure hope it's another good year!

A Cosmetic Junkie

Anyone who knows me, knows that I'm a fan of make-up. Always have been. Not sure why or when it started. I just am! The opportunity to transform oneself with dime store products has always intrigued me for some strange reason. Before I was allowed to purchase my own, I used to raid my older sisters' stash-once to the point that my dad put a lock on my sister's make up cabinet to deter this cosmetic addict.

Once I got the okay to make some modest makeup purchases of my own, I was on my way! Seldom did the tip money from my waitress jobs make it home because of my stops at whatever dime stores and drug stores were along the way. Revco, Kreske's, Super X-they all offered so many delightful options! The fact that I probably looked like a trollop or a clown when I left the house some days, didn't matter - I was hooked on makeup!

I'm also a big fan of nostalgia. Even more so, as I've gotten older when there's even more to be nostalgic about. So, what was I to do when I saw an online ad for an item from my past-an item that combined my love of beauty products and nostalgia?

This will date anyone who answers this question. Who remembers Tangee Lipstick? (It was my first "legal" purchase of what would become a lifelong addiction.) I'm thinking - if they're remaking it available now, sixty years later, I CAN'T be the only one who remembers it! Tangee Lipstick - "It changes to the perfect color to compliment your skin." That's what they said. So, I caved and purchased a tube online.

I gotta tell ya -when I applied it, the years melted away. That lipstick tasted the same as it did when I was thirteen, and it had the same scent to it, too. To make my trip down memory lane complete, I kind of wish it would've come in the metal tube like it used to - the kind with a slit on the side and a little button that raised the lipstick up when you wanted to apply it. And the cost these days? I could NEVER have bought it at Bartel's Drug Store years ago at the current price! (I wasn't THAT good of a waitress!) But when's the last time you brought something from your past up to the present that it didn't disappoint just a little?

I know all the beauty experts suggest that old(er) broads need to use a lighter hand when applying make-up. I guess that's so the makeup doesn't creep into the wrinkles and lines and have you looking like a madam running a brothel. And I'm working on it. Old habits die hard, but as long as I have the energy and the presence of mind, I hope there will always be lipstick on my lips. Tangee or otherwise.

Yep, nostalgia is good for my soul. It's fun to think back on how many words have passed through these lips, how many kisses have been given by them, how many different colors of lipsticks have been tried-starting with Tangee. What can I say? I'm a sucker for nostalgia!

Now, if I could just get my hands on a soft, fluffy, pastel Mohair sweater, I'd be all set!

I'm Good Enough!

I went and did it! To start the new year off on a positive note, I cancelled all the subscriptions to my magazines! And why you might ask?

Because I'm tired of reading them and then feeling that I'm not good enough! Not the articles so much but the ads! The slick, beautiful pictures of obviously air-brushed models trying to convince us that expensive creams will have us looking like them, that their makeup tricks will give us chiseled cheekbones, plump, moist lips, and eyes that will mesmerize anyone within ten feet, or that we'll have voluminous, shiny hair with just a few drops of whatever they're peddling.

I'm tired of it!

I've birthed three sons, raised those sons to be contributing (and fun) members of society, held numerous jobs, helped care for aging parents, have been blessed with great family and friends, and have been a loving and attentive wife. And I think I'm "good enough."

And so are the younger and more impressionable women they're trying to suck into thinking they're not. Leave them alone! They're already beautiful and "good enough".

Sure, I'll continue to slather on cheap face cream, drug store cosmetics, and hair color like I always have. But I've found in my advancing years, that having a smile and a kind heart makes me "good enough" to those who matter.

So, magazines, you're out! I'm done with you - except for the HGTV one, and that one's on probation. I don't need a $300 ottoman either- because my comfortable, well-worn furniture is "good enough," too.

Scars-Proof that We Have a Past...

"Scars are proof that we have a past." No one gets thru life unscathed. We all have scars, whether inside or out.

Anyone who knows me knows that I would HAVE to have external scars, as I am far from graceful. Through the years, I've been hung up on barbed wire-that's on my chin. Also, on my chin is a scar from doing a star-turn-some dumb move where you spin around when jumping into a pool. Key to that is making sure you jump out far enough from the ledge. My legs have been banged up countless times: walking into furniture, tripping over stakes, falling up steps and falling down steps. My nose has been broken, twice, that I know of. We've joked around here that if they ever do an autopsy on me, hubby will probably be arrested for domestic abuse. If you're still around, please, tell them that's not the case. He's a sweetheart and I was just a klutz!

Most of my internal scars probably came about the same as everyone else's. Losing a loved one, being left out, hurt feelings, and criticism over something. A kid in grade school once called me Meadowlark Lemon (one of the Harlem Globetrotters) not because of my prowess on the basketball court, but because of my height. I think I slouch to this day because of that scar.

Stitches took care of most of the injuries that produced my many external scars. But there's no plastic surgery for the internal kind. I guess that's where age, gaining confidence, or granting forgiveness enter the picture. I'm comfortable in my skin now, scars and all, but it's taken about five decades. That's not to say I don't secretly hope that some unkind fifth grader never grew past his fifth-grade height. (I didn't mention revenge, or holding a grudge, did I? Yeah, there's that, too.)

What? Me Worry?

Worrying...I keep reading that it is really bad for you, health-wise. Maybe because I'm getting older, I pay more attention to such information. But really, I've known that forever! I'm a worrier-always have been, probably always will be. If I can't find something to worry about, I'll worry about the fact that I have nothing to worry about! It's probably genetic. My Dad was a worrier. Of all his wonderful attributes, it figures I'd inherit the worry gene!

I think it's probably normal for moms to worry about their kids. What they eat, where they go to school, or who they're with. And when they grow up and move out, the worrying doesn't just stop. Are they happy with their jobs? Are they enjoying their lives? Are they healthy? Are they worrying? Throw parents, in-laws, grandkids, and friends into the mix and you have enough to worry about for a long time.

Prayer is my first "go-to" when I'm worrying. For years I've been saying, "Trust in the Lord, but lock your car." You do what you can and then let Him handle it. I figure the good Lord has heard it all before and I should just turn it all over to Him. He doesn't have to hear it in church (I'd be in church all the time, if that was the case!) I can pray anywhere-especially at night when the worries really come out. Another worry-He's probably getting tired of hearing from me.

Hubby has the healthy attitude that things always work out. And they do. But who's to say my worrying and praying isn't the reason? He also thinks I need to see a therapist. Yeah, that'll happen!

I need to work on this. I know that. My health and life may depend on it. I need to start adopting the attitude that someone else is driving the bus and I'm just along for the ride. Anyone else wanna go?

Focus, Woman, Focus!

I certainly hope I'm not the only one who is finding, as the years tick by, that I'm losing more and more of my daily focus. It'd be funny if it wasn't so darn time-wasting or troubling.

I can start out in the kitchen, loading the dishwasher, look out the window, see some leaves and go out and rake-before the dishwasher is loaded! Or I can be carrying laundry to the bedroom, look in the mirror as I pass the bathroom, and end up plucking my eyebrows-laundry now the furthest thing from my mind. Or changing the dog's water and stacking the water bowl over the food one - and then spending four hours looking for the mysteriously absent food bowl! I've noticed too, if I'm working on my laptop, I jump around from site to site, and forget what I'm looking for when I get there.

I've become a big note writer-to myself. If I'm leaving the house, I have to list, in order, the places I intend to visit. If I don't make that list, chances are good that one of my stops will be passed up. And God help me if I enter a store without list in hand!

What is going on? I'm blaming it on keeping track of the kids' and the hubs' schedules all those years-and all the minutia I've held onto for so long. I can tell you information from a past job I held twenty years ago, but please don't ask me how many bananas I just bought at the store! There's no room in my head for current stuff anymore, like how to finish a task, without distraction.

This exercise in writing, I hope, helps me with my focus-trying to organize thoughts, come up with words...oh, wait a minute...those curtains need straightening...

Let's Talk Hair...

I've never had a lustrous mane, but what's with this thinning hair? It's not like I've treated my hair well through the years, but come on! One more thing to chalk up to the aging process, I guess.

The first time I turned my locks over to Clairol, (Loreal and any other haircoloring brand) was forty-five years ago, and it's been an adventure ever since. I have had every color in the hair color spectrum, and some haven't even been a human hair shade! But I just do it over, and over, and over. I'm not even sure what my real color is, but I'm pretty sure it's peppered with grey by now.

I've been blessed with a wonderful hairdresser (for the past thirty years) who never cast judgement on the color and has steered me through decades of hairstyles. She *could've* steered me away from the perm decade in the 80's, but we made it through that phase and I'm still with her.

It's funny how we lose hair in one place and sprout it in another. I'm not as bad as the woman who remarked that she went to brush a hair off her lapel

and realized it was attached to her chin! Not yet-anyway. And thank good-
ness, we're not like the male species who, sometimes, develop eyebrows like
Andy Rooney, or get a healthy crop of hair growing out of their ears or noses.
Not yet, anyway!

There's really no good reason for me to have a hair my head. But I'll keep
on coloring, cutting, growing, plucking... This aging process is EXHAUST-
ING, isn't it?

Jump Suits-A Terrible Idea!

Please tell me I heard wrong! That jumpsuits are trending in women's fashions
this year??? That's a TERRIBLE idea!

Maybe because today's designers weren't around the last time jumpsuits
were "in" in the 70's, so how would they know? But I know I'll never forget
them!

For those of you younger than forty-a jumpsuit is a top, with slacks
attached, fashioned I suppose, from what fellas who jumped out of planes
wore, hence the name "jumpsuit." I always thought they resembled a mechan-
ic's uniform from the 60's or maybe prison garb now. I don't know, but whoever's idea that this is a good look - well, you're an idiot!

The fact that I was tall, back in the 70's, when some other idiot thought
jumpsuits were a good fashion idea, didn't help matters. Finding a jumpsuit
that fit was difficult...the pants legs were too short or the crotch too high.
Going to the restroom was a big production, too, as the entire outfit had to
come down when nature called.

Years ago, I managed to find a cute baby blue jumpsuit that fit perfectly!
It was pricier than I would normally pay, but I had started working earlier in
the week at the very store that had it! Employee discount!!! The best part of
working retail! I was so excited! I had some nice new apparel that I could pay
off gradually.

Well, that was until they had the audacity to ask me to work a weekend!
Can you imagine that? Them expecting ME, who had absolutely no skills
and no talents, to give up a part of my life on a weekend? I told them that

perhaps this job wasn't for me, and I quit! The bad news was that I owed the store more for that damn jumpsuit than I had earned working there!

If jumpsuits really do make a comeback, I'll be reminded of two things every time I see one:

1. Why was I such a "sheep," following a trend I didn't particularly like-nor could afford?

And

2. How sorry a work-ethic did this bratty old self have?
The designers or yours truly-really, now, who was the idiot?

Turn Around!

"Don't feel sorry for yourself
if you have chosen the wrong road
--turn around!"

It's time for me to "turn around." Yep, I've been a slacker this year. There I said it! Not that I didn't get a lot accomplished. There were so many projects to oversee around the house and some transitions to help with. But, plain and simple, I got out of the habit of working out. I just couldn't get revved up about it, like I did before. Having a son's wedding as an incentive in 2013 certainly helped. Yep, I'm committing to becoming more fit this year. Maybe writing it down for all to read will be incentive enough. Hope so!

Really, I haven't been a total slouch. My walking friend is a beast and wouldn't allow it- making me get up and go out walking at 7:00 or 7:30 in the morning, year-round! Armed with flashlights, we haven't let the time change alter our schedule, either. We solve all the problems of the world while getting a nice workout to start our day. My legs are fit, but I'm thinking I need more now. Did you know one of the biggest problems, as we age, is a lack of arm strength? Your legs can function like an NFL running back, but if you can't lift yourself out of a chair, what good are those legs???

I think there's a direct correlation between my addiction to Facebook and blogging and my lack of fitness. It's so relaxing-catching up on everyone's lives and writing about mine. But I'm going to try to strike a balance. Walking, blogging, working out at the gym- I'm ready to stop "feeling sorry for myself if I've chosen the wrong road. It's time to turn around".

That Realization......

The absolute worst thing about aging, I've decided, is coming to the realization that you can't do what you used to do- or what you used to love doing! It can be a gradual process and sneak up on you or WHAM! It can be brought to your attention in a sudden way-like hurting your back or having achy muscles for days.

I have never been one to shy away from heavy work. In fact, working in the yard three seasons out of the year is my favorite activity. Cutting grass, cutting trees and bushes, (although hubby isn't a fan of my using power saws because of the accident-prone thing I have going on…) hauling stuff, digging-I love it all-or I used to. That was before that old enemy named Aging had to remind me that I'm not the girl I used to be.

Now, I have to do things in dibs and dabs, and with my loss of focus these days, that could be problematic. Bending over to pick up sticks…"Oh, that garden statue could use some paint." I used to be able to knock out a lawn cutting job in an hour or so. Now, I dawdle around and set a goal of getting done before sundown-and our yard's not that big! Getting the lawn and porch furniture out for the season used to be cause for celebration! Spring's Here!! These days, I spread that task out over a week! And I used to be able to plant tomatoes on a nice spring morning. Now? Kroger's has very nice tomatoes.

It's not that hubby's a sloth or anything. He's always there to give a hand, but after forty-eight years, he knows I like things the way I like 'em and it's best he stays out of my way.

Maybe it's time I loosen my grip on some things-not an easy realization for a control freak-but is having a well-cut lawn, well-arranged and newly painted porch furniture, and tasty tomatoes worth the hard work and subsequent aches and pains? I'll have to get back to you on that.

Pessimist, Optimist, *or* Realist?

"The pessimist complains about the wind.

The optimist expects it to change.

The realist adjusts the sails."

I don't know a single soul who is just one of those. I am all three, depending on the day, the topic, or the mood. And I bet most folks would agree.

Many times, I'm a pessimist when I return from a store where the service is awful. Or when someone rudely misses a traffic light because she's yakkin' on her cell phone. Or when a kid is disrespectful to a parent when I'm within earshot. I'm pretty sure, during those times, I'm convinced our society is going to hell in a handbag. The world news on TV usually leaves me in a pessimistic mood, longing for the good old days. It's these instances -and more - that leave me "complaining about the wind." Pessimists attract other pessimists because pessimism is a great conversation starter, isn't it? Folks love to grumble and share their woes. Maybe I'm a magnet in the line at the store because of my pessimism?

I'm an optimist when I'm in church because, there, I'm reminded that there's something more than what we have here. I'm an optimist when I'm around certain people-usually other optimists. Friends who always see the good in others or give others a second chance because we don't know their circumstances. I'm an optimist when I'm around my kids and grandkids. They have so much going for them-so many opportunities within their reach-so much promise. Maybe, just maybe, they can "change the wind."

I'm a realist many days. I'll see things as they are-pure and simple-no rose-colored glasses here. I may not like what I see, but to use an over-used phrase, " It is what it is." During those times, I guess I better just "adjust my sails."

Which one are you most of the time?

Always Listen to Your Mama

Remember as a kid, when your mom would remind you to "always wear clean underwear, in case you're in an accident?" Whether it was said in jest or if it was one of those serious life lessons, I'm here to tell you to listen to your mama! Something happened to me recently, but with a little variation to that theme and I'm sharing it, only so you don't make such a dumb mistake.

I'd had something working on me for a few weeks; I had been to the doctor's and had some tests run. Still no diagnosis. One day, I felt too lousy to even get dressed, so I laid on the couch, just hoping to feel better. That wasn't going to happen, as things got worse as nighttime came. I was doubled over in pain, unable to get up. My hubby had been concerned all along, but this startling change in my condition really had him worried. "We're going to the hospital," he said, and I was too sick to argue with him. Only problem was, as I mentioned before, I was unable to get up and walk. Against my protests, he called 911.

Those who know me well, know I've been active in our local school community and know quite a few of its graduates. And I'm proud to say, quite a few of those grads are in law enforcement and on our fire department, manning the police cruisers, fire trucks, and life squads in our town. Those who know me also know I'm a fan of animal prints.

And here's where our moms' warning came to mind. I could hear the sirens and I could hear my husband letting the EMT's in, talking, a bit too familiarly with them. As I lay there in a grungy, raggedy old leopard print nightgown (I TOLD you I love animal prints!) I could hear them walking down our hallway, pushing a gurney. They entered our bedroom and I'm telling you, I knew every one of them from their high school years! I could have died! Not from the pain, but from embarrassment in how I was dressed!

Here I was -looking like some sixty-three-year-old old haggard hussy and you'd have thought, in my sick condition, I wouldn't have cared less. But I remember mumbling to one of the paramedics that if word ever got out about my choice of nightwear, I'd hunt him down and hurt him. And the night wasn't over yet, as the embarrassment continued in the emergency room. I'm sure they see some sights far worse than me, but I certainly wasn't accustomed to being seen in public that way. Shameful! Ha!

There are a few lessons that were reinforced that night and I wish to pass along to you. Number 1. Take care of your health. Number 2. Be prepared for anything, if that's possible. Number 3. After age sixty (some would say even earlier) lose the leopard prints. And, finally, number 4. Always, ALWAYS listen to your mama! And you're welcome!

An Open Letter *to* Clothes Designers *and* Manufacturers

Hey, clothing industry!

What in the hell are you thinking when you're designing clothes for women? Another summer and another season of my not buying tops or dresses-and why? Well, for starters, I don't have Jennifer Aniston arms - all toned up and buff. No, my arms have "sleavage," that scrunched up skin that forms cleavage that, in the right spot, I would covet. And cellulite? Ugghhh!

Anyway, back to my rant. The tops and dresses are darling this season. Cute, some frilly and lacy, some tailored and sharp. But they share a common feature. They're all sleeveless! The younger gals all look fabulous with their tan, toned arms and bodies that haven't seen six or seven decades. Oh, sure, some of the middle-aged ladies look all right in their sleeveless garb. Maybe they've just given up and said, "The hell with it," and have caved to your marketing. But not this old-er broad! I am too kind to do that to my fellow men and women. And I couldn't do that to the dairy industry either. Were I to go sleeveless, they'd be faced with an abundance of unsold cottage cheese from the loss of appetites. Count on it!

Sure, I could hit the gym more, but I really enjoy gardening and walking more. No worries though, aside from my vanity. My arms are strong enough to hug my grandkids and the hubs, to swing a hammer, to hold a paintbrush, to push a lawn mower, (and soon, a baby stroller for another grandchild) and lift my old butt out of a chair, if need be - and that's okay.

I'll continue to wear the three-quarter sleeved tops from many seasons ago or throw on a sweater (in the summer, no less.) The stores will have racks of unsold sleeveless wear come August because, once again, you've missed the mark. And oh yeah, I'll be praying that I live long enough to see if Jennifer Aniston has "Jennifer Aniston" arms when she's pushing sixty-eight. I highly doubt it!

Deader than 4:00 - NOT!

How I wish I could sleep like I did as a kid! I really didn't appreciate it then. In fact, I think I fought sleep-a nap mat in kindergarten, having to come in from playing when the streetlights came on as a youngster, getting into the house before curfew as a teenager- they all signaled a time to sleep, but I don't think I savored it then like I would now. Of course, back then, the biggest worries I had were which cereal I was going to have for breakfast or who was going to come out and play. The good old days!

For years, hubby has used the term, "Deader than 4:00." That meant the carousers and party animals are usually in bed by then, workers aren't up and at 'em yet, (unless they're shift workers) and all is quiet for that brief hour of the day. Unless you're in our house where I'm wandering around or lying awake, trying to find that elusive peace.

It's not like I have huge worries now (although you never stop worrying about your kids, your grandkids, your spouse, your future, or your friends, do you?) The truth is I can't do a damn thing about any of it at 4:00 in the morning! But it doesn't matter. I remain awake.

I try different techniques in the hopes of nodding off. First, I start with praying. If that doesn't work, counting my blessings, of which there are plenty, is next. If I'm still awake, I play a game of, "If I won the lottery, who would I share the riches with?" The answers vary, depending on how I feel about that particular relative (hear that, boys?) or institution on that particular night. Then I start worrying about family members and friends I left out of the lottery game! Oh, heck!

My husband, who doesn't suffer from this malady as much as I do, swears I need help. And I probably do. But I know I'm not alone. From conversations with others, it sounds like a lot of folks struggle to go to sleep and stay asleep.

Maybe some entrepreneur out there could start marketing adult-size kindergarten nap mats. Any takers?

My Wish for Women

When did celebrities and the media dictate how we look, how we feel about ourselves, or how we live? Maybe back to the days when Marilyn Monroe and Elizabeth Taylor graced the covers of fan magazines...maybe back even further?

I don't know, but it has to stop! With that in mind, I humbly have some wishes for the women reading this. They may seem insignificant and fluffy, but it's a start in realizing that we can be ourselves, on our own terms, when it comes to womanhood.

I wish teenaged girls realized that they may not have clear skin all the time. It'll come someday perhaps, but it's one of those things you go through to get to the good stuff of life. And your body's not going to look like Rihanna or Jennifer Lawrence's, either, unless your parents are Rihanna's or Jennifer's. Most of that's all genetic.

I wish young moms realized that their bodies are not going to snap back into shape like Jennifer Lopez's. It'll take time, if it happens at all. And if it doesn't, who's going to love you any less? And your kids aren't always going to look like her picture-ready kids. That's not reality either.

I wish middle-aged women realized that cellulite and expanding waist-lines are a fact of middle age life-unless you have a personal trainer and a nutritionist, like Halle Berry. Same with wrinkles -unless you take the botox route and look like you've stood in front of a jet engine all day long. Your wrinkles are a testament to all the smiles and laughs you've enjoyed. Treasure them!

And older women -of which I'm one. I wish for you good health and peace-no easy task some days, I know. During a time when bra sizes should maybe read "38 Long" instead of "38 with a B Cup" and your knees ache at the thought of walking a mile, we have to rejoice in our track record and smile that we've all made it this far.

I'm not suggesting that we all throw in the towel and slob it up the rest of our lives. Nope, we still need to maintain -with exercise, moisturizing, putting on some blush and lipstick, a smile on our faces and carry on, like we do.

God made all of us in all shapes and sizes and gave us all different life experiences. To strive to look like an unrealistic face or body on a magazine cover isn't fair to us, no matter the age. Maybe the Hollywood types would do well to emulate US for a change. They'd see women, happy with their lives, with their strengths and with their beauty. That's my wish anyway.

Turn the World on with a Smile

In my real life, there have been some very sad losses lately, so the way I took news of a celebrity's recent passing, surprised me. Oh sure, another part of my past is gone and that makes me realize how quickly time's going. But it was truly a bit of melancholy that touched me when I read about the passing of Mary Tyler Moore.

It was more than the fact that she was a class act-an attractive actress who seemed genuinely nice. It was what she represented, at least on screen, as Laura Petrie on The Dick Van Dyke Show. And then, during a more tumultuous time in our history, as Mary Richards, on The Mary Tyler Moore Show.

I wonder if the young women who have watched either show on Nick at Night realize what a pioneer Mary was? She was, to me, as much a comedic icon as Lucille Ball and Carol Burnett (and easier on the eyes, for the hubs, who was always a fan.) But she was even more than that; she was a pioneer.

Simpler times... the early 60's-in the days of Laura Petrie, when twin beds were a prerequisite on sitcoms, because, God forbid, viewers realized what went on in bedrooms across America! Her sing-songy, "Oh Rob," and the batting of her eyelashes got her out of the doghouse in many a domestic conundrum. Laura's capri pants and ballet flats, in a previous world of house-dresses, made a fashion statement.

Then in the early 70's, here came Mary Richards into our homes. It was a time when the American scene wasn't quite as tranquil as New Rochelle, NY-the home of Rob and Laura. The Vietnam War was going on...demonstrations in the streets against that war.... Watergate.... The Pill. Life wasn't so simple anymore.

The Women's Movement was in its infancy, too, during that time. I'm certainly glad the Gloria Steinems and the Betty Friedans of the world took on the fight for feminism. Truly. They fought hard. They were brash and confrontational-kinda "hit ya over the head" or "burn your bra" kind of hard. But I was more aligned with Mary Richards' soothing way of showing women every Saturday night, in the comfort of their family rooms, that women didn't HAVE to be married to have fulfilling lives, but that they could have careers and that they could climb the corporate ladder and be more than school teachers and nurses - both noble professions, for sure - but maybe there were more choices out there? Many times, in that fictitious newsroom at WJM, she was more on the ball than her male counterparts, Lou Grant, Murray Slaughter, and Ted Baxter, combined. She showed that women need friends, like Rhoda, Phyllis, and maybe even the rather loose Sue Ann Nivens to get us through things in life, with humor.

Mary Tyler Moore, aka Laura Petrie and Mary Richards, taught us a lot, if we were paying attention. She was a pioneer in the television comedy world, in feminism, and in femininity, just by "turning the world on with a smile."

We could all use that, right about now... And Mary's missed.

She's
Gonna
Fall

Not sure why I fall a lot; maybe it's that I've always been a tall girl who got tall too quickly. Maybe it's because I'm always in a hurry or maybe the shoes I wear aren't always suitable for the task at hand-maybe I'm just a flat-out klutz. But I fall a lot! I fall up curbs. I miss bottom steps. I misjudge obstacles. I trip on air.

And this isn't a recent condition. It's been a lifelong problem. And I'm probably too old to change now. My most recent fall occurred when I was trimming some bushes. Loppers in hand, I backed up to view my work and just went down. Luckily, there was no electricity involved. We have a rule around here (and with good reason) that I'm not allowed to use power tools. I used to bounce up quickly, looking around to see if anyone witnessed my mishap. Now, I take my time, looking for something to hold onto while I hoist myself up. (The loppers came in handy as a cane in this latest instance.)

As a young mom, my falling was so frequent that the young sons would either walk over me or pile on, like I was in the mood for a WWF wrestling match, ala Hulk Hogan! Once, while the boys were down in our rec room watching cartoons, I slipped and fell down our outside steps. It was a cold wintry day and our back door had a tendency to stay ajar, unless you pulled it shut. In a heap at the bottom of the porch steps, I could hear from the basement, "Mom, close the door! It's freezing down here." I'm happy to report that it was only a broken tailbone and not "A frozen corpse found on Tiffin Avenue" police report! I'm also happy to report that my sons developed some compassion as they matured-but my falling STILL doesn't alarm them.

Same can be said about our friends. Once a group of six couples rented a lake house. I was in the kitchen of that beautiful place and went down, behind the island that overlooked the room where the crowd always gathered. Not one friend rushed to my aid. In fact, a dear sweet friend could be heard to say, "She's gonna fall." Yep, he coined the phrase that has become my trademark. "She's gonna fall."

I've fallen in the shower before - once as a teenager who required stitches because I kicked the faucet on my way down. Another time, as an older gal, I went down in the shower, but was able to kind of slide down the wall. I remember, staying there awhile, too embarrassed to call for help. Sorry about that visual- some things you just can't unsee.

Except for the tailbone thing, I've not suffered any broken bones-knock on wood. I'm pretty sure it's because of the padding I've maintained for most of my life. But this old(er) body feels my history more and more every year. Who knows what damage has been done? We joke that an autopsy would probably see the hubs being hauled in for questioning! Ha! I figure I'm a broken hip away from a nursing home so maybe I should slow it down a bit, wear sensible shoes, and take more care in where I'm going. Oh, who am I kidding? I've been doing it for so long, I'm not sure I'd even know how to stay upright for long.

So, if you drive past our house and see a woman lying in our front yard, or you spot some commotion in a parking lot at the grocery store, don't be alarmed. It's just me - in a pretty familiar position. No worries-I'll get up eventually, but more slowly than years past-ready for the next time, cuz "She's gonna fall!"

Chain, Single Stitch, Percocet...

Add another craft to my list of things I'll never master. I'm talking crocheting!

I've long been an admirer of the beautiful handwork of those who HAVE mastered it-the beautiful colors and the exact precision in their stitches. I'm blaming it on my being a left-hander. And if that fails, I can always fall back on my dislike for following directions. Have you ever read those things?

My grandmother was a wonderful crochet-er, and we all had the bed-spreads, afghans, and house slippers to prove it. When I first attempted to try my hand at her craft, she was more than willing to teach me. I remember her loving instructions and her trying to adapt them to a lefty. I promised to practice, which is what it takes, but I hadn't planned on falling and breaking my tailbone that winter. Bad for my hubby and kids, but good for my intentions to master crocheting. Couldn't do much else, as I was laid up for a week. I learned something more than crocheting that week, though. I learned that prescription drugs can be wonderful things.

That week, while under the influence, I was cranking out crochet squares like I was possessed. When Grandma witnessed my progress, I'm sure she was proud. But when the drugs ran out and my tailbone healed, a strange thing happened. No longer relaxed, I regressed, tightened up and it showed in my stitches. Truth be told, nothing has come out straight or even ever since.

Friends have tried their best (Thanks, Sherry.) to help me produce the beautiful pieces I've admired for years. I just can't do it! Things come out too tight or too loose; scarves come out too long and crooked. And my afghans are laughable...seriously!

Crocheting just seems like a cozy thing to do. I really wish I could have made my late grandma proud, replicating the fine things she made. But I also know she'd be proud that I "just say NO" to drugs and accept the fact that I need to find something else to do on these cold winter nights.

Get Me A Filter!

One thing I'm noticing more and more is that folks, particularly those my age and older, are in need of filters. We (myself included) sometimes give our opinions, judge, or criticize-whether it's solicited or not. Sometimes it's needed. Other times? Get me a filter!

I guess I need to realize that it's a different world now and so much of what I think or have to contribute, isn't relevant anymore. Do you think that maybe it's that we think we're running out of time, so we have to get it all in? Or maybe because we've "been there, done that" that we think we have all this wisdom to impart?

I hope my input is always needed - we all want to feel needed. I just pray that I'm not some judgmental old shrew, in need of a filter. Instead I want to be a part of a support group, cheering people on to better things. We'll see how THAT goes!

Gratitude - More Than an Attitude

I like to think that I'm an appreciative person - I may not express my gratitude enough, but believe me, I am grateful for my blessings every single day.

Like

* Good health - mine and that of my family. After seeing so many dealing with health struggles, it's been reinforced how precious good health truly is.

* My hubs. As we grow old(er) together, his ability to make me laugh every day has, perhaps, been the best gift he could give me.

* All the grandkids! Whoever said, jokingly, if they'd have known how much fun grandkids were, they'd have gone straight to that chapter and skipped the "kids" one, was correct! Ha! (Just teasing, boys!)

* Having raised three terrific sons, (sometimes, you never know how that will go,) and to have in our family, two daughters-in-law who make them happy every day is a blessing for sure.

* My faith - good times and bad, not sure what I'd do without it...

* My parents. I know it wasn't always easy raising me, but I'm glad they persevered and hope they were pleased with the end result.

* Friends - old and new. We've had so many good times and great memories. And although we don't get together as often as we used to, (kids and grandkids see to that!) friends have certainly made life fun!

* The fact that I live in this place -nation, city, and home - at this time in history. Oh, I know. Politics drive us crazy, but we're still here! And things will be fine.

* The places I've worked and the people I've worked for and with. I can't recall one job - whether it was as a waitress or as a school's development person, that I didn't enjoy.

* The opportunity to go places. I've seen a lot of the town I love, this great nation, and some beautiful parts of the world.

* My siblings.... I have four terrific ones. We had great childhoods and continue to enjoy each other's company.

* The men and women who unselfishly defend us. Sometimes, I truly question whether we deserve it.

* My ability to see humor in almost everything. It's gotten me through some tough times, especially by using the self-deprecating kind.

* The internet. It has changed the way we live, the way we do business, and the way I've reconnected with old friends and made some new ones. And social media makes me smile daily.

* Kind people. Life's too short not to be one and not to have them in your circle.

* My Family. Immediate and extended. They make it all worth it, right?

Gratitude IS more than an attitude, and it's kind of useless if you don't let others know you appreciate their presence in your life. So that's what I'm going to do every day in Lent. Pray for what I'm grateful for. And say thank you to you all. "Thank you!"

Flip Flops

or

Thongs?

I was cleaning out my closet, making way for my summer stuff when I came across something-and the question begs to be asked… So why did a comfortable rubber summer shoe of our childhood have to take a backseat to a specific style of ladies' underwear? Yep, I'm talking "thongs."

I still refer to flip flops as thongs, much to the amusement of my grand-daughters. I don't do it often, but I get this look, like, "Oh, Grandma,"when I do.

Old time "thongs"were quite innovative when they were first introduced. I mean, who ever had colorful rubber shoes before? Thinking back to them evokes great memories of throwing on a swimsuit, a cover-up, putting on my thongs, (the shoe kind!) grabbing a towel, and walking to the public pool with my sisters and friends.

I guess thongs, the new kind, evolved from strippers. (Sure, they're attrac-tive on THAT body type!) And I guess places like Victoria's Secret saw the chance to bring them to the general public- and then Walmart, K-Mart, and everyone else followed suit. Honestly, I don't get it. I bet most of us spent our entire childhoods and most of our teen years, pulling our underwear out of "there." Why in the world would we want to go there again? Spoiler alert: you won't see me in pasties or using a stripper pole any time soon either.

Don't worry, kids-when I say I'm going to put on my thongs, I'll be wearing rubber shoes on my feet. Count on it!!!

Sometimes Subtle, Sometimes Not

What the heck are these? These purplish marks on my hand??? And when did this happen? I remember Grandpa having similar marks on his hands, but I'm too young for that, aren't I? Or am I? I'm exactly the age he was when I started noticing things like that! I noticed, back then, he took a lot of naps, too. "Gulp!"

These little things are sneaking up on me, almost daily, reminding me that I'm getting old(er). And the not so little things-like a recent highway incident. After turning a corner, I put my signal on to change lanes. A loud horn sounded....a long, loud horn. We get to the light and a fella in a truck, has his window down and yells, "That's why old people shouldn't drive!" Ah, the impatience of youth. I thought that calling me old was rather harsh, and if I knew I'd done something wrong, I would've apologized. (Just kidding! As is always the case, I have a snappy comeback-about two hours after the fact! Mine, this time, would've been, "I sucked at driving when I was younger, too, you jerk!" THAT would've shown him, wouldn't it? Ha!). Who am I kidding? I AM getting old.

Yep, there are little, subtle things that tip me off- like wandering area parking lots looking for my car, only to find it three aisles over from where I thought I parked it-or telling a son something, only to find out I've told THAT one the same story twice (or three times) and neglected to tell the others, at all.

And there are in-your-face moments, that remind me that time is marching on-like stepping out of the shower. Whoever thought big bathroom mirrors were a good idea? Where my old, round jack o lantern body (YOU figure out the eyes, nose and mouth! Ha!) smiles back at the reflection. Some sadist, I'm sure!

Oh, I'm not ready for the house dresses my grandma favored (although I WAS in my robe a lot this winter.) I walk with a friend almost daily and hit the gym three times a week (Okay "hit" is a strong word.) I "go" to the gym where my trainer/friend helps me work on strength and balance. I hope to age gracefully, but those who know me, know that I seldom do anything "gracefully." But I'm trying.

And anyway, there are worse things than aging. I can think of several - like NOT aging. Or being an asshat who takes pleasure, yelling at old(er) women drivers. (I HOPE I run into that clown again - you can bet your arse I'll have a comeback ready this time!) Be well, friends...

So-Called Disasters

A friend of mine recently sent me a list of tips-all really good ones. But one jumped off the page (or computer screen) because it truly spoke to me as one that I really should try to incorporate into my everyday life.

"Frame every so-called disaster with these words: 'In five years, will this matter?'" That's a good one, isn't it?

You see, I'm a worrier. I fret over many things- imagining worse-case scenarios all the time. I thought once the kids were raised, it'd get better, but it hasn't. I've just found new ways to worry about them....and their spouses... and their kids.

I'm also a do-er and it's hard to avoid disasters if you're one of those. Countless home projects that I screwed up, convinced I'd be in the doghouse for, turned out fine. Events I've worked on in my past careers would have me lying awake at night. One potential disaster, in particular, was sending a letter to a gentleman telling him of an honor he was to receive. Then I found out that out that there were two identical names in the database, and I sent the letter to the wrong guy! Disastrous mistake that turned out to be funny, because the mistaken fella didn't even qualify for that honor -and he knew it! Crisis averted, but it took its toll on me for two days!

Even my Facebook usage has been fraught with potential disasters that never happened, but I sweated about for some for days. Case in point-some may wonder why I don't share posts or pictures under the name of the one who originally posted it. Well, in my early days of Facebook when I was still learning how it all worked, I thought I was on my page, Marysue Wright, and I posted a risqué cartoon. Turns out I posted it under the Facebook page that I manage for my employer! Good lord! Worried about it all night before I found out how to delete it. Whew, spared from getting fired!

I could go on and on about other disasters that I envisioned - I don't want to give up TOO much. But looking back, it turns out, many of my potential disasters turned out to be some of my finest hours. And if they were so awful, who would care in five years? I'm still going to try to frame every disaster with, "In five years, will this matter?" Who knows? That little gem could add years to my life!

DDIY Projects (DON'T Do It Yourself!)"

I can state, with absolutely no hesitation, that I removed the last speck of wallpaper that I will ever remove in my natural life! Sure! Wallpaper looks good (usually) when it's up and it's kinda fun to hang. But its removal? Grrr!

I decided it was time to refresh a room-no big deal. The wallpaper was very cool when I applied it seven years ago. I still liked it, but I was ready for something more neutral. I had forgotten that, in seven years, the body can't always do what it used to do-like climb ladders, bend over 300 times in two hours, or kneel for long stretches of time. Figured I'd be in traction for a week after this DIY project.

While I was spritzing, scraping and tugging at my nemesis, I thought back to the countless rooms, in our many homes, where wallpapered walls were the norm. Our first home- decorated in the 1930's-even had the ceilings papered. The master bedroom ceiling paper had little metallic stars in it. It was supposed to cast a romantic nighttime feel to the room, I guess. As I mentioned, this was our first home, and we were sort of newlyweds. We didn't NEED that kind of romantic ambiance in those days, and it had to go.

I was a DIY novice back then; I had gouges and holes everywhere. No problem. I could pop the ceiling (a process where plaster was applied in a decorative pattern.) I've probably mentioned before how I ended up with a Mammoth Cave type pattern - stalactite looking things, dripping from the ceiling. Not the look I was going for! Plus, I had a stiff neck for a week from looking up for three straight days!

There has been wallpaper with wildflowers from the 70's, boys' plaid bedroom wallpaper, stripes, metallic, and grass cloth-all kinds of wallpaper. Some of my own doing. Some not. It was a way to make a place our own, but it was always more fun, going up than coming down.

Wallpaper fell out of decorating favor for a while. I guess the contemporary style dictated it. Clean lines and all that. But I understand wallpaper is making a comeback now. Good for you all! But this old(er) broad will not be lured back into THAT trap! All the beautiful colors and pretty patterns in the world won't have me dealing with that diabolical, gluey stuff again! You can have it!

From now on, wallpapering and its removal will be a big, fat "DDIY" project - a "DON'T Do It Yourself" one! (Unless they bring back the metallic star pattern for the ceilings. We're no longer newlyweds and a little romantic ambiance couldn't hurt! Nah, never mind...)

Under the Same Roof

Is there a nicer holiday than Thanksgiving? It's my all-time favorite! It's about family, friends, food, and giving thanks -four of the most important things in life. (Well, the food's not THAT important, but I'd be lying if I said I didn't enjoy the heck out of it!) Thanksgiving doesn't have the sometimes-crass commercialism of Christmas -no distractions of gift-buying, hectic schedules, and filled with things to do and places to go.

It's a more serene time for us and I love that! In years past, I had the luxury of having others do the hosting and cooking. My oldest sister could cook a mean bird for my side of the family and my mother-in-law couldn't be topped when it came to a turkey dinner (for the hub's side.) So why wouldn't I be a slacker when it came to Thanksgiving entertaining? But we were together, all under the same roof, and that's what the holiday's about.

My being lazy in the food prep department would soon change. As our families grew and loved ones passed, our traditions had to change. Families have to be flexible that way. The siblings began their own traditions with their own families and, soon, the torch was passed. Our house soon became the Thanksgiving hub for our own crew, and it was wonderful. Not that I didn't have kitchen mishaps, like cooking the turkey with the innards still in the bird (who didn't do THAT?) or figuring the timing wrong and having to wait, impatiently, for the turkey to finish cooking. Lumpy mashed potatoes, runny gravy, tasteless pumpkin pie-it didn't matter. We were together, all under the same roof, and that's what the holiday's about.

Like I said, with families you have to be flexible, and although I'm a traditionalist, we, once again, needed to switch things up a bit. For a few Thanksgivings, we travelled to what was more of a central locale for all of us - middle son's place, two hours away. I hadn't shed the cooking responsibilities yet. Nope, we just loaded up the car-sort of a "meals on wheels" trip, with the daughters-in-law bringing along their contributions, too. But we were together, all under the same roof, and that's what the holiday's about.

We've once again become the Thanksgiving site for our crew. I know it's not easy - the travel and packing up the babies and the teenagers-the hubs and I appreciate it and will never take it for granted. But we're together, all under the same roof, and that's what the holiday's about.

Oh, I've never fooled myself into thinking we were that family, from a Norman Rockwell painting, with the hubs at the head of the table, carving the bird, while everyone sits in quiet anticipation of the feast. Nope, ours is a pretty raucous group. Catching up with each other's lives, reminiscing about past holidays-and I swear - the boys - now men - still plop on the couch, tease each other and tell stories on one another, like the old days. But we're together, all under the same roof, and that's what the holiday's about.

I know it won't always be this way. Like I said, families have to be flexible. The grands are getting older (so are the kids) and the traditions we have will change again. Already, they don't stay as long as they used to -basketball schedules, naps, and sharing them with the in-laws make it tougher. But for one more year, barring any bad weather or sickness, they'll be here again.

And I feel blessed. Because we'll be together, all under the same roof, if for even a brief time. And that's what the holiday's about.

I hope you're with loved ones, family or friends, all under the same roof, giving thanks for all the blessings in your lives-recalling old memories and making new ones. And if you have to unbuckle your belt a notch or two because of all the terrific food, that's alright, too. Happy Thanksgiving from this old(er) broad!

Lofty Goals

I had such lofty goals when summer began! Okay, so I didn't get the next great American novel written over the summer. Neither did I finish the completion of several chalk painting projects I'd aimed for. I'm reminded of that every time I walk into the garage and see four pieces of sad looking furniture staring back at me. I didn't get the bountiful garden or the beautiful flower beds I'd invested in during the spring. And I didn't lose the twenty pounds I'd promised myself, when trying on summer clothes, back in March.

All of those would have taken time - that precious commodity that becomes even more precious as the years go by. Try as I might, there never seemed to be enough of it this summer. In past years, I'd have labeled myself a failure, of sorts-a slacker. I had such big plans that never came together! But I'm not going to beat myself up over it.

Perhaps, because...

I spent precious time with my grandkids. One-on one time, seeing how they're developing their own strengths, setting their own goals, and enjoying their own lives. (Whether eighteen, one or in between, they've made the passing of time enjoyable, but they can slow it down some now!)

I had the blessing of strolling the streets of Caesar on an incredible trip to Italy with the hubs, the middle son, old friends, and new. (And the reason my garden didn't thrive? One has to be present to water and weed, it turns out!)

I got to enjoy friends, laughing about old times, or planning some new chances at making memories. I was able to witness the growth and the good qualities of my sons and their wives. (Is there anything better than the realization that you had a hand in giving the world good people?)

I was able to visit my mom - who no longer knows me, but I know her. (A chore, some days, to visit her in that awful state, but if the roles were reversed, she'd do the same.)

I got to spend time with the hubs. Whether traveling the world or just watching *Jeopardy* (a nightly staple. Yeah, we're THAT old!) or *Everybody Loves Raymond,* (we're inching closer to identifying with the old folks in THAT show) We're a pretty good pair.

I have outside interests, like meeting with women who have common interests, gardening, the gym, (don't get excited. I'm far from fit or buff- ha! I am just going for flexibility and balance now.) our kids, and grandkids...

The darling pictures of kids, growing up on Facebook and returning to yet another year of school and the countless familiar names in the obituary column serve as a constant nudge for me to get busy-or busier.

But there's that pesky thing-time. Usually a friend, but not when I don't have it!

I hope I always have goals - lofty or not. Seems I'll have given up on life, if I don't. So maybe the fall will give me time to write-or organize-or paint-or plan next year's garden-or lose some weight. But the Summer of '19 will be noted as a summer of achievement, not because of the things I did or didn't get done, or how I spent my time, but just that I had it.

When It's Over, It's Over!

Well, another Christmas is behind me. I always love the holiday season. Getting the house and yard all prettied up, the entertaining and seeing friends we don't see often enough, putting thought into who needs or wants what, the kids and grandkids all making the trip "home," despite the miles and their busy schedules. (That's the BEST part of all!) The shopping, cooking, cleaning, and preparation are even pleasant when I'm getting ready for this wonderful time of year.

But you ask anyone who knows me well, they'd tell you, for me, when it's over, it's over! I don't want to hear a Christmas carol on December twenty-sixth. I don't want to eat a Christmas cookie! I don't even want to check out the Christmas clearance tables! Most years, you'd be hard pressed to find any traces of Christmas in our home on December twenty-seventh! My Christmas treasures that had been lovingly placed throughout the house, the ornaments that had been meticulously hung on the tree, and the tree itself! All practically thrown into boxes to come out again in 325 days. (I get ready for Christmas at Thanksgiving, so cobwebs on the tree aren't unheard of! Ha!) The only part of Christmas I will acknowledge, after the fact, are the photos from this year's celebrations and the memories of that particular Christmas.

But things are a little bit different this year. I'm not sure if it's an age thing or what. What used to be a "breeze thru the house" task, takes more time. (Oh, I know THAT's an age thing!) But it's more than that. Seems I'm savoring the exercise more. Packing things away more carefully and more neatly, recalling, more often, the origins of my Christmas gems-who they came from, the memories they evoke, and the thoughts of folks no longer around, to be a part of making this year's Christmas memories.

And speaking of memories-there was a family, with three little boys, seated behind us at Christmas Eve Mass. You could tell how the excitement was building for them, in what would be under the tree, when they got home. I didn't need to be reminded of how quickly time is going, but I was. It doesn't seem like it was that many Christmases ago, that I was in the same position as that mom-calming the boys down and trying to keep things under control for a few more hours. It was an "in my face" reminder of how I need to savor things, because, although Christmas traditions stay the same, Christmases don't. "Life" assures that.

Yep, I think I'll leave my Christmas things up a little bit longer this year. I mean, what does it hurt? When everything is packed away, the house looks dark and naked, anyway, so what's my hurry? Maybe, this year, it'll even prolong the joy for a while.

But don't you dare offer me a Christmas cookie-and I mean it!

Ramblings
and Rants

We have a dog. We've had several in the course of our marriage. It always seemed right -boys and dogs, man (or woman's) best friend. We fell for it. Sometimes we took a shot at the local dog pound, but once we got one through an owner. THAT nightmare lasted three days. He was returned because he just wasn't nice - We named him Damnit. We thought it was funny - "Come here, Damnit; go lay down, Damnit." (Maybe he wasn't nice because of the name?) Anyway, he went back to his original owner and few tears were shed. No use having a mean dog around the kids.

Our most recent dog daughter came to us via a place that trains service dogs, using a prison program. These animals, trained by prison inmates, go onto living productive lives, and helping those in need of aid in performing daily tasks. It's a very cool program. The dogs who don't make the cut are adopted out. Maybe because they were stubborn, anxious, or quirky.

Well, that's how we came upon Tansy. She never made the cut, because she's all three. I was never a fan of her name, but we were afraid to change it for fear we'd confuse her and lose all the valuable training she DID have. (Plus, our record with naming dogs was pretty dismal - Boo, Boo 2, and the aforementioned, Damnit.)

We needn't have worried about losing that training. We knew we had a nut job when she stood like a statue on the floor of the back seat of the car for the entire hour and a half trip home from the kennel!

Okay, she was housebroken. She goes to her crate when we say "kennel up," and she rings a bell at the door when she wants to go out. But after that, all bets are off!

This is a dog who goes all Cuejo on anyone who has the audacity to step onto our front porch. But once you make it into the house, after some skittish scrutiny, she'll be your best friend for life.

This is the dog who would take a bullet for me before she'd allow that dastardly mailman to do us harm. She has saved my life on a daily basis for eight years now.

This is the dog who will welcome treats all day long, going so far as to nudging open the closet door where treats are kept for an owner who's too blind to see that she's clearly starving. But she won't eat her real food until her real master (we let the hubs THINK that...) returns home from work each night.

This is the dog who will wait to see which shoes I put on for the day. Gym shoes? Excitement builds over a possible walk. Loafers? Head to the crate. She's going to work. Slippers? Oh, good! Looks like it'll be a couch-potato kind of day.

This is the dog who didn't like a car on her first car trip to her new home eight years ago, but now jumps into the car if the door's left open while I unload groceries or hangs out the car window, slobbering and savoring all the smells that dogs savor. She stands in the driveway, surprised that we have the audacity to go someplace in the car, without her.

This is the dog who will whimper at our bedroom door when it rains-not loud storms-just hard rain. And when I come out to sooth her, ("I get the couch, pal!") rather than lying down to be comforted by a compassionate master, she starts her pacing. Dog toenails and laminate flooring are a bad combo. I'm trying to get back to sleep and she's tap dancing across the floor like she's auditioning for a 1930's Broadway musical!

Quirky? Stubborn? Anxious? What we have here, folks, is a pooch with even more issues than one of her owners! A real headcase!

But you know what? In spite of all her sometimes-moronic behavior, I'm glad our goofy dog wasn't placed with someone who needs help getting through daily life. Or was she?

Being a Left-Hander

For my entire life, I've felt like I'm a klutz, very ungraceful, a spaz. I've blamed it on my height, my need to get places in a hurry, and my just-not -being-very-coordinated. And I would have gone through the rest of my life feeling that way, if I hadn't happened upon an article online. Finally, I have a reason for my condition! My failure to look poised and feel graceful can be directly attributed to the fact that I'm a lefty!

From the first time I tried using scissors in kindergarten all the way to dipping ice cream with an ice cream scooper at my first job, I've known being a left-handed person in a right-handed world was difficult. But after finding out new information in this article, it isn't any wonder I come off looking awkward!

Like, did you realize that a tape measure's numbers are upside down if held by a lefty? Or that can openers are downright dangerous in the hands of a left-hander? You know the pens that get handed out, the kind with advertising on them? In the hands of a lefty, their message is lost because the printing is upside down. And the pens attached on a chain at the bank are on the wrong side for someone of my ilk. Same deal with credit card scanners-wrong side! The countless letters and cards I've written that were smeared from dragging my hand across the fresh ink? Unavoidable for a lefty! And don't get me started on spiral notebooks and binders! It's downright painful for a left-hander to write with those wires jabbing into your hand!

I could take solace in the company of famous left handers, like President Ronald Reagan, the great actor Robert DeNiro, and basketball whiz Larry Bird, but gloss over some of them, like the Boston Strangler, Jack the Ripper, and John Dillinger, all lefties. But I, perhaps, should just own it and face the fact that things are just a bit askew for someone like me.

So, do me favor. The next time you see someone wrestling with their credit card at the check-out line, writing upside down at the bank teller's window, or bleeding from using a spiral notebook, don't look at them with disdain or pity. Just know that they're doing the best they can with something they never asked for-being left-handed!

I Hate Nature! Ha!

Okay, I wasn't going to do this for fear that folks would think I'm a nut job or that I live in a shack, down in the holler. But I'm about on the edge, so I'm going to rant, once again. If for no other reason, I'm writing this down to document things for my future insanity hearing.

Anyone who knows me, knows that I'm no fan of nature. I used to reserve my hatred for the trespassers into my house, (mice, squirrels, flies, ants…) but after this summer, I am extending that to ALL of nature…inside and out! Except for my dog, who's on probation, I'm saving all my love for humans (and some of them are on probation, as well.)

Because my memory is clear on most recent events, let's start with the spring/summer of 2016. The horny robin that kept trying to procreate with our bedroom window? You remember him. He hung around a week, making the grating noise that comes from repeatedly cozying up to a screen-until he wised up and realized he was an egomaniac, attracted to himself. The perv!

And then it was the squirrels, deer, birds, and rabbits that laid claim to my garden. In spite of the commercial deterrents I bought and the Facebook advice I took, they still had a summer-long garden party! Note to self: Don't hang red Christmas ornaments around the garden - a Facebook suggestion - to trick the birds into thinking that, if they peck at those, they won't peck at your tomatoes. It didn't work-plus the neighbors think I'm some kind of over-anxious goof, ready for a neighborhood Christmas Walk! And whoever posted that a red cardinal in your yard is really a loved one just saying "hello?" Baloney! If that's true, my late dad has had his fill of afterlife tomatoes!

Which brings me to my most recent dealings with critters. Yesterday, I spotted some mouse droppings. I know. I know…I have a wooded lot. I'm going to have an occasional mouse. Well, that doesn't mean I have to LIKE them! In the spring, I followed someone's Facebook advice about keeping mice out of my house. "Just sprinkle peppermint oil in your doorways. They hate it!" So, I ventured into a foreign aisle at the grocery story - the baking section (I hate baking, too, remember?) and bought the peppermint oil and followed those instructions. Well, they neglected to tell me that the peppermint oil in the doorways also keeps those creepy varmints IN your house if they've already set up residence there. Thanks for that sage advice! Anyway, we set the traps and the Hubs went to bed. I was too jacked up about Mother Nature intruding yet again, so I watched a bit of TV, and that's when the trap went off. Well, (here's a surprise!) I'm a wimp about such things, so, of course, I went in and woke up The Bear to dispose of the thing. He was less than pleased with his crazy wife.

I know I overreact over all this nature business, but I am truly tired of "nature" trying to take my stuff. I want to be the sole proprietor of this house (along with my brave hubby, of course) and enjoy my homegrown produce, unscathed. If that's being selfish, so be it. I'm on the edge here, I tell you!

A question: Does an insanity plea work in Divorce Court? Just wonderin'...

Timberrrr.....

"If a tree falls in the woods, and no one's there to hear it, does it make a sound?" Well, I'm here to tell you, "Yes it does!" And I have plenty of experience with falling trees!

What used to be a beautifully wooded back yard has been decimated by that damn ash borer. We have pumped up the local economy by supporting the tree removal guys for a few years now. Doing it in phases has made it more manageable for our wallets. And we're not done yet! Seventeen down and about twelve more to go. And those are just the ones that pose a threat to the house.

It saddens me to see the trees go. My Dad planted many of them forty years ago, confident, I'm sure, that they'd be around forever. And when we became stewards of his beloved woods, we did, too. But Mother Nature had other plans. She must have gotten the idea that we didn't love the cool shade those trees provided, the gorgeous colors of the leaves in the Fall, or the beautiful greens of the spring. Well, Mother Nature was wrong!

Now we have a sunny area in the back of our home, where once a beautiful, shady stand of trees stood. It's so sunny now that I've moved my garden back there. I guess that's what you call "making chicken salad out of chicken sh**!" At least the former woods are being put to good use now. Not as pretty, but productive...

I read a while ago that, "Planting a tree is having hope in a future that the planter may never see." I think that's what I'll do. Plant some trees to replace the ones we've lost. Hope. I'll never see them grow to the grand state of our lost trees, but it's comforting, in a way, knowing that someone, some-day, will appreciate their woods as much as we once did.

So, if you hear the buzzing of saws and grinders in our neighborhood, just know that after "Timberrr!" there's hope.

Bucket List or F......it List

Whoever came up with the term "Bucket List?" That wish list that we're supposed to fulfill before our days are over? Probably some malcontent, unhappy with his life, who just HAD to plant the seeds of discontent in everyone else's minds about their own lives. Well, I say, "Enough already!" There's nothing wrong with my life, yet I was sucked into thinking I needed to check something off my bucket list. It just about killed me!

Let me set the stage. I was recently blessed to go on a girls' trip...boating, shopping, dining, laughing, hiking, and drinking, with some delightful gals. It was a lot of fun. So why wasn't I satisfied with all of that? No, I had to go and push for a stop at a zip lining park. I've always wanted to try it. It looks so free-ing, so youthful, so fun. So, our thoughtful hostess obliged. I was the one who wanted to do it and the other gals agreed.

The first tipoff that there was some peril involved should have been the form we had to sign. There was more writing on it than a real estate contract! Of course, I signed it! I hadn't come THIS far to back out. (There'd be time for that later, I guess.) Another clue that things may go wrong was the youth-ful fella, outfitting us in ropes, pulleys, straps, and helmets. When we'd heard enough of his, "It's all good," and " No worries," we were all set. So up the steps we went (no easy task for this old(er) broad, loaded down with all the gear that had us looking like we were linemen working for the power com-pany!

Our adventure was set to start as the attendant hooked me onto a line and I was told to walk off the platform. With a leap of faith, I followed his instructions. Everything was smooth sailing at that point-and it WAS lib-erating...it WAS fun-until everything just stopped! My zip lining pal flew past me and there I was, hanging above a lake, going nowhere. Just a'dangling in midair, kind of afraid to move, but sooo ready to. The jacket, the heat, the helmet... I felt like one of those big, big salamis hanging in the butcher's window! I remained there for fifteen minutes, (but felt like an hour!) while they worked on getting me to the platform with a rope. Turns out I was put together all wrong by the aforementioned youthful "no worries" guy. My so-called friends, who were now safely on the ground, were alternating laughter with concern, but filming all the while! The young employee was publicly chastised by the main dude. I sure hope he didn't lose his job over my mishap.

But I have to ask the question...Do you know what an atomic wedgie feels like? Have you ever worn a strait jacket? Have you ever thought that falling into a lake from high up may just feel better than what you're feeling, hanging uncomfortably by a rope? Well, I now can say I do!

I can also now say that bucket lists are probably over-rated. What's wrong with being happy with the way things are, with the hand I've been dealt? I have a very sweet life and I count my blessings every single day. Throwing in a little extra excitement isn't going to change that. But would I do it again? Although my sore bum would say "no," I hate to admit that this old(er) broad would say, "No worries; heck yeah!"

Crisp Nights and Golden Days

We live in Ohio, and I love the change of seasons. It's one of the nicest things about Ohio for me. Living in an area where it's always warm or always cold would be boring - and although last winter put my love for this place to the test, I still love Ohio.

I especially love fall in Ohio! I love the thought of cooler temps, after a long, hot summer. I love the thought of jeans and sweaters. I love the crisp nights and the golden days. I used to love the thought of the kids (and me) getting back into some kind of routine. I love the thought of putting the lawn mower away for a while and getting out the rakes to rid the yard of this year's beauty and bounty.

The fact that we're a "football family" puts a positive spin on shorter days and longer nights. Years ago, Hubby, a coach, and the boys would trudge in after practice, the smell of dirt on their uniforms still a vivid memory of the season. Game day, when the boys were young, game nights when they were in high school, and game weekends when they were in college, made fall a busy and fun season in our family life.

Another upside to fall is that cooking becomes more fun for me. Sure, the fresh fruits and vegetables of the summer are hard to beat, but, for me, making hearty soups and stews, and long-simmering meals, trumps anything fixed on the grill. I'd like to say that the fragrance of fall baking would be a nice, too, but you should know my track record with that by now. I'll just leave that to those who enjoy and excel at baking.

Aside from the occasional surliness that comes from hubby going to work and coming home from work in the dark, the biggest downside to fall is what comes after it! Winter! Except for the holidays and the fact that there are no mosquitoes or flies, I can't think of one redeeming reason for that season! I think bears have the right idea and hibernating should be an acceptable option. (Oh, wait! I'm an insomniac! That wouldn't work!)

The seasons come and go; it's all pretty remarkable to witness. I guess I should feel very blessed that I've been around to see so many of them. It'd be a boring world if we all loved the same things, so I get it -some folks prefer the fall over spring or summer. But whether I love it or hate it, it's here, so I'm going to bundle up and enjoy it. What else you gonna do?

No Vacancy

We don't live in a holler. We live in a brick, well-sealed (or so I thought!) home that backs up to a lovely wooded lot. Any creature of the wild would be happy to live out back. Trees, nuts, berries......

But if you, arrogant squirrel, think you're better than your brethren and that "movin' on up" means taking up residence in our attic, you're wrong! Just because we shared a kernel of corn with you during the past year doesn't mean we want to house you and your family now!

And those dance parties you're hosting have to end, too. I can appreciate the fact that you can't sleep - I share the same malady - but I don't twerk all over the house at four o'clock in the morning with total disregard for those who CAN sleep!

Yep, you and your kin may think you're living the high life now, but that's about to end. You probably think you're entitled to enjoy the warmth of our home. Others of your kind have had the same thought and have met with tragic endings.

I'm not usually so inhospitable, but this is our home and you have the entire outdoors! So, save yourself and get out now! And spread the word! The Wright Place can get wild sometimes, but we don't need your kind around here-indoors anyway.

I'm really starting to think, maybe, that I'm a big-city kind of girl.

Some Questions I've Pondered Lately

- Why is it that so many things that taste so good are bad for us?
- Who had the nerve to take the first selfie? And who thought it was a good idea? What ever happened to folks taking pictures of each other from a bit of a distance? Nostrils and bags under the eyes really aren't my most attractive features.
- Who was the first person to think an oyster was edible? Those slimy globules are the least appetizing-looking things God ever made-and people eat them!
- When did celebrities and the Hollywood-types become so darn important? Many probably couldn't hold a job anywhere else.
- Why do boys' bikes have that bar across them? Shouldn't it be the girls' that have them? Or why have them at all? Unless it's just so you can tell the difference between a girl's bike and a boy's bike, but it seems unsafe either way.

- Will we ever run out of websites, email addresses, or passwords? Think of all the passwords you have or that you've changed–now multiply that by how many people use computers.

- Why is it oldsters drive too slowly and youngsters drive too fast? Wouldn't you think we old-timers, who have fewer years ahead of us, would speed up a bit to get it all in, and the kids, who have many years ahead, would slow down and enjoy the ride?

- Has it hit anyone else that, after all the expense of buying big screen TVs, more and more people are watching movies and shows on laptop computers and little phone screens?

- Why am I still getting so many phone calls from businesses and organizations when I'm on the Do Not Call list?

- Whoever decided Christmas should be celebrated in December? Wouldn't be as nostalgic, I grant you, but summertime would be nice shopping weather.

- Where did the pioneers get the courage and stamina to "Go West," encountering mountains, rivers, and God knows what else? I have to think twice about driving all the way to Fairfield, five miles away, so I would've been left behind for sure!

If anyone has the answer to these queries, I'd love to hear 'em!

"Hello" or "H...E...L..L..O".....

I guess we're a couple of the dwindling number of folks who have a landline phone in our house. Sure, I have a cell phone and it pays for itself in convenience. I get it. Being able to call someone when I'm out and about is terrific!

I also get texting-sorta. Contacting someone, without really interrupting them, is pretty neat. But telephones were invented AFTER typewriters, so it seems like we're going backwards, doesn't it? I personally like the sound of a voice in my conversations. There's something warmer about hearing a friend versus hearing FROM one. Plus, my spastic fingers make texting a long, drawn out process. I can talk a lot faster.

I may be wrong, but without a landline, I think our home would lack a connectedness. No central station. I'm glad cellphones weren't around when our kids were young. They could've said they were somewhere and not been there at all. Our folks, years ago, knew who we were talking to and for how long because they were right there. If that sounds mistrusting, it is! I was a kid once, and I had three of my own.

To this day, if one of my friends calls our landline and the spouse answers, there's a good chance he'll engage them in conversation. And I do the same with his friends. Maybe that's not so enjoyable for them, but I enjoy it! That would be missing if we're always using our own cellphones.

We'll have a phone at the old homestead for as long as they allow them. I think it gives the place permanence and represents something tangible-an address. I'll keep using my cellphone, too, and who knows? Maybe someday, I'll be a convert and lose the landline, but for now, we can be reached at the same number we've had for over thirty years, sitting in my comfy chair. "Hello"?

Things I'm Giving Thanks For

I am very blessed in my life, and thankful every day, for things like family, friends, my faith, my home, etc. That's a given, not just during the holidays, but year-round. Well, the holidays are in the distant past and I have come up with a list of mundane things that probably don't get any appreciation but make my life a bit nicer. So here goes...

- Queen or king-sized beds. My marriage of forty-eight years would not have lasted in anything smaller.
- The Invisible Fence for my dog. I wouldn't have a dog without it.
- True dollar stores- I can always find something there and usually have a buck to spare.

- Yoga pants-so comfortable and it looks like I'm working out-or going to.

- Mr. Clean Magic Erasers-where the heck were those when our boys were young?

- My dog. Another heartbeat in the house, and she never judges-ever.

- Face Time or Skype-I couldn't live three hours away from my grandkids (and be pleasant) without it.

- The 1960's era snowblower that my father-in-law left us twenty years ago and its flawless performance this past winter.

- Coca Cola-anyone who knows me knows that I'm a fan-nectar of the gods.

- Makeup and hair products- How fun to reinvent oneself every once in a while!

- Pierced earrings- I would never have stood for those clip kinds!

- The game of golf-makes hubby happy (most of the time) and it's something we can enjoy together, occasionally. (Okay-I can enjoy occasionally, playing with him; I'm pretty sure it's not that enjoyable for him.)

- Fast food-Once in a while-come on, you know you like it, too!

Well, that's it for now. Feel free to add to my list or make up your own. What little things in your life do you under-appreciate?

Four Quarters or a Hundred Pennies

Read an interesting quote online recently that said, "As I get older, I'm becoming more selective of whom I consider a friend. I find that I would rather have four quarters than 100 pennies."

Is that true with you? It really got me to thinking about the folks in my life.

I've been blessed with great friends throughout my life. Some are the kind that, no matter how much time has passed since I saw them last, we pick up where we left off. Some are the siblings I grew up with. Some are the wives of hubby's friends who've become best friends of mine now. Some are the parents of our kids' friends -our relationships forged as we rode herd on a bunch of boys. Some are newer friends, brought into my life because of a common interest we share. Some are old school friends -our friendships renewed because of class reunions. Some are "friends" because of the amazing technology that is social media.

The above quote suggests that, as we age, we don't have the need for so many people in our lives. But I want to challenge that. Sure, hubby and I don't feel the need to party with big groups of friends, like we used to. It takes too long to recuperate, but I hope that we always have friends-and all kinds of them in our lives. When it's all said and done, whether they're "quarters" or "pennies," you can't put a price tag on friendship.

The Time Change

Who came up with the idea of time change? That silly practice of falling back one hour during one part of the year and springing forward another hour during another season of the year? Well, it's happening again this weekend!

I was surprised to find out that Benjamin Franklin was the culprit who decided that messing with our clocks was a good thing. Prior to learning this information, I thought old Ben was a brilliant guy. Now? Not so much.

As you may have gathered, I'm not a fan. Sure, I understand the reasoning. We get some extra sunlight during certain parts of the year -and that's not a bad thing. Farmers love it, I suppose, but I have to tell you that the time change wreaks havoc on my body that first week after it goes into effect (and I'm not sure it ever gets caught up after that!) The day after we change our clock, I don't know if it's 12:00, 1:00, or 11:00! I know, you're thinking, "What difference does it make?" I can't answer that-it just does!

Before Ben thought messing with time was a good idea, we had standard time. From caveman on, we've looked to the sky and when the sun's at its highest point, it's noon. And you go on from there. How can we take an hour and store it somewhere for a few months and then magically bestow it on another day, months later? And who are we to mess with a fundamental structure of the universe, anyway?

Now, if they'd come up with a way of jockeying weight around -taking pounds away, magically, and bestowing them on another person -then they'd HAVE something! And I would certainly get behind THAT!

Just Thinkin'

- We start the political stuff way too early! Been sick of it for months and it's still a ways off!
- Watching TV the night before a colonoscopy is a bad idea. Fasting? With all those delicious-looking commercials-wow.
- Just because the calendar says April doesn't mean the weather is going to be terrific!
- Wallpaper always seems like a better idea going up than coming down.
- Why are the Kardashians still here?
- When and why does toilet paper need a marketing campaign and so many tasteless commercials?
- Our seafood choices have become so much more than the fish sticks of the '70's.
- Who decided weeds are weeds?
- Why have toasters never been improved upon? Everything else in the kitchen has changed, it seems.
- Are marijuana dealers in states where its use is now legal allowed to advertise in magazines, like cigarette companies used to?
- Why do some folks in our neighborhood have to fix their cracked sidewalks when others don't have to have sidewalks at all?

- Food Network Chef Bobby Flay looks like Howdy Doody to me. How has he landed three wives?

- How bad must some product have been, to be "new" and "improved" almost every year?

- Funny how your day can go to hell in a hurry - all because of a computer.

That's it for me! What have you been wondering about?

Hot Tubs, Lava Lamps and Water Beds

The mention of those three items conjure up thoughts of the '60's and '70's- the days of "Make Love, Not War," bell bottoms, and fringed vests, LSD, campus demonstrations, and Viet Nam.

Not that I was actively a part of any of it. (Okay, I wore bell bottoms.) I was a strait-laced, conservative girl in the 60's and, by the early 70's, I was married to a pretty strait-laced, conservative guy. But no one escaped the influence of the 60's and 70's. It was everywhere! Turning on the TV every night brought all these strange and foreign images into our family rooms. To me, the 60's had a kind of sleazy feel to it. I don't know. All these new things: beaded curtains, "turning on and tuning out," water beds, (whoever thought THAT one up?) the psychedelic colors and patterns, Twiggy and the London Look- I really wasn't a fan.

So why do I even bring this up? It probably has everything to do with the fact that we've sprung for a hot tub! But no worries. There won't be any wild parties here like I imagine took place in the days of free love. Nope. Sad to say, it's for therapeutic purposes now. These old bones and muscles crave its warm massage and I thought we'd better get one now, when I can still climb into it! I suppose there would've been more of a fun factor to it years ago, but maybe having relaxed and loose muscles will be fun now.

If you drive past our place and see the glow of a lava lamp, (one of the boys left one here from their college days -I guess they made a brief resurgence in popularity) know that I'm having a "groovy" time in my hot tub about 40 years late. And if you hear someone hollering, do me a favor and come and help me get out of it!

A Dog's Life

As I lay awake another night - thinking, worrying, praying - our dog, snoring beside us, I've decided, in the next life, I want to come back as our dog.

He sleeps without a care in the world; his biggest decision is, "Should I go after that ball or just chew on this bone." I'd have someone to pick up after me and have my meals put out before me. I'd have an occasional pat on the head for the most mundane thing, and I'd never have to give a thought as to how I look or what I should wear.

Our dog greets folks a bit more ferociously than I would, but she'll follow you to your car, after the slightest friendly attention, hoping for a ride, windows open, ears flapping in the wind. An occasional treat, chasing birds instead of deadlines, and a chance to run back and forth in the yard at the sight of a UPS truck is all it takes to make her happy. If only life was that simple...

Yep, if there's such a thing as reincarnation, I wanna come back as my dog!

The "F" Word

You know which one I'm talking about-the foul word that has crept into our everyday vernacular? And for what reason? Because it's one syllable? Because it's a strong word? Because our vocabulary is so limited that we can't come up with a better one? Because it makes us sound cool and grown-up? (although that reasoning doesn't work if you're already old) I just don't get it.

I'm not going to act all holier-than-thou and pretend I haven't used the word; it's an easy, go-to word when things aren't going right. But I've noticed that it's become totally acceptable in today's music, movies, and television (on the premiere channels) and why? I remember when saying the word "shit" was enough to get me grounded. When did things change? Are parents doing anything to their kids when they utter that word? When they use it frequently themselves?

I've never understood how or why the F-word is used in the first place. Why use a word that represents something beautiful, like lovemaking, when we're angry or want to hurt someone?

Let's try an exercise. Where we might use the F-word, let's substitute it with the real word, okay? I'll start, "Aw, Intercourse you!" or "He is so intercoursing cute!" How about,

"I don't give an intercourse!" or perhaps "Intercourse you and the horse you rode in on!" There, that's enough. You get my reasoning, right?

I know that my writing this isn't going to change anything. That dumb word will still be overused, but I, for one, find it boring, redundant, and I think that its use makes folks look like they lack the skills to express themselves any better.

Perhaps you're thinking, "Aw, intercourse you, you old woman." To which I'd respond, "Get a dictionary...a whole new world awaits you."

National Grouch Day

I have tried to be quasi-positive in my posts, but sometimes, I just have to let it out. So, in observance of National Grouch Day, (Yeah, I made that up) I am going to list a few of the random things that tick me off.

1. Grey days -I can almost take cold and I can almost take hot, but I can't stand grey!
2. Folks who talk or text while driving- you're handling a 2000-pound weapon there. And you're not that great at multi-tasking.

3. Cashiers, waitresses, or nurses who call me "Honey" or Sweetie." First of all, you don't know if I'm sweet (many days, I'm not!) and it's condescending to an older woman.

4. Large portions at restaurants - how about serving us half of that and charging us less?

5. Most commercials on TV- especially, the feminine product ones, the erectile dysfunction ones, and any that make dads look like idiots.

6. Gasoline prices- How can they be so different from gas station to gas station? One part of town can differentiate as much as fifty cents a gallon from another part of town. Who sets these prices?

7. People who illegally park in handicapped spots-really? Get some exercise and park where you're supposed to. On the other hand, excessive handicapped spots. Does a roller rink really need ten of 'em?

8. Unkind people- life's hard enough for a lot of folks without adding being treated shabbily to their list of things to contend with.

9. Pet owners who walk their dogs and don't clean up after them. I have my own dog and, after the winter we've had, I've got plenty to clean up myself.

10. Vendors who rush the seasons- I get it- you have to be a bit ahead of things, but I don't want to buy a winter coat in July or a bathing suit in February! (Truth be told, I don't wanna buy a bathing suit EVER!)

There! I'm done with my grumbling til next year's National Grouch Day. Oh wait- and I can't stand liars!

"If Wishes Were Pigs, Bacon Would ALWAYS Be on Sale."

Or as an old and dear friend used to say, "Wish in one hand and sh*# in the other and see which one weighs the most." You get what I'm saying? Wishes are always there- we all have 'em - but they're just that -- wishes. They seldom go anywhere. With that in mind, I'm posting my end-of- year wish list-an inconsequential tabulation of wishes I've had lately. Feel free to add to, okay?

- I wish they made Big Wheels for adults.
- I wish that there was a big tube of ointment that could be smeared all over this nation to heal the scars from such a vile election.
- I wish my eyelashes were as lush as they used to be.
- I wish all the systems in the government which are broken would magically be fixed.
- I wish that my dog wouldn't get any older.
- I wish that those with computer smarts would use their talents for noble causes or for fun-nothing sinister.
- I wish I could rake or blow leaves without ending up with more mulch in the yard than in the flower beds.
- I wish I could bestow experience on my kids and grandkids so they wouldn't make the mistakes that I have.
- I wish the spirit of Thanksgiving and Valentine's Day lasted all year long.
- I wish the hubs and I slept all the way through the night, just once!

- I wish those who "have" shared with those who "have-not" without the government's involvement.
- I wish they'd park the street cleaners from August until March. What's the point, when there are leaves everywhere?
- I wish our government wasn't so big.
- I wish January and February went by as quickly as June and July seem to.
- I wish I could shower off pounds-you know, go into the shower at one weigh and come out ten pounds (or twenty) lighter?
- I wish my mom didn't have dementia. It's like she's not my mom anymore.
- I wish folks communicated more, face-to-face or voice-to-voice.
- I wish I understood the coloring books for adult" craze. I could never stay in the lines so that's one craze I'll not partake in!
- I wish I'd never picked up a cigarette-ever!
- I wish those I love knew how much.
- I wish people (me, included) would just be kind-always.

See how that works? Well, I'll keep on wishin'. "The bacon's always on sale" in MY world and FYI: The sh*#" weighs more. Have a great day!

"Hello...You've Been Selected..."

I usually try to be upbeat about my age-stage in life, but age- specific telemarketers are making it very hard! I can't tell you how many times I answer the phone to hear a recorded message, geared toward the elderly. I know we have special needs but come on!

One that really irks me is, "Did you know that eighty percent of seniors will fall in their homes this year?" Yes, I know that. I'm a big part of your statistics already. Or the weekly call telling me that I've been chosen to test a new security system that will keep us safe from those "who prey on the elderly." Particularly offensive are the calls asking me to serve on a panel regarding incontinence. I'm not THERE yet, either!

And my aggravation isn't limited to telephone marketing either. I bet we receive a piece of mail daily, asking us to give THEIR health insurance plan a look, or have we given any thought to long-term nursing home insurance? Geesh! Quit rushing me!

I know that the number of baby boomers makes us a very sought-after demographic in terms of sales, but please! It's almost like they're trying to talk us into being needy. The constant reminders that I need this and I need that, strengthens my resolve not to need any of what they're selling.

And NO! I'm not interested in a plot in your burial park!!! We already have our plot!

Just Wondering

When did eyebrows become so important? Have you seen all the products in the makeup aisles, devoted just to them? I figure, if I just pluck the strays and don't look like I have two big wooly caterpillars on my forehead, I'm good.

Why does August seem to go so much faster than February when August has thirty days and February only has twenty-eight? Is it the impending end of freedom that August brings and the impatience for spring to arrive, that just makes it SEEM that way? Hmmmmm.

And along those same lines, why does the school year begin so early now? I'm sure it's because of testing. But tourism dollars lost because August is now an in-school month, for the most part, seems kinda dumb to me. Go back to starting after Labor Dad and end after Memorial Day schedule!

How come brussel sprouts are so pricey now? Is it because they're popping up on chic menus everywhere? Same with skirt steak or flank steak. Even chicken wings. Used to be "garbage" cuts- couldn't give 'em away. Now? Wow!

In these days of cell phones, do kids still act up when their moms are on the phone? Seems when our old home phone would ring, that would signal the time for the kids to either act up or to need mom for something.

I love the splash pads that have provided cool refreshment for kids throughout our fine city this summer, but I have to ask. Are kids still learning to swim? And if not, how silly will it look when our future adults are just running around beaches and pools, giggling, instead of actually being IN the water?

Why are airlines still demonstrating how to use seat belts? Haven't we been using them in our cars long enough now? We get it! The one end snaps into the other! What I REALLY want to know is how does that heavy plane stay up in the air?!?

Why do clerks in stores refer to me as "Sweetie?" Must be an age thing-have they seen me walking around, aimlessly, looking for my car in their lot? Okay, I'm old(er) but that's a pretty big assumption they're making - that I'm sweet. Ask the hubs if that's the case. Ha!

How many occupations are around now that weren't so in-demand thirty years ago? Besides computer-related ones or cable TV ones (grrrr!), I can think of a few. Tattoo artists and manicurists. Oh, they've been around for years, but the numbers of those needed to keep us all tatted up and gel-nailed now must be remarkable!

Okay, we have ground beef and we have ground pork. So why do we have pulled pork and shredded beef? And who got to decide that? Both are delicious, but pulled sounds rugged and shredded sounds kind of wimpy, don't ya think?

Who types in all the information we find on the world wide web? And do they actually type it or is it scanned? It's taken us hundreds of years to accumulate all that knowledge and now it's all there, at our fingertips! Amazing!

Why don't they make really wide eaves and really wide, round downspouts for our houses, so the leaves would be flushed out when it rains? Sure would eliminate the awful (and dangerous) task of cleaning out the gutters. Yuck!

I have a skewered way of looking at things, I know that. Perhaps too much time on my hands? But how about you? What have YOU been wondering about?

If You Think You're in A Hole, Quit Digging

It's funny, I think, how the beginning of the new year always brings out all the experts, offering their versions of how we can improve our lives. Whether it's physical fitness, healthier eating, or financial security, they all have new ways of making our lives better.

I've been paying special attention to the financial wizards and their advice, and I think I've come up with an even better and more innovative way to ensure good financial health. I'm titling it, "If You Think You're in a Hole, Quit Digging" program.

I'm old school, I know. I came late to the party that had folks using ATM's and debit cards. I still write checks (you know, those antiquated pieces of paper that represent cash?) I don't bank online (except to check my balance) and I pay off credit card balances in full each month, faithfully. I'm not being snotty about it-that's just the way we roll.

When one reads about the amount of debt in this country, it's obvious that we're very much in the minority. I'm so afraid that so many are living beyond their means, with homes and cars they can't afford, taking trips that take a year to pay off, and credit card balances that would keep me awake at night. I even read about a couple who was in debt trouble and were using credit cards to pay off credit cards! Stop it! "If You Think You're in a Hole, Quit Digging!"

If you're spending money on things you can't afford, stop it! Who are you trying to impress? If people judge you on what you have, you don't need 'em! If you aren't squirreling away money for the future, you better change your ways. Start paying yourself in the form of a savings account. You have a lot of years ahead of you and who knows what the future holds?

I'll retire now from my financial advisor role - I'm really not qualified, but, to me it's just common sense- "If You Think You're in a Hole, Quit Digging!"

Maybe, next up, I'll become a personal trainer at the gym. Nah, never mind.

The Art of Casual Observing

Well, I'm trying something new. I'm trying to master the art of casual observing. That's going to require watching the world go by without being judgmental or vocal. This is a challenge for someone who seems to have an opinion on just about EVERYTHING!

Some recent casual observations:

- I see a cute couple at dinner, each intent on concentrating more on their phones than on each other. I so WANT to say, "You have a gorgeous lady with you! What could be more important?"

- I see someone taking credit for something when they had nothing to do with its success. I WANT to tell them a popular online saying, "Takers eat better, but givers sleep better." How about giving (credit) for a change, hon.

- I see countless motorists, who instead of paying attention to the road, are looking at their phones (do you sense a theme here?) I so WANT to yell out my car window at them, "Pay attention to driving, you jerk!"

- I have dealings with a company that said they'd do something and didn't come through with their promise. I WANT to tell their rep that, I deserve better!

- I'm sitting in a doctor's office for an hour or more past the scheduled appointment. I WANT to ask the receptionist, "Isn't my time just as valuable as yours?"

I could go on and on with things I've observed recently and felt the need to speak out about. Maybe just getting along with people is better than getting all worked up about their lives and how they live them. And a wise man DID once say, "It's better to remain silent and be thought a fool than to speak up and remove all doubt." Maybe I'll keep you guessing, for now. I'll be quiet THIS time and casually observe, but just so you know, it's very hard.

Another One in The Books

Another Christmas in the books and it was a dandy! The family, the friends, the food, the gifts, the music, the fun -all outstanding!

Now I don't share the retailers' enthusiasm for the season when they have Christmas trees in the aisle by Labor Day, but I AM an early bird. I decorate the house early (Thanksgiving weekend early.) We have an annual party the first week of December and that gets me moving-and done!

I must ask though -why is it that putting up the Christmas decorations is so much more fun than taking everything down and putting them away? Is it the kid in us that makes us excited about the upcoming season? Is it the kid in us that's disappointed when it's all over?

I LOVE Christmas and everything that comes with it, but by Christmas, my things have been up so long that I have cobwebs on the tree! When Christmas is over, it's over! I don't want to hear a Christmas song one day after the twenty-fifth. I'm not sure our decorated tree has ever seen New Year's.

I envy those who luxuriate in the season after the actual day. The trees and lights do look pretty into January, just not in our home. I do hate how the house looks so dark and empty when the holidays are over, but I have the warm memories of another wonderful holiday season to carry me through until next December-and the hope that everyone I hold near and dear will be here then, too.

I guess it's just in my DNA-hurry through things, get to it, and be done with it. If I was fortunate enough to have any superpower of my choice, it would be to blink my eyes and just skip through January, February, and March. Except for a trip to Florida and four family birthdays, there's nothing I like about that time of year. Just fast forward me to spring.

I hope you all have a warm and wonderful winter. Me? I'll be hibernating, and I will see you in the spring!

International Flavor

Does anyone remember the first time they had a slice of pizza? Unless you count french fries or french toast (and I don't!) I'm pretty sure that pizza was the first international flavor most of us tasted.

Back in the 50's and 60's, unless you were Italian, pizza was pretty exotic, wasn't it? Certainly, not something that we dined on at our family dinner tables on a regular basis.

My first taste of the gooey stuff was from Pasquale's, one of the first pizza chains in Cincinnati. We were at my grandparents' home and my aunt, who was a bit of an eccentric, ordered a pizza pie. We all tried it; some of us liked it a lot and some, not so much.

I remember, as a young girl, making Chef Boyardee cheese pizzas. That was a new product that came in a box. It supposedly contained everything you needed to make your own tasty pizza at home, but it was not even CLOSE in flavor to my first taste of real pizza! It was a good alternative, though, to the fish and the grilled cheese we ate in the days when Catholics refrained from eating meat on Fridays-so Chef Boyardee it was!

Look how far we've come! Neighborhood pizza parlors, pizza chains, and pizza delivery. Our eating habits and our family lives were forever changed by pizza. Many probably can't remember a world without pizza. But I can.

I got to thinking of all this, not because I was chomping down on a pizza, but because I needed chorizo sausage for a Mexican dish that I was making. At the store, all the different ethnic foods that are available now it amazed me. Our country became a melting pot for so many cultures and they all brought their cuisine and flavors along with them-and our neighborhoods and grocery store aisles will never be the same! Restaurants that serve exotic fare are the norm now. My spice rack includes spices I'm pretty sure my Mom never heard of.

Our world has certainly gotten smaller and our menus reflect that. Italian, German, Chinese, Japanese, Vietnamese, Thai, Mexican, and more-all for the taking.

My comfort foods are still the standards like meatloaf, a good pot roast, or a tasty chicken dish. But it sure is nice to have expanded our repertoire, both at home and dining out. And to think it all started with a pizza.

Broken Fences and Beautiful Gardens

"True friends overlook your broken fences and just admire your beautiful garden."

Not sure if it's because we've been looking forward to spring for so long and the gardening that comes with it or if it's because I've been thinking of friendships a lot lately. Really, no matter the reason, but that saying really caught my eye recently.

I've been fortunate to have some great gardens through the years. Good soil, enough watering and effort-it's not that hard. Those gardens have yielded some wonderful tomatoes, huge cucumbers, and flowers galore. It's not always pretty- weeding is a constant chore and the deer sometimes wreak havoc on my fences trying to get to those tasty treats. But it's worth it.

I've been blessed with wonderful friends through the years, too. Whether those friendships go way back, are more recent, are friends in the flesh or through social media, it takes effort and as much nurturing as any garden.

Keeping up with friends, conversing with them, and picking up where you left off when you DO get together- all take time, but it's also so worth it. I can't imagine my life without my friends, and I love 'em for loving me.

Sometimes, we have to decide if a friendship is worth that effort, though. Sometimes, things just change. It's nobody's fault and that's okay. It's never taken lightly, but we move on and hopefully have other friends to help fill in the void.

Sometimes, I'm not as thoughtful or attentive to those dear friendships as I should be. Sometimes, I'm surly or self-absorbed, getting caught up in my own stuff. But I hope my true friends overlook "my broken fences" and feel that I'm worth the effort, care, and nurturing that friendships take, and I hope that they at least see SOME beauty when they look at "my garden."

Yard Sales 101

Springtime! When the trees are turning green, almost seemingly overnight and the flowers are popping up out of nowhere! Also popping up are yard sale signs, as folks are ready to unload their treasures onto others. I know Ebay and online sites are probably favored by many now, but, to me, there's nothing like seeing and touching what I'm buying. So yeah, I'm a fan.

I should make it clear: I'm a fan of GOING to yard sales. I LOVE finding a furniture piece to breathe new life into! But my days of HAVING yard sales - dragging everything out, pricing it, getting up at the crack of dawn to hang poster board signs all over the neighborhood and dealing with the early birds? Those days are over!

My desire to HAVE yard sales may be a thing of the past, but my NEED to go to them isn't. I still tend to accumulate way more stuff than we need. That's where editing comes into play. My new method of editing was learned from a sharp friend. When going through my things, they now have to pass the *Love it? Use It? Need It?* test. If my things don't say, "Yes" to those three questions, they're gone. As I was going through my things recently, I thought back to the many yard sales I've had over the years. So, consider this "Yard Sales 101." The musings of an old(er) yard sale veteran, passing along tidbits to newbies.

* If the first purchases of the day paid for the aforementioned poster board and ad in the local newspaper, I was in the black already (unless I count the carry out dinner we're going to have because I'm too worn out from the yard sale.)

* The things I want to sell the least will sell first. I once put a sweet memory thing out to sell, thinking it would never go and, sure enough, it was snatched up. Wish I had it now.

* Some of your junkiest stuff is still desirable to someone. Just because YOU think something's useless, doesn't make it so.

* If you're choosing a date for anything outdoors, don't ask for my input. I could plan a June yard sale and it would be cold, rainy, or windy-or all three. Take it from me, fetching your blown away merchandise from down the street sucks!

* Some old folks just want to talk and reminisce-let them. I love the stories about the things they have, what they're looking for, or what I was selling-and you might just learn something!

* Yard sale folks are early birds. If the signs say 9:00 a.m., they'll be there at 7:30 a.m. -or maybe, even the night before!

* Folks love to dicker! If you have something marked $10.00, it may be an, "I'll give ya $1.00," from some ballsy customer. I didn't want to GIVE my stuff away, but I always figured the nice folks who shopped my yard sale would give my old treasures loving homes, so I'd cave and dicker.

* And expect a lull, a business slow down, about two hours in-maybe three hours, since they were there an hour before the advertised time! Not sure why, but the early birds are done pickin' and the others take their time to arrive. That's a good time to have that coffee you missed because of the over-anxious early birds.

* I have never made it to the advertised end of my yard sale. Seems 1:00 was my limit. Not sure if I'm a slacker or what, but yeah.

* My rule is if an item makes it to the yard sale, it doesn't go back into the house. Some organizations are always going to be the recipient of some pretty nice stuff.

* I always set a goal for what to do with the profits from my sale-like mulch and flowers for the yard or some new, cute summer shoes - something! And oh, the carry-out dinner I mentioned before.

* Some years I made my goal - other years not. (Some years, I just had better stuff.) But I always made my goal of clearing out our stuff -to make room for more "stuff" that I'd find when I am on the buying end of a yard sale. Makes sense, right?

I should probably not say that I will never have a yard sale again-you never know! But I'm old-school - I'll leave the digital marketplace to those who know what they're doing. If I get an abundance of stuff to unload, you may just see me hammering posters onto telephone poles that already have a nail or two (or three) of mine imbedded in them. Honk and wave! But please don't be an early bird and follow me home! I'll need that cup of coffee! Happy selling!

Lucky in Love, Unlucky in Lottery....

Well, we didn't win the Power Ball; some folks in other states did. Really, no matter how much I'd win, I'd still write because I love to write- but things would have gotten crazy, I'm thinking. Hasn't it been fun, though, the past few weeks, thinking about what you'd do or wouldn't do if you were the one whose numbers were drawn?

I personally don't think ANYONE should win that large of an amount. A billion dollars? I can't even fathom all those zeroes! To my way of thinking, that kind of wealth for someone who's not ready for that kind of wealth (and who is?) would ruin ones' life. How much does one person need anyway? Split it up-draw several winners and make more folks happy.

If I were to ever win, the first thing I'd do with the Hubs, would be to hire a financial advisor and tax attorney. After getting their counsel, we'd make a list of those who would share in our good fortune. For years, one of the ways I've tried to lull myself back to sleep after a bout of insomnia, (and if prayers aren't working,) is to make a list for that. Depending on how I feel about a particular son (just kidding, guys!) or organization, on that particular day, determines their gift.

I would never want to complicate my kids' life with too much wealth all at once. I'd set it up so that they're stress-free about money, but not overdo it. Some struggles in life are lessons-blessings, even, and I don't want to make things TOO easy for them.

Next on the list would be my grandkids' college educations-and great nieces' and nephews', too! (Not sure how folks do it these days. It was costly enough when our fellas were college boys, and it's even more now!) The organizations that hold a special place in my heart would get the nod next. My alma mater, the hubs and boys' colleges, the parishes and schools in our town- they'd all get a piece. Homeless shelters, health organizations, like the heart or cancer associations, and friends in need, all benefit would our number be drawn. I'd even start a foundation for kids, education, or health issues. I'd certainly have the money for it. And to assure that funding for all of these would go on forever, I'd bank the bulk of it.

It's fun to think about, isn't it? I truly doubt that I'll ever win a lottery -of the money kind, at least- and I'm okay with that. Like I said before that kind of wealth could ruin lives. And I like my life too much to risk that. Plus, I've already won the Life Lottery. My family, my health, my friends, my faith-all blessings and all things that money can't buy.

I truly hope that whoever wins large amounts of money, like the Power Ball, is a good and generous person, surrounded by good people to guide them through that life change. But what I REALLY wish for YOU is that you, too, are blessed in the "Life Lottery"- blessings that no Power Ball winnings could ever top.

More Observations on the Road

I can still see the look on my dad's face-the disdain and the shaking of his head. And this was all because of the length of The Beatles' hair on the magical night they made their first TV appearance in America.

It's been many years since Dad made it apparent that he thought we were all going to hell in a hand basket. Somedays, I feel that same look come over my face, that shaking of the head- quite certain that things are headed in the wrong direction, but I can't help it!

It became most apparent when I was on the road last summer. Perhaps because I could sit back and take it all in? Because I'm getting old and crotchety? Or because things really ARE that disturbing? Maybe a little of all three? You decide.

1. I noticed at nearly every place we were, how so many parents are missing out on life. Their faces were buried in their phones- at the pool, at the restaurants-everywhere. They were not answering their kids' questions or acknowledging their swimming accomplishments. Please, parents- I can tell you that life flies by, and unless you want your child's memory of you to be looking down at an inanimate object, like a phone, instead of their sweet faces, put the damn thing down and savor life - yours and your kids'.

2. Is it any wonder we've become a nation of fatties (myself included...)? The portion sizes of food is ridiculous! "A Little Burger" (that's how it's billed at Five Guys, a popular burger spot) is about as big as my head. And their Little Fries could feed a family of four! Soft drinks, everywhere, all look like Big Gulps (and this is from a true Coca Cola aficionado.) Food places would do all of us a favor by toning it down and pulling back a bit on the portions. It'll benefit them if we, their current and future customers, live longer. That'll be pretty unlikely if we keep chowing down on their mega-sized grub!

3. Being outside the listening area of any familiar radio stations, we pulled out the old trusty CD's and listened to music of our

younger years. It still amazes me how Neil Diamond could write such poignant lyrics and beautiful melodies. Or the voice of Whitney Houston! Adele is terrific, but I doubt we'll ever hear anything as pure as Whitney. There's fine music out there now-I know that -once you sort out the songs that have grunts that used to be heard only in the restroom, and foul language that was oftentimes only heard in locker rooms. I suppose the current music will be someone's oldies someday.

My dad was shaking his head fifty years ago over the supposed impending doom, brought on by a few mop tops from England. And here I am, doing the same thing-a different scenario, but shaking my head, just the same. "At times like these, it helps to recall that there have always been times like these." Some brilliant philosopher came up with that years ago. I hope he knew what he was talking about!

Okay, what's the consensus? Am I too old and crotchety? I KNEW it!

Time for An Upgrade?

I heard the craziest conversation on the radio recently and, naturally, that had me thinking back to how things were compared to how things are now.

First the set-up...I'm driving along in my car and two radio personalities were talking about the new iPhone 7 and some of its features. "It can do this, and it can do that," and, "The jet black one is on back order because it's so heavily sought after." Jeesh!

It seems to me that they change and upgrade those darn things so often and lure folks into thinking they just HAVE to have 'em! And I feel kind of sorry for those people. Oh, I know the technology is great! And they have new and better features that enhance the texting, phoning, and picture-taking experiences. Throw in a little vanity and there you are.

Now think back to the phones of old-not the simple cell kind. Further back than that. I'm talking about the old, black rotary dial ones with a cord that was seldom long enough to escape our parents' curious ears. Yeah, THAT one!

Can you imagine a segment of a WSAI radio program with Dusty Rhoads or Jim Scott being dedicated to a discussion of that wall-mounted black phone in the kitchen? "Oh, yes, I just think the jet-black color is divine." or, "And the cord is just the right length to allow me to lay on the floor and chat," or perhaps, "And don't get me started on the sleek rotary dial! It's so cool!"

Back then, the phone was a utility-not a status symbol. It provided a very valuable service of connecting folks, quite simply. And sure, folks were excited to have a phone in their homes but come on! It was a phone!

True, the technology is fabulous for our kids and grandkids. And that's a good thing. But as parents, they'll never have the ease of calling someone's home to check and see if their kid is REALLY where they're supposed to be. They'll never experience the sheer joy of making an older sister wait for her boyfriend's call while the younger sister ties up that old black phone, chatting away, just to make her mad! And they'll never have the fun of pranking people, calling and then hanging up on them. Caller ID will see to that!

Sure, the newest phones are pretty spectacular. And those will be what our kids and grandkids reminisce about. I just hope the kids, in their quest to have the best and the latest, never lose sight of the fact that words spoken INTO a phone are much more important than the phone they're speaking into. We can only hope!

And You're Wearing?

If there is a profession that pats itself on the back more than the entertainment industry, I don't know what it is!

Yep, it's the award season-that time of year when countless programs are on, extolling the accomplishments of actors, directors, sound editors, singers-all of them! And although I sneak a peek, I always ask myself the questions, "Why?" And "Who cares?"

I guess we've created the problem - reading the magazines, watching the talk shows, buying the movie tickets. But the so-called celebrities' feelings of self-worth are so over-inflated, it's ridiculous-and it starts with the dresses.

As they parade down the red carpet, hounded by the paparazzi, just once, I wish one of these celebrities, when asked, "What are you wearing?" would respond,

"Wal-Mart" or "J. C. Penney."

"And your jewelry was designed by?"

"My kids"... How would that be for striking a blow for the common man? Oh, who am I kidding?

I've also noticed a recent trend that has the celebrities, using their time at the podium, to tell us about their political leanings, their thoughts about equality-like they should be our morality cheerleaders. Puleeze! I'll get my information from folks far wiser than you! Just act, or sing, or whatever you're paid to do.

We'll continue to watch the shows and follow them like they mean something. Maybe, for a change, an awards program for people who truly have made a difference - like a Mother Teresa or a Jonas Salk? Nah, that would probably never air, and if it did, would we even watch? Hard to imagine Mother Teresa in something by Oscar de la Renta...

A Final Resting Place

So, you know you're getting old when you and your hubs buy a cemetery plot! Yes, we went and did it. Have been talking about it for a while and recently, we finalized it.

Not that anything's looming (that we know of) but who's to say? We're thinking of it as a gift to our kids-kids who shouldn't have to deal with such things, when we're gone. They certainly don't even like talking about the topic, so I think we're doing them-and ourselves-a favor.

We met the friendly cemetery representative (now THAT would be a hard job, don't ya think?) at the place, walked around, found our final resting place and put our money down. Fact of the matter, I've spent more time shopping for shoes! It was easy- and it's done!

I've always wanted to be cremated. With my claustrophobia always on my mind, the thought of being in a box forever didn't excite me. It really would be more appropriate to be planted next to hubby, getting on his nerves for all of eternity-side by side forever. But with the help of the cemetery rep, I found out I can have it both ways-cremation and not far from hubby. Problem solved.

The subject of death, dying, cemeteries, burials isn't one that I've relished. But as I've gotten older, I've become more of a realist-some would say fatalist. We're all gonna go sometime. I'm also a control freak and having a say on where I'm going to end up is, in a bizarre way, comforting. Getting to choose my neighbors, some of whom were wonderful friends in life, is the way it should be.

Please don't think I'm being maudlin writing about such a thing. I hope hubby and I aren't going anywhere anytime soon, but I really do view this as another step in the aging process, an investment in the future, or a down payment on eternity, so to speak.

Next up? A headstone! Nothing too big or extravagant. Just something to say, "I was here." At least, if I have a say in that, my name will be spelled correctly. I TOLD you I was a control freak!

The
Friendship
Garden

Those who know me know that I've been whining and griping about our dead trees for a few years now. Our woods used to be beautiful, but then became a wasteland because of some dumb bug. Yada, yada, yada. You know, too, that I undertook a restoration project of those same woods. It was kind of my duty-a duty thrust upon me, not only because it used to be my parents' woods, but also because I was sick and tired of looking out the window and seeing ugliness.

I learned a long time ago that gardening is having hope in the future. You never know what may bloom, season after season. But you keep at it and hope it's something beautiful. You don't know if you'll be around to see the fruits of your labor, but you certainly hope that you are.

Last summer, I asked friends on social media if they had seeds or starts that they would be parting with and would like to donate to my project. Oh, heck. Who am I kidding? I posted pics of the ugly woods and practically begged, pathetically, for whatever I was too cheap to buy. My history with critters and my record of not finishing what I start loomed in the back of my mind. In addition to lacking confidence, I AM thrifty!

Well, I was amazed by the response and the gifts of seeds, starts, and support that I received. Folks calling and messaging me, with offers to help and some even dropping donations off at the house. Others, giving me their addresses for pick up. It really drove home that social media is remarkable in its scope and usefulness for such things, and that my world is full of truly nice people.

I probably should mention that most people would ready their flower beds before planting. Not me- I did it kind of ass-backwards, as one might expect. Last summer, I dug, planted, watered, and waited. This spring and summer, when things began to thrive, THEN I made the move to create beds around my *gifts*.

What is it about determining the amount of dirt one needs, that's so perplexing? On delivery day, the dump truck kept dumping and dumping and dumping. That was a lot of dirt! The way I was posting pics on Facebook of dirt piles, you'd have thought I was really doing something great. And in a way, I was. It really wasn't my goal to haul seventy wheelbarrows of soil by the time I turned sixty-five, and all in one week. But I did! And it's done!

Now, I promise to cease carrying on about my restoration project. I promise. But only because it's been renamed "The Friendship Garden." For although I hauled that dirt alone, it was the gifts of friends that are making a formerly ugly spot a beautiful and hopeful one. Thanks, friends!

P.S. Next Spring, I'm pretty sure I'll shamelessly be forming a Weeders Club for any friends who wish to continue to *"give."* And thanks, in advance, for your consideration!

Oh, For Gawd Sake!

I have a real grump on, and I hope you'll allow me to vent. Please know that, "OH for gawd sake," isn't me taking the Lord's name in vain. It really isn't. It's just my overused go-to comment lately, used as a substitute for the also overused "Seriously?" and "Really."

"Oh, For Gawd Sake," Our cable bill is now higher than the mortgage payment of our first and second homes! How did that happen?

"Oh, For Gawd Sake," Swimsuits! Nuff said!

"Oh, For Gawd Sake,". Why did God make cicadas? They live underground for years and emerge, only to have folks despise them. Hardly seems like a life with a purpose.

"Oh, For Gawd Sake," How many television stations are there? And not one thing worth my time to watch-which makes that aforementioned cable bill even more aggravating!

"Oh, For Gawd Sake," What possesses a person to take that first dose of heroin, knowing its addicting qualities? Desperation? Stupidity?

"Oh, For Gawd Sake," What are these guys, with ear expanders thinking? You know, those things they put in a pierced ear to make the hole bigger and bigger? Do these kids know what that will look like when they're in their 60's? Reminds me of the childhood song, "Do Your Ears Hang Low." They don't HAVE to, ya clowns!

"Oh, For Gawd Sake," How many brands of bread are there in the shopping aisles these days? Remember when Rainbow Bread, Rubel's Rye Bread, and a few store brands were the only choices we had? Some days, I long for simpler times.

For all the grumping I've done, you'd think I'm an unhappy woman. You'd be wrong. Most days, I'm all sweetness and light. (Okay, maybe THAT'S a stretch.) But some days, you just have to say, "Oh, For Gawd Sake!"

Real Estate -Really?

I'm sure many are unaware, but I was a realtor for a brief period of time back in the late 80's and early 90's. I succeeded, because I had a brother-in-law in the building business, and I had family and friends who decided to move during that period of time. I enjoyed it for a while-loved meeting people, but I also blame it on the beginning of my sleeping disorder. The night before a closing I'd toss and turn, "What if I crunched the numbers wrong?" The mother in me would try to talk kids out of a pricey home, "Are you sure you want to be married to your house and not have money to do other things?" Yeah, I was some kind of saleswoman! Ha!

I got out of real estate when I was offered the best job I'd ever have, in a totally different role. It was probably in everyone's best interest, and my timing was good because it was before the dawning of HGTV-the birthplace of so many real estate shows! Whoever thought that we would be entertained by folks, trudging through houses, in search of their dream home?

Well, we apparently are, as those shows are some of the top viewed among evening choices. I'm thinking those shows have created an era that has been torturous for those in the real estate biz now. Yep, it's good that I got out when I did. Back then, my biggest beef was driving an out of town couple around with their three toddlers for two weeks, showing them properties, their kids, slopping fountain Cokes and baby formula all over my car, only to have them go to an Open House by another realtor and sign on the dotted line. No commission...and still a gas and car cleaning bill to pay! Grrrrr!

That was nothing compared to what would be going on now! I would probably be in jail if I had the word *realtor* on my business card nowadays. I'm afraid that I'd have to bitch slap the gal that whines, "It doesn't have a screened-in porch for my cat." or "Our dog would just love this yard - if it had a fence." Are you kidding me?!?

If I were a realtor now, I'd be losing clients, left and right because I'd really let 'em have it! Seriously!

"Look, you've been living in your in-laws basement for three years, so are you REALLY going to let a paint color keep you from buying this house?? I'm sure your in-laws would gladly help you paint!" Grrrr!

"You have this much to spend. A house in that price range doesn't come with granite countertops, hardwood floors, or an in-ground pool." Jeesh!

"Folks in the early 1900's didn't have the wardrobes we have now so, no, there is no walk-in closet in this 1920's house." And same deal with a double sink vanity. They didn't need counter space for their makeup and hair appliances back then. Get over it!

Yep, it was good that I got out of the real estate profession. And if I hadn't? Maybe I'd be one of those crusty old pros who wouldn't pussy-foot around, telling it like it is. And maybe I wouldn't make a dime in commissions because of that candor. Maybe I'd be in the county jail for assault. Who knows?

One thing I DO know is that the folks I know aren't as demanding, spoiled, or self-absorbed as those portrayed on those programs. But I do tip my hat to those in the real estate business now. I'm sure *House Hunters* and shows of their ilk haven't made their jobs any easier.

And me? I'll probably still watch that dumb show, marveling at how shallow some people are, griping to the hubs that it's a stupid show and how I'd like to deck those jerks. Not sure why it draws me in to watch another episode. Oh, now I know why? I still have that sleeping disorder! (And I have tons of episodes dvr-ed.)

Stay tuned! You never know what I'll be griping about next!

Rooting for The Underdog

So, there was a horrible incident here locally. It was so awful, it even garnered national attention. Seems a puppy was abandoned by some asshat and was tragically hit by a train. This little guy's injuries were so horrendous that it warranted the amputation of two legs and his tail. The force of the trauma even caused the loss of an eye!

Turns out, some good samaritan grabbed up the dog and took it to our local animal shelter. One would think that would be the end of the poor creature. Euthanize the thing. It was so badly injured and so unwanted.

Hold on there! Not so fast! A movement was started to save the dog, as funds were raised for its treatment and care. The story grew and grew, and many were rooting for the pooch's recovery. Turns out that with the assistance of a rear walker-type contraption, the dog, now named Trooper, zips around seemingly unaware of its disabilities. People were lining up to adopt Trooper, and I'm happy to say that he's been placed in a loving home, with folks who deal with special needs dogs. Trooper even has his own Facebook page now, allowing us to watch his progress and gain even more fans.

I gotta tell ya. I was one of those who favored putting this poor animal down. I LOVE dogs but, seriously, what kind of life awaited him? He looked like Popeye with one eye stitched close. His mobility, even with his walker, is far from dog-like. Who would even want to deal with a future with such a dog?

And then it hit me! Folks, me included, are desperate these days for feel-good stories- for the chance to root for the underdog (literally and figuratively) and for happy endings. I think Trooper represents the tenacity and drive we all wish we had when our lives suck. Even when he didn't look or feel well, he's moving forward-something we humans often fail to do. Trooper doesn't realize the stir he's created, nor does he care. Dog-people may argue with me on this, but I doubt he even knows how blessed he is to even BE here.

I'm going to follow Trooper's story like many others will. It's nice to be able to see something that started so awful end with a bright conclusion. Good luck, Trooper! And thanks to the good people who saved him and will see to it that he has a good dog's life. He deserves it.

I can state, with little reservation, that there's nothing sadder than a garden store in September or a swimming pool closed for the season. I love the fall, but can anyone disagree?

Oh, I know, I had little use for a swimsuit this year. I think I was brave enough to put one on this summer to jump into a lake in Michigan. More of my suit-wearing takes place in the winter when we are able to head south. But gone are the carefree days of joining the neighborhood gang for a walk to the neighborhood public pool, flip flops on, (or thongs if you have any sense or age to ya...something went between toes long before it went between butt cheeks!) beach towel and quarter in hand. Those were such great times! But the voices and laughter of the neighbors' backyard pools are silenced for another year. And it's evident, another summer is gone. Maybe, I'll use the off-season to work on things a bit and trying on a suit in spring of 2017 won't evoke laughter from the reflection in the mirror. There's hope!

And perusing the aisles of my favorite garden stores will have to wait, too. What was, a few months ago, beautiful displays of plants that I couldn't wait to plant in my yard, are now withered, overgrown, or gone from the shelves. They say, "To plant a garden is to believe in tomorrow." And I do! Despite my dismal crops this summer, I'll be back at it in the spring! Planting, weeding, and cursing the pests that insist on sharing my poor bounty. There's hope!

And there's always hope that the rich colors of fall, the camaraderie of the holidays, and the peaceful quiet of the winter get all of us through to another pool and garden season.

Hoping!

Time - the Great Equalizer

Everyone remembers their high school years. Some fondly, others, not so much. Let's face it. Those years were awkward ones: new bodies, new feelings, new kids to meet, trying to figure out who and what we were going to be.

Fast forward a few years and it's time for class reunions. I get it-the early ones are awkward, like high school was. Who's doing well? How many kids do you have? Will anyone remember me? Who still looks good? And a lot of people stay home.

As a seasoned veteran of these get togethers, I can tell you that time is a great equalizer. Some of the kids who were on the fast track to success in high school may have gotten derailed. The mousey girl in your math class may be the swan of the class now. The knockout maybe isn't such a knockout anymore. The star athlete struggles to tie his shoe now. You get my drift?

The best news is, as the years go by, that none of that matters anymore, if it ever did. Our value to our family, our friends, our community, and the world, is far more important now than income, titles, or belongings. Our health is a blessing that has become more valuable than any position on the team, ranking in the class, or popularity in the school. Our high school years are far behind us, but they've given us all our foundation and a history with so many good people-people who had some of the same struggles back then and perhaps now. I want to celebrate that history and the fact that we're all still here!

Our high school class took a "What are we waiting for?" approach a few years ago and started having get togethers more frequently than the usual five-year increments. We've found fun excuses for it. A Social Security Picnic, when we reached that magical (eligible) age was one. We even had one that was a "What Are We Waiting For?" party.

We noticed that we were losing classmates at far too fast a rate- nineteen by the time we hit sixty. Now, we just pick a spot, set the date, let folks know about it, and whoever wants to or can make it, comes. I've never had a bad time.

I guess the message I'm trying to share here is that high school was a long time ago. Things really do have a way of evening out. Life is short and reconnecting with those from our pasts really can be fun. Tick, Tock, Tick, Tock...

To All the Moms and Dads Sending Your First Child Off to College

I feel for you-that feeling in the pit of your stomach-a bit of an ache in your heart as the day approaches. Your family unit will never be the same. The dynamics change. The number of places at your table will be reduced by one, for now.

But you know what? You've done your job and are ready to launch one! How exciting is that? You've spent their lifetime preparing them for this milestone and it's time to share them with the world!

I haven't always been so upbeat about this topic. I was a mess when we sent our first one away to college. Cried all the way from his school to our driveway, and arriving home, I threw myself on his bed and sobbed. But I'm here to tell you, they come back, better than they were when they left. New experiences, new knowledge, and new friends-what a terrific opportunity you're giving them!

You gave them roots. You can't be selfish-now let them fly! Good luck to your college bound kids, and congratulations to you, who got them there!

"Be a Fountain...Not a Drain."

Who'd have ever thought one could get inspiration at a place as unlikely as a Cracker Barrel restaurant? Sure, I've enjoyed their chicken and dumplings for years- it wouldn't be a trip to Cumberland Lake or Norris Lake without a stop at one along the way. And their shop out front while you're waiting to be served? Who can resist that? But getting inspiration for everyday living? Hmmm!

But that's where I saw a cute yard ornament that served as a reminder of how I should strive to be. "Be a fountain, not a drain." That's what it said. Nothing terribly profound, but it got me to thinking.

To me, a fountain is a thing of beauty. It can be functional or decorative. It's refreshing. It can reflect light, recirculate and make water useful and ready to be spewed into the air again. And the drain? Isn't that kinda the end of the road for water? After it's collected debris along the way?

I really hope, as I get older, I'm a "fountain." Some days, it's hard-the aches and pains and aggravations of daily living make it difficult to be positive or even pleasant. And it'd certainly be easier to be "a drain" sometimes. Just sitting there and accepting whatever life sends your way. But I so hope I'm always useful-someone who refreshes others instead of "draining" them.

And the next time I have a need for inspiration and a hankering for chicken and dumplings, guess where I'm heading? You got it!

My Hometown

"Your hometown's not just where you're from.
It's who you are." (Arnold Palmer)

Turns out old Arnie was not only a terrific golfer, but a rather astute thinker. "Your hometown's not just where you're from. It's who you are."

If that's true, I'm certainly glad my folks decided to make Hamilton, Ohio their home when I was born! That would mean I have good midwestern values, a fine work ethic, a lot of terrific people in my life, and a positive attitude that, no matter how things are, they can get better.

My hometown has, like most, an ever-changing landscape, both figuratively and literally. As a young girl, my mom would hold my hand as we got off of a city bus in a busy downtown. Neighbor kids had to head for home when the whistles of the many factories signaled that it was soon suppertime. The homes were neatly kept, and the yards of grass were ideal for games of Spud or Tag.

But just as wonderful as things were, I've found, as I've aged, that everything in life is cyclical and then it was our towns turn for harder times. Downtown wasn't so bustling, factories and businesses shuttered up or left, and a lot of the kids who had played Spud left, too, seeking their fortunes elsewhere. The homes looked tired and the grass is gone.

But another cycle has begun. There's a new energy in my hometown. A busy downtown is emerging. It's not the same as the old one was, with the big stores and the countless eateries. But with cute niche shops, parks, and a craft beer brewery. In place of the factories of old, technology-based enterprises are popping up. Cool flea markets and concerts are drawing young folks in. Neighborhoods are being spruced up, old eyesores torn down to make way for green space or new developments. Yep, folks, life is cyclical. It's someone else's turn to be tired and in need of renewal. Because my hometown is BACK!

Oh, sure-some find amusement in its diverse citizenry and criticize it for being a bit backward or hick. I'll grant you-the roads are in need of repair and getting around in the traffic is a pain. Things aren't perfect, I KNOW that! But you'd best not be too hard on this place I call home within earshot of me because as Arnie said, "Your hometown's not just where you're from. It's who you are." And I'm proud of who I am.

Oh, For Gawd Sake – Part Two

It's been awhile since I've publicly vented. But I have a grump on again and I hope you don't mind. A disclaimer - "Oh, for gawd sake" isn't me taking the Lord's name in vain. It really isn't. It's just my overused go-to comment, used as a substitute for the also overused "Seriously?" and "Really."

- Hollywood and sexual harassment- if a lecherous old man welcomes you at his hotel room door in a robe, who in the hell goes in? "For Gawd Sake!"

- Being a weatherman in Florida has to be the most boring job in the world! "We have a cold front moving in that will bring our temps down to seventy degrees. There will be a cool breeze coming off the gulf. Be sure to take a sweater." But they get just as excited as our Ohio ones do when something unexpected (like rain ...ha!) crops up. "For Gawd Sake!"

- Tide pods - Now I'm not talking about the teenage asshats who are eating them on a dare! I'm wondering why we aren't questioning the need for something so strong and poisonous just to clean our clothes! "For Gawd Sake!"

Why aren't women's slacks sized like men's, with an inseam for different sizes? Not all twelves (or fourteens) are the same height or require the same length! And especially if one needs extra fabric in the seat -THAT shortens slacks even more! (Or so I've been told. Ha!) "For Gawd Sake!"

Oh, For Gawd Sake – Part Three

Normally, I look at failures as opportunities in disguise. So what opportunity is being disguised by my failure to lose weight? Who knows? "For Gawd Sake!"

Did anyone else notice that nothing catastrophic happens when the government shuts down? Maybe we can do without the high-priced clowns who SAY they represent us, after all. "For Gawd Sake!"

I'm trying to be upbeat about the winter weather this year. We can't do anything about it, and without it, what would a lot of us have to talk about anyway? "For Gawd Sake!"

Please don't tell me we're starting political campaigns already! How about working on the problems we elected you to do before worrying about your future job security! "For Gawd Sake!"

Well, that does it for me. I feel better already! Thanks for obliging me. Now, is there anything that has you saying "For Gawd Sake!"? (besides my nonsensical ramblings?)

The Pigeon or the Statue?

"Some days, you're the pigeon-some days, you're the statue."

Last week, there was a day I was definitely the statue! I had doo-doo dumped on me the whole day!

The day started out innocently enough. I had my morning coffee and was on my way. Granted, the holidays have everyone moving at a faster pace and I was in a holiday hurry. At least, that's why I think I took out our car mirror when backing out of the garage! That, or my vision really IS that bad of late. That daggone garage door frame just wouldn't get out of my way!

I work part time for a local car dealership, so it was no big deal to run into the service department and tell the guys my plight. They said they'd order a part and let me know when they could repair it. Good enough. Off to my next destination-probably in a hurried state.

Now, what are the chances the hubs would be bringing his company car into that same service department that morning? And what are the chances the service fella would hand the hubs the estimate for MY car (which the hubs knew nothing about yet) to give to me? The service guy was just doing his job. I know that. And I was EVENTUALLY going to tell the hubs... Just not yet. Was the hubs mad? Naa...he's used to my ways and, after forty-seven years, I don't think he'd kick me to the curb over a broken car part. A $400 repair. I sure hope not anyway.

Okay, so my next destination was in a part of town that had parking meters. No biggie - I put my money in the slot and went on to my appointment. The way my day was going, of course, I would return to my car to find a parking ticket affixed to the windshield! (Damn pigeon!) How come I'm in a hurry, except when getting to my car in time to avoid a ticket?

I'm home now and I think I may just stay put until things settle down a bit and the need to hurry is over. Curled up in a chair, with a blanket, causing no harm or damage. Who am I kidding? I'll be out and about racing around again, like everyone else. But would someone please answer me this?

Aren't pigeons supposed to fly south for the winter? I sure wish they would!

The Nose Knows

In these days of Febreeze, Glade plug-ins, and my favorite scented candles, (especially the fall season ones!) I got to thinking, "When did we, think we needed all these fake fragrances?" What are we masking?

Okay, I know-we have a dog-an animal whose hygiene and manners are questionable, and sometimes my cooking gets away from me. Some dirty laundry may sit a bit too long. But is all this covering up, overkill?

Of course, this had me thinking back to the scents of the past. As a kid, I remember the wonderful fragrance of burning leaves in the fall. That was before the days of the EPA and, although I know they're around for our health, I think they're killjoys- at least, in this case. That's the way all of our neighbors disposed of the leaves they had raked up, and it was wonderful! And nothing evokes warm memories of my childhood more than when my dad would build a fire in our fireplace at home or the family sitting around the campfire at the pond where we ice skated.

For spring and summer scents, it has to be the beach and the ocean smells for me! Because the fishy, briny smell really isn't all that pleasant, it must be the memories of great beach vacations that makes it special. And the smell of chlorine takes me back to the carefree days of the neighborhood swimming pool and the kids we hung with. The fragrance of carnations bring back good and bad memories for me. The good was when the carnations were in the bouquet I carried as a flower girl in a family wedding and the bad was when the floral arrangements at my grandfather's funeral also had carnations in them. Smelling God's earth, when I'm gardening, is wonderful, but not so much when that "earth" is mixed with sweat on football uniforms.

It's funny how it all works-fragrances, scents and smells are complex and personal, aren't they? How different people interpret them differently. I know that, as we get older, our sense of smell diminishes somewhat-that's a fact. So, I think I'll pull out the plug-ins and put away the Febreeze, so I can enjoy the real fragrances of life while I still can. Our dog better behave!

Progressive AND Nostalgic

Well, we went and did it! The hubs and I have subscribed to Netflix. In addition to some terrific original tv series, they also offer up complete seasons of some of the great old ones. We've been enjoying old shows, like *Cheers*, *Twilight Zone* and *Wonder Years*. Oh, the memories the old shows evoke. I can blame my dislike for ventriloquists on a *Twilight Zone* episode. And just hearing the theme song to *Cheers*, "Where everybody knows your name," brings back memories of rustling up the boys and getting them to bed so I could enjoy some me-time in front of the TV.

What Netflix has made me realize is how different program viewing is now. I remember, talking at school and work about the shows we watched the night before. If it was a popular one, we all watched it at the same time and had a common point of reference. Nowadays, with hundreds of channels, DVR-ing, computers, and phones, that's no longer the case. Seems that everyone, now, watches different programs in their own time, in their own way.

I think it would be interesting to see how the reporting of President Kennedy's assassination would be handled today. I can remember how Walter Cronkite, "The most trusted man in America" reported it with tears in his eyes. His strong presence surrounded us as we were glued to our televisions, all viewing the same program-all discussing the same coverage. Would that be the case now, with today's 24/7 news outlets? Unlikely. Standing on the playground, chatting about last night's episode of *The Donna Reed Show* or, during a lunch break at work, talking about the *M.A.S.H.* finale, probably wouldn't happen now either.

Cable TV, with its tons of channels, and VCRs were the beginning of the end of communal viewing. Tape something, watch it later, zoom through commercials, keep it forever. Who wouldn't like that? And then DVR-ing came along, so an episode of a show like *The Walking Dead* (a favorite of the hubs that sends me to the bedroom for a DVR-ed episode of *Flip or Flop*) isn't missed.

So, sure, I miss the good old days, when everyone crowded around the TV, watching, laughing, or crying at the same program, at the same time. But there's this thing called progress and we move along to something better. Maybe that's why I'm a fan of Netflix. It allows these two old-timers to be progressive AND nostalgic at the same time. So, when I hear the theme song of one of the old shows playing on Netflix, I'll appreciate the way things were then AND are now. Yep, I'm goin' with that!

It's Kool Inside

We knew it was going to happen. They were living on borrowed time. And at the age of twenty-eight, they really surpassed their life expectancy. But are we ever really prepared to say goodbye? Luckily, their time didn't come in the heat of the summer or during the coldest of days. Yep, our heating and air conditioning system bit the dust. Air Conditioning put up a fight-sputtering and clunking to the end. Her brother, Heating, wasn't quite ready to go, but since they've been together since 1986, we figured they'd want to go together. Instead of taking the Band-Aid approach and pouring more money into their sad conditions, we're going to pull the plug on both of them. What choice do we have?

This decision got me to thinking, "When did we become so addicted to such comforts as air conditioning?" Heating has always been a given. Since the age of cave men and the creation of fire, we knew that keeping warm was needed if we were going to survive. But air conditioning? It's a luxury that we all have to have now. And I have the checkbook balance to prove it!

Kids today, and even some of their parents, just assume that air conditioning is a right of life because it seems that we've always had it, but that wasn't always the case. When we were kids, sleeping in a hot upstairs bedroom with the night breeze coming thru an open window, was what we had. A box fan in the window was a welcome addition to the household and if it was blazing outside, the basement provided a cool spot. Perhaps not having air conditioning was the reason for our crowded public swimming pools, and air conditioning's growing popularity was part of the reason for their demise. Okay, maybe that's a stretch, but think about it. Sitting in a cool home is less strenuous.

As a kid, I remember the mom and pop stores, like Hessler's Market and Jim's Corner Market, (both on Benninghofen Avenue) had window air conditioners. They weren't pretty, stuck in the window, but they kept the customers cool when we were shopping there. Avenue Pharmacy, on the corner of Pleasant Avenue and Hooven Avenue, is my first recollection of an all-out air conditioning system. They even had a sign on the door that said, "Come In. It's Kool Inside." Clever marketing, I'd say, as they advertised a popular brand of cigarettes, as well as cool, comfortable shopping. (Why in the world would I remember that?)

Thinking back to simpler times is always fun, but the fact of the matter is- we are spoiled. It won't be long 'til I'm scurrying from my car (okay, you can stop laughing at THAT image!) to reach my air-conditioned nirvana that is home. Maybe, one of these days, a flea market find from simpler times is in my future-one of those signs that says, "Come In. It's Kool Inside!" Now, wouldn't THAT be Kool?

Fifty
Shades
of
Grey

So much press and hype for books and movies like *Fifty Shades of Grey*! Yikes!

I read that book and I'd be lying if I didn't say it was (hmmm...what word do I use?) hot. I didn't quite understand the need for much of their behavior but to each his own, I suppose.

I was reading the book when it first came out, on a flight with our son's women's college basketball team. Under the cover of a magazine, I saw no need to advertise the fact that I was reading, what most would consider, a trashy book. Sitting next to me was a team member-an inquisitive little thing-and spying a page, exclaimed, "Mrs. Wright! You're reading Fifty Shades of Gray?"

"Why don't you get on the intercom and announce it, you little snip!" I didn't say that to her, of course, but, jeesh, how about a little discretion?

What's always interesting to me is how someone can take the written word and transform it into a movie. That would be such a daunting task-trying to stay true to the author's beloved words. I'll see the movie -much like I saw *Romeo and Juliet* after I read the book. Who am I kidding? It's going to be a lot hotter than THAT movie!

It's no secret that I enjoy writing, and anyone who writes dreams of commercial recognition and success, much like the Fifty Shades' author has received. I can assure you; my first novel won't be as steamy as hers. They say you should write what you know, so I'd have to write something tamer, I'm thinkin'.

Let's just say maybe MY Fifty Shades of Grey should reference the paint chips I'm pondering for a room redo or maybe a hair dye job. Yep, that's more my speed...

Bacon and Cigarettes

I read that a recent medical study has found that taking a baby aspirin daily is no longer considered to be as beneficial as was once thought. What? For years, the medicos have been telling us that one of those little pills would protect us from cardiac problems. Now they're saying that it helps only if you've had a cardiac episode already. So, do I continue my daily regimen? Do I stop, only to be told in a few years that my first heart attack could have been prevented if I'd have taken a baby aspirin every day?

This got me to thinking about all the dietary advice that we've been offered in the past. And now I have to ask: What are we to believe? Who has the right answers? What is going on?

Folks have been sucking down Diet Cokes, thinking they were less fattening than the regular Cokes. Now "they" say that the sweetener itself can cause weight gain and health problems. It also turns out that butter isn't as bad for you as "they" once claimed. "They're" now saying that it causes fewer heart-related illnesses than margarine! And dark chocolate is touted as a health food? Sure, eat a piece of dark chocolate a day! It's good for you! We're supposed to reduce our sodium and fat intake, says one group of doctors-only to be countered by a group who say that our bodies NEED salt and fat in our diets, and not having enough of them in our daily diets can result in health problems.

I really wish everyone would get on the same page. I know that studies are challenged all the time. New findings disprove the old ones. "They're" only looking out for us, but they sure don't make it easy. I guess the best chance at having a crack at a long life is everything in moderation and to keep movin'.

It's wishful thinking here, but I'm holding out for the day "they" reverse their stance on bacon and cigarettes and say they're really not that bad for us! Now THAT would be a good day!

I suppose it's because of the town I live in or maybe it's the position I held at a local school. But I've been blessed with so many wonderful people in my life. That makes for a wonderful life! It also means that you see many terrific people go to their eternal reward. The following are three of those...

Rest in Peace A Community Icon...Gone.

It's funny how someone can come into your life, in a strange way, and leave such an imprint. Such was the case of Terry Malone, a legendary football coach and an iconic figure in this area, who passed away recently. Now, keep in mind - I am perhaps the least athletic person on the planet. So how has a football icon impacted someone's life in such a profound way? Here's the backstory.

Terry Malone was the football coach - history teacher - drivers ed instructor at the high school I attended. Sure I've heard the stories - false teeth, coming out when he was steamed about something on the field..... Calling students "rubes" in class.... things that would be considered politically incorrect today. But Terry was also considered a second dad to many of his players, a pioneer in the game of football, a stellar teacher and guy who made the high school world, sit up and take notice, just by walking down the school hallway or across a football field.

I am personally grateful to coach Malone for luring my future hubs back to his alma mater to coach and teach, after college. Dean was a player and captain of one of Terry's teams and wanted nothing more than to return to his hometown to coach with The Coach. Terry made that happen. And how would my life have turned out otherwise?

When this younger broad and Dean started dating, Terry and his wife, Betty, were the least judgmental people I've ever met. I was this young thing, entering their circle, 20 years their junior, a few years older than their oldest child. They were so welcoming and made this young lady feel like she belonged.

My husband was fortunate to stand beside (or behind him, pulling Terry's coat or shirt when he was going after a player or a ref was one of Dean's duties) this high school coaching great for so many years. My sons - all three

- were blessed to be on teams coached by this legend. I worked with Terry, in his later years, at the same high school he put on the football map. I came to know he was a man of deep faith when I'd see him, sneaking into the chapel of his beloved high school for a quick prayer or two. Or after his retirement, where he could be found at daily mass at Saint Anne's.

The impact of Coach Malone's influence is vast. I like to think of a stone, hitting the water in a pond. The ripples and waves go everywhere, and you never know who or what they touch. No one knows how many lives were changed because of Terry Malone. But I don't have to look any further than across the breakfast table and see my hubs . Or see my sons on the sidelines, themselves, now coaches. Or witness the character my sons and so many former players and friends display in their lives - to know that Terry Malone was, indeed, here.

Yep, Terry Malone left a huge imprint. My heart aches for his kids, for his family, for his friends, for his players and students, for his co-workers. His presence will, indeed, be missed. And this world is a better place, for having had The Old Coach in it. Rest, easy, Coach. You've won the greatest victory of your incredible career.

Hooven Avenue to Heaven-He's Earned His Wings

I don't want you to think I'm depressed or maudlin. But when you live in a town like we do...where everyone knows everyone... the losses of those you know can be frequent and they can hit you hard.

Such is the case with Bobby Schuster. The world lost one of the good guys with his passing yesterday and plenty of folks are feeling it. Gosh, we loved that guy! And what a human being he was! He overcame such odds to live a life with humor, grace and strength. Something we should all try to emulate...especially when we don't have the hardships and health problems he did.

I went to school with Bobby and I loved him, even though he was kind of a turd! Nothing evil or sinister...just an ornery kid who knew his charm would get him out of any trouble he'd get into. I came to know him even better and love him even more after a softball accident left him a quadriplegic. His emails, visits on his deck or sitting with him at different functions, gave me such insight into the beautiful person he was. Never one to complain about his fate, he was usually the one who did the cheering up. He and my hubs had a sweet bond and I could listen for hours about some of the teacher/student stories they had. Gosh, we're going to miss Bobby!

You can't think of Bobby Schuster without thinking of his family. In this world of dysfunctional tribes and selfish people, one would have a hard time finding a more loving family than the Schusters, when it came to Bobby's care. Generations of them... They have been chipping in and taking care of business for forty-four years! Bobby felt their love every day of his life, I'm sure, and was lucky to have been born a Schuster. But Bobby's family and friends would probably tell us that THEY were the lucky ones. That's the kind of family they are.

I guess I should be sad about Bobby's passing. Oh, I'll miss his occasional "just checking in" emails... And he'll be missed at class reunions, where he would jokingly offer his services to me, one of the organizers, "to control the crowd", when the reunions were sparsely attended and there WAS no crowd... (still a turd, right?) His sometimes-raunchy Facebook posts will be missed. His concern, when others were going thru a tough time, will be missed. His offer to share his cigarettes, if you'd help him smoke one, will be missed... Yes, I should be sad because Bobby's gone. But I'm not. I'm sad for all those who loved him, because we've all lost such a terrific spirit... I'm sad for those, in the world, who never knew him, because they really missed out on knowing one of the best.

Yep, Heaven gained an angel with an ornery gleam in his eye. I like to think Bobby's walking, for the first time in 44 years, getting into trouble, hoping to escape the wrath of the recently deceased Terry Malone, our school's vice principal. I can almost see it now.

Prayers for Bobby's family and friends, because I truly believe Bobby doesn't need them. He earned his wings here on earth. Rest in peace, old friend.

The
Memory
Maker

Another icon from my high school is gone. Another man who has left a huge imprint on the lives of the thousand of students he taught and all those who had the good fortune of knowing him. Another example of someone who, like tossing a stone into a pond... You never know where or how far the ripples go. Joe D was like that. Who knows how many people's lives he has impacted?

Everyone should love their workplace as much as Joe did. He was a proud ambassador of the school for over 50 years. Think about that! 50 years!

Some would say you can't work at a place for fifty years and NOT have an impact on people, but Joe was one of those characters that, I'm pretty sure, if he had worked there only 2 years, you'd remember him.

I will remember Joe as a memory-maker for the school. In addition to teaching countless classes, Joe was The Prom Guy.....making sure students had a fun, safe memory of that special weekend. As the DIstributive Ed guy.....he exposed kids to travel, taking them on out-of-town adventures and competitions that would change their lives and again...the memories. As the Variety Show guy....he could convince kids that they had talent, when they didn't even know it themselves, urging them onstage. (Thanks, Joe, for THOSE memories). As the Spaghetti Guy...Joe brought folks into the school, every March, to partake of his meal, to enjoy fellowship and to give his kids the experience of serving others.

Yep, Joe D. touched many lives...maybe even saved a few. He was the same to some of the "stinkers" in the school as he was to "the top of the class" kids. When I worked at the same high school as Joe, I soon realized that, when alumni returned to the school on a school day, it was usually to see Mr D. And he was always welcoming, interested in their lives. I'm certainly sad that Joe's gone, but I'm even happier that he lived. This loss is going to hurt.

Joe was a man of faith so I'm thinking he's already planning and organizing things in heaven, catching up with those he knew, but still keeping an eye on all of us he's left behind...just like he always kept up with the many whose lives he touched here. Yep, this one's going to hurt.

So that's it! All I've got. I suppose the take-away from this attempt at writing is that, if there's something you want to do, do it! I may be the only owner of this book (maybe the hubs and my sister will buy one...) but I DID IT!

If you're read this far, thanks for coming along.

Love,
The Old(er) Broad

Photo Credit: Shawnda Corder Partin